# THE ASIAN LEGACY
# AND AMERICAN LIFE

© Most Serene, Serene, most puissant, puissant, high, illustrious, noble, honorable, venerable, wise and prudent Emperors, Kings, Republicks, Princes, Dukes, Earls, Barons, Lords, Burgomasters, Counsellors, as also Judges, Officers, Justiciaries & Agents of all the good Cities and places whether ecclesiastical or secular who shall see these patents or hear them read: We the United States of America in Congress Assembled make known, that John Green Captain of the ship call'd the Empress of China, is a citizen of the United States of America and that the ship which he commands belongs to citizens of the said United States and as we wish to see the said John Green prosper in his lawful affairs, our prayer is to all the beforementioned, and to each of them separately, where the said John Green shall arrive with his vessel & cargo, that they may please to receive him with kindness, and to treat him in a becoming manner, permitting him upon the usual tolls & expences in passing & repassing, to pass, navigate and frequent the ports, passes and territories to the end to transact his business where and in what manner he shall judge proper whereof we shall be willingly indebted.

In Testimony whereof we have caused the Seal of the United States to be hereunto affixed. — Witness His Excellency Thomas Mifflin President this thirtieth day of January in the year of our Lord one thousand seven hundred & Eighty four and in the Eightieth year of the Sovereignty & Independence of the United States of America. —

Thos Mifflin

Cha Thomson Secy

The "Sea Letter" of the Empress of China, Inaugurating the China Trade in 1783-84. From the Library of Congress.

# THE ASIAN LEGACY AND AMERICAN LIFE

ESSAYS

ARRANGED AND EDITED BY

ARTHUR E. CHRISTY

*Illustrated*

GREENWOOD PRESS, PUBLISHERS
NEW YORK                    1968

First Greenwood reprinting, 1968

LIBRARY OF CONGRESS catalogue card number: 68-9541

# CONTENTS

*Illustrations will be found in three sections following
page 76, page 100, and page 244*

# FOREWORD

THE occasion for this book is the rise in recent years of numerous governmental and private agencies sponsoring educational programs in intercultural relations. Enlightened statesmen and private citizens have at last recognized the fact that isolationism is politically untenable, economically unsound, morally preposterous, and intellectually parochial. One of the most urgent tasks of our day is to arouse interest in the life of foreign peoples, and to dispel ignorance about the interdependence of all the tribes of the human family.

There are three ways in which the study of foreign peoples may be conducted. One is to study them *in vacuo*, with a sense of complete detachment. Another is to explain the differences between the world's peoples and their cultures—a study which unhappily leads to invidious contrasts and contributes little to man's sadly needed store of good will. A third is based on the assumption that as long as the peoples of the earth have some similarities, are blessed with intellectual curiosity, and sincerely share a desire for something approaching the brotherhood of man, mutually beneficial relations can be developed among them. This final approach involves knowing other peoples intimately and acquiring ability to see their interests as well as our own; but above all, it emphasizes the process of cultural interchange.

The question "What can the East give the West?" has long been asked, but few have sought to answer. Some scholars have devoted themselves to the question in terms of European life and civilization, and have sought in such works as the Oxford *Legacy* series to show the exchange chiefly among peoples of the Mediterranean littoral. No concerted effort has yet been made to answer the question in terms of American life. At no time in history and in no area of the world has there been greater need of such study than in America. The peoples of the New World, a fluid mixture of races, look out upon the life of the earth from a continent whose coasts are washed by both of the great oceans, beyond which, in ancestral Europe and ancient Asia, are the fountainheads of their traditions.

The legacies of Israel and Rome in Occidental civilization have been described as the Jordan flowing into the Tiber. In more recent times the Yangtze has flowed into the Thames and the Ganges into the Mississippi. We do not minimize the basic contributions of Israel, Greece, and Rome to Western civilization, or the modern European traditions upon which American culture is founded. But we recognize the fact that as the earth has shrunk with the scientific conquest of distance, the world's peoples no longer live unto themselves and many Asiatic peoples hitherto remote from us have been brought into our intellectual orbit. Indeed, they have in many ways, without many of us being aware of it, influenced our sense of spiritual values and enriched our workaday lives.

Paradoxically, the shrinking of our physical earth has also meant the enlargement of each individual's world. The neighbors of modern man are no longer those who live in familiar parishes, but those who inhabit the ends of the earth. No one can safely predict, if a world civilization is ultimately to arise, whether it will conform mainly to the standards of Europe. Spenglerian prophets of doom for the West have thought too exclusively of domination or decline. They have ignored the fact that a shuttle of interacting influence is ceaselessly weaving the warp and the weft of the world's cultural fabric, while other forces are laying foundations under man's dream of universal brotherhood. It was not sentimentalism that impelled Sisley Huddleston to write in *In My Time:* "What we must have is a genuine cosmopolitanism, and that means a growing body of really civilized individual men and women in a number of countries, sufficiently enlightened to . . . admire whatever is lovely and of good report in every country, and sufficiently numerous to leaven and color the thoughts and feelings of the masses."

This book is intended to be a modest contribution to knowledge in a generally neglected field of Western cultural history. That it is not exhaustive and does not presume even to survey many important problems in the history of Oriental-Occidental relations must be emphasized. Its stress is mainly upon processes and values which politicians and economists generally ignore. The contributors are officials and scholars who have been asked to agree upon only one principle, namely, that intercultural exchange involves *more* than the commodities or bric-a-brac which cross the oceans on the bottoms of ships, the records compiled by attachés in consular offices overseas, and trade treaties favored by chambers of commerce. That this emphasis needs to be made in American relations with Asiatic peoples cannot be too strongly stated, if we are ever to be fully absolved from the charge of being essentially a materialistic people or curious about the picturesque details of foreign life alone.

The emphasis of the book is, furthermore, on contemporary American life, on living issues. The past has not been ignored, however, since historical perspective is needed; and European backgrounds have been emphasized, since what America owes to Asia in many instances came indirectly through our European relations. Following the editor's contribution, the chapters are arranged in turn to present a varied sense of such vital details of our debt to Asia as the fruits and cereals which have become staples in the economy of American life, the social institutions and the arts which are the chief channels of cultural interchange, and the religious and philosophical issues implicit in the relations between the cultures of the world's hemispheres. Finally, Dr. Coomaraswamy contributes to the series as a citizen of the world, an Oriental by birth and an Occidental in training and professional life, stating what seem to him the crucial needs and issues.

Readers will discover much information hitherto inaccessible. But the contributors while pointing out trees have also described forests. Skilled at taking pains, they have not forgotten for what purpose alone research and the scholar's cares are worth the effort, and they have not neglected either the broad view or the deeper understanding and larger interrelations. Since each contributor worked independently, free to select his own facts and draw his own conclusions, the separate chapters reflect individual points of view arrived at through long years of observation, study, and personal experience. The cumulative result is a rich assortment of facts, stimulating ideas, and approaches to one of the most vital issues in international life today. The editor is confident that both the general and the learned critic will realize that the purpose is not rhetorical effect but the awakening of the American public to a comprehensive view of all that is involved in our relations with non-European peoples.

Among the many satisfactions, encouragement, and help the editor has received in his work, his chief debt is to the internationally known authorities who have contributed to the pages which follow. To speak of their eminence is unnecessary for those who know their work. For those unacquainted with it, the chief facts of interest to the reader have been noted on the contents page. The editor is confident that men who share a common interest and are willing to spend themselves for international understanding cannot fail to find mutual satisfaction in the advancement of the cause. Among collaborators, therefore, the silence of simple pleasure at tasks completed contains a deeper note of satisfaction and gratitude than can be conveyed by words for the public eye. To Pearl S. Buck, founder of the East and West Association, the editor tenders his thanks for the gracious manner in which his first proposal for this book was received and for the chapter which enriches its pages. Finally, to the John Simon Guggenheim Foundation and the American Council of Learned Societies the editor is under debt for encouragement and aid in the development of the field of study which this book represents and of which it is a hint of work in progress. Representative materials quarried from the records of the East India trade in European and American archives are included in the opening chapter or kenneled in an innocuous appendix. Since most of the facts are either new or from unpublished records, specialists may find them informative; and the general public, for whom this book is intended, may be introduced through them to the history of the cultural discovery of the Orient.

ARTHUR E. CHRISTY

*February 1, 1945.*

# THE ASIAN LEGACY
# AND AMERICAN LIFE

*Arthur E. Christy*

# THE SENSE OF THE PAST

## I

IF IT is true, as Savigny said, that history is the only way to attain a knowledge of one's condition, a sense of the past is needed in the conduct of cultural relations between European and Asiatic peoples. Indeed the civilization of our modern world is in many ways a product of the interchange between the eastern and western hemispheres; and there are peculiar reasons why the American manifestations of the reciprocal contacts are particularly worthy of study. The New World, from the time of Columbus, has stood midway between Europe and Asia. It is the laboratory in which many values are tested, the field in which everything from Oriental flora and fauna to exotic modes of life and thought is being domesticated. In John Buchan's *Pilgrim's Way* appear pertinent comments on the antiquarian habit of mind which belittles the present and looks backward. It is a vicious business, he wrote, to look backward unless the feet are set steadfastly on the forward road. Change, inevitable with the passing generations, must be welcomed. Open and flexible minds will recognize the need of transformation and set themselves to apprehend new conditions. But they will also recognize that the past is "the matrix of present and future, whose potency takes many forms but is not diminished." They will cherish it scrupulously, labor to read its lessons, and, realizing fully that "in the cycle to which we belong we can see only a fraction of the curve," will appraise it properly by looking both ahead and backward a few centuries to its beginning.

The vastness of our subject precludes a detailed historical discussion of the Occidental debt to the Orient. Intercourse began in Graeco-Roman times, and it included everything from the commodities of the early caravan trade to modern circus freaks and chinaware, from the art of printing to the mariner's compass, from gunpowder to the game of chess, from Arabic mathematics and science to the Aristotelianism which Averroes and Avicenna transmitted to the thinkers of the European Renaissance, from Hindu fables to theories of art, from loan-words in our vocabularies to *materia medica*, from wallpaper to theosophies. The historian might also consider the beginnings of all "comparative" studies, including linguistics and religion; and if he elects to consider the most modern of all problems, he would delve, as has C. G. Jung, into the psychology of the unconscious in the light of the ancient scriptures of the East.

The question of the Occidental debt to the Orient is thus of the greatest significance. The vital issues which it raises for the future were suggested by the Irish poet George Russell (AE) in *The Living Torch*. "If Europe," he wrote, "is to have a new renaissance comparable with that which came from the wedding of Christianity with the Greek and Latin culture it must, I think, come from a second wedding of Christianity with the culture of the East." Romain Rolland in his *Prophets of the New India* raised a somewhat analogous question as he viewed American life. "It would be a matter of deep interest to know exactly how far the American spirit had been impregnated, directly or indirectly, by the infiltration of Hindu thought during the nineteenth century," he wrote, "for there can be no doubt that it has contributed to the strange moral and religious mentality of the United States. . . . It is . . . a psychological problem of the first order, intimately connected with the history of our civilization."

For a brief survey, we do well to begin with the opening up of the world by Columbus and Vasco da Gama and to restrict ourselves to a few of the purely intellectual consequences. The first fact to be noted about the voyagers of the late fifteenth and sixteenth centuries is that they opened the way to self-discovery no less than to unknown lands ripe for economic exploitation. They disclosed to Europeans as never before their ignorance, their poverty, and their limited intellectual horizons. At first they appear to have been most impressed by the wealth of the Indies, and the flora and fauna of Oceania and the New World. The Occidental mind, even that of Western Europe, was adjusted to a time when the Mediterranean was the center of civilization. Centuries were to pass before the historical record of all that the various branches of the human family had accomplished and thought were to be unfolded. The discoveries began at a time when almost all Europeans regarded the Pope as God's vicar over all the known races of mankind. The record, furthermore, must be viewed against a background of momentous changes in the intellectual life of Europe itself. It embraces all that Occidental peoples have found overseas, domesticated in their homelands, learned about foreign ethical and political systems, sought to formulate for the conduct of their own lives, and finally, are studying with the critical apparatus of modern scholarship.

In the early pages of such a record, wild guesses, errors, and misconceptions are to be expected. But to ignore or minimize the work of the early explorers of Oriental culture is ill-advised. One does well to remember that at first:

> Geographers in Afric maps
> Make savage pictures fill their gaps,
> And o'er inhabitable downs
> Place elephants instead of towns.

Ignorance of the physical world before arduous and dangerous exploration led to the inner secrets of unknown continents has never been regarded as a mark of weakness in the European intellect. Similar ignorance of the inner spirit or meaning of foreign cultures cannot be fairly regarded as a mark of dullness of mind and insensitivity of soul. Marlowe in *Tamburlaine the Great* put into the mouth of his dying hero words which clearly epitomize the spirit of the first European explorers:

> Give me a map; then let me see how much
> Is left for me to conquer all the world,
> That these, my boys, may finish all my wants.

> .    .    .    .    .

> Look here, my boys; see what a world of ground
> Lies westward from the midst of Cancer's line,
> Unto the rising of this earthly globe;
> Whereas the sun, declining from our sight,

3

Begins the day with our Antipodes!
And I shall die, and this unconquered?

Shakespeare in *Much Ado About Nothing* also suggested what such exploration did to the European imagination: "I will go on the slightest errand now to the Antipodes that you can devise to send me on; I will fetch you a toothpicker now from the farthest inch of Asia; bring you the length of Prester John's foot; fetch you a hair off the great Cham's beard. . . ."

Clearly the Europeans who opened up the world were avid for knowledge. While many were lamentably intent on economic exploitation of foreign peoples and lands, not a small number valued more the cultural legacies slowly and simultaneously made known.

## II

The persistent ignoring by cultural historians of the Oriental contribution to the imaginative and spiritual life of Europe stems of course from their sense of values and their home-keeping tendencies. It rises no less from the sentiment that the record consists chiefly of manifestations of credulity and ignorance. Such manifestations are, nevertheless, useful suggestions of the realms of human experience in which Orientals and Occidentals will in time discover common ground and realize what they may contribute to each other. For perspective, one may turn to the dawn of modern European history and illustrate through a book, a writer, and a saints' legend, the varying ways in which European thought, literature, and institutions, have been influenced from abroad.

It is a little known but surprising fact that the first book printed in England, entitled the *Dictes and Sayings of the Philosophers* and published by William Caxton in 1477, was basically Oriental and reflected the centuries-old European debt to Indian folklore and Arabic wisdom literature. The first compiler, according to the editor of the version published in 1941 by the Early English Text Society, was Abu'l Wefa Mubeschschir ben Fatik, an Arab philosopher living in Damascus probably about 1053 A.D. No question in the history of Oriental-Occidental cultural relations is more intriguing than the origin of the popular sentiment that the East is the treasure-house of wisdom, of profound insights, and of

4

occult knowledge. The celebrated *Dictes* may be taken as significant evidence of this belief in the literature of Western Europe.

Behind the book is a very complex collection of sources which stem through Arabic and Greek versions of fables, parables, and moral apologues migrating westward from India, of Alexandrine Neo-Platonism, and of the work of Arab philosophers who served as mediators in the intellectual life of Mediterranean peoples. The work on which Caxton based his text appears to have been compiled in Latin about 1350. It was translated into French in 1410, and the English version was made by Anthony Woodville, Earl Rivers, tutor to the youthful Prince of Wales, who thought it "full necessary to my said lord the understanding thereof." The time was the tumultuous period of the Wars of the Roses, when the partisans of Edward IV sought refuge at the court of Charles the Bold of Burgundy. Caxton had served as "Governor of the English Nation abroad," that is, as business agent for the Merchant Adventurers, and had been able to render frequent aid to his expatriated countrymen, who with him found ample opportunity to acquaint themselves with Oriental fables and proverbs transmitted from Moorish Spain into France. They were doubtless also introduced to Latin collections of Oriental lore circulating on the Continent. Under these circumstances, it was not by accident that Caxton's first book should be representative of the literature which had caught the attention of men who lived in days when the changes and chances of life were unpredictable, and when on all sides individuals sought stability. The popularity of the *Dictes* in England is indicated by the fact that Caxton himself brought out three editions. Its title is perhaps deceptive, for it was in no sense an exposition of Oriental philosophy. On the contrary, it contained numerous pleasant stories for the seasoning of conversation, many quotable maxims or proverbial sayings such as one finds appended to Æsopic or Buddhist tales, and parables which are reminiscent of the Apocrypha. This curious and historically significant book marks the beginnings in English publishing of hundreds of volumes which have presented to Western readers the distillation of ages of human experience in the East. It marks the beginning also of that vague exoticism which has never ceased to be an element in our popular literature. In every subsequent generation some writer of note has sought to satisfy the demands of his contemporaries for the exotic.

Sir Thomas North, the translator of Plutarch and Marcus Aurelius, is an excellent example. In 1570 he published *The Morall Philosophie of Doni*, a book whose title unfortunately fails to suggest its Oriental origin. North used for his translation the Italian work of Antonio Francesco Doni, a journalist of Florence whose interest was in the ancient fabulists of the East and who, like Boccaccio, wove many an oriental tale into the popular *novelle* of his time. *The Morall Philosophie* is an English version of an Italian adaptation of the Pehlevi version of original Indian collections of Buddhist birth-stories and moral apologues. Here is clear indication of the popularity of such stories in the West and of the knotty bibliographical problems involved in tracing their origin, various adaptations, and extensive diffusion. The Oriental materials in such collections as the popular *Gesta Romanorum* and *Seven Wise Masters* of the Middle Ages reflect the same interest. In the East had been discovered a storehouse of narrative and maxims which contributed to the *exempla* of monkish preachers, to the tales of a writer as great as Chaucer, and to later Elizabethan dramatists. But North's *Morall Philosophie* was more than a collection of incident useful for later writers in the construction of plays and tales. It came from the hand of a great English stylist, who possessed the art of saying great things simply, and who contributed richly to the development of Tudor prose. One is tempted to extensive quotation, no less than to an exposition of the ways in which Doni's Italian vivacity tempered the Oriental gravity of the originals. But brief lines from the apostrophe "To the Reader" will suffice to indicate its foreign source and character:

Of wordes and of examples is a sundrie sort of speache
One selfe same thing to mindes of men in sundrie wise
    they teache.
Wordes teach but those that understande the language
    that they heare:
But things, to men of sundrie speache, examples make
    appeare.
So larger is the speache of beasts, though mens more certaine bee:

6

But yet so larger as conceyte is able them to see.
Such largenesse yet at length to bring to certaine use and
  plane,
God gaue such grace to beasts, that they should Indian
  speach attaine.
And then they learnde Italian tongue, and now at length
  they can,
By help of North, speake English well to query English
  man.

It is customary to illustrate the appeal of the Orient to the European imagination in the Middle Ages by the popular travel books and diaries of Marco Polo and his contemporaries. There can be doubt neither of the stimulus of such works, nor of the fact that the fictitious *Travels* of Sir John Mandeville owed its being to the current demand for more works like those of the monks and merchants who on overland journeys to Cathay observed the wealth of unknown peoples and reported the wonders they had seen. But the legend of *Barlaam and Josaphat*, with variants in Greek, Latin, French, German, Swedish, Dutch, and even Icelandic, reveals in a different fashion what the European mind wished to believe and could do with a few meager facts. The legend has been called "the first religious romance published in a Western language." It contains much of the life of Buddha himself, birth stories from the Buddhist canon, tales from the *Panchatantra* and other Oriental myths, combined with Christian traditions. Whatever the version by which it entered the Western world, beginning with a Sanskrit prototype and passing from Pehlevi to Arabic to Georgian to Greek and finally into many other European forms, the moral tone of the legend pleased Europeans. It appears in the *Exempla* of Jacques de Vitry and also in the *Gesta Romanorum*. And of all unexpected results—it led to the canonization of its hero, Buddha, as a saint of Rome and Byzantium.

The gist of the story can be briefly told. Christian teaching had found its way into the East, and many converts had been made in the dominions of an Indian king. To this king a son was born, at whose birthday feast Chaldæan oracles prophesied that the infant would grow in wisdom, abandon the religion of his fathers,

7

and embrace the true faith. The distressed father tried to keep his son ignorant of the miseries of the world, built for him delightful palaces, surrounded him with all that was beautiful, and, as in the legendary life of Buddha himself, gave instructions that the youth should never be shown sickness, old age, and death. A Christian hermit gained access to the young prince and instructed him in Christian doctrines. The prince, converted and baptized, resolved to give up all his wealth and pleasures. In some versions he even converted his own father and many of his subjects. Eventually he followed his teacher into the desert, became a hermit, and died in the true faith, a Christian saint. Within the frame of this simple tale, there was offered opportunity for storytellers to interweave innumerable parables and Oriental apologues, especially at the debates before the king's court on the merits of the various religions of the time which preceded the prince's renunciation of the world. In these disputations one may find evidence of an early attempt at "comparative" religion, although the real object of the book was manifestly a simple exposition of the principal doctrines of the Christian faith.

Many scholars besides T. W. Rhys Davids in his work on *Buddhist Birth-Stories* have examined the records which pertain to the canonization of Buddha as St. Josaphat. Barlaam, the Christian hermit of the story, need not concern us here. What is significant is that the legend of the converted Indian prince became widely accepted as authentic, and his name was included in various local lists of deceased saints and martyrs which were recited in the so-called Canon of the Mass. Religious men of local celebrity were often included for that purpose in the local lists or Diptychs, and their names in time became honored throughout Christendom. The confessors and martyrs thus honored in the 'Canon' were in that sense said to have been canonized. For a long time local ecclesiastics were permitted to insert such names in their Diptychs. After 1170 Pope Alexander III decreed that the power of canonization, so far as the Roman Church was concerned, would be confined to the Pope himself. With the passing centuries the names in various martyrologies were thus no longer inserted in the Canon but were repeated in the part of the service called the 'Prime,' although the term 'canonized' was still applied to the holy men mentioned in them. Finally, as the increasing number of martyrologies led to confusion and raised doubts about the exclusive power of the Pope to canonize, in 1585-90 Cardinal Baronius drew up a *Martyrologium* which was to be used throughout the Western Church. In it were included not only the saints canonized at Rome but also those already canonized elsewhere who were then recognized by the Pope and the College of Rites as saints of the Catholic Church of Christ. Included in this list were "The holy Saints Barlaam and Josaphat, of India, on the borders of Persia, whose wonderful acts Saint John of Damascus has described."

Behind this story of the Christian canonization of Buddha lie two facts. The first is the legend itself, so impressive in its account of the conversion of the Oriental prince that its authenticity was not questioned and the hero became a saint. The second factor involves early linguistic confusion of names. The name Ioasaph is derived from Bodhisattva, the title of one destined to attain the dignity of a buddha. In Arabic Bodhisattva became Bodasaph. Later, since Arabic B and Y differ only by a single diacritical point under the character, Bodasaph was misread as Iodasaph in Georgian and Ioasaph in Greek. These names were later rendered by Western European adapters of the legend into the more familiar Josaphat or Jehoshaphat.

The amazing vitality and adaptability of Oriental myth, legend, and wisdom-literature are also clearly suggested by the bare facts noted about the work of Caxton and North. The synthetic character of Christianity itself is likewise indicated in the saints' legend of Buddha. These popular signs of 'orientalism' in Medieval Europe are a meager suggestion that the East had contributed to its thought and imagination before the opening of the sea route around the Cape of Good Hope. As navigators and merchant mariners in increasing numbers returned from far voyages with the wealth of the Indies in their galleons to enrich the material civilization of Western Europe, they may have been ignorant of the significance of the mystery cults of the eastern Mediterranean world and of the extent to which Arab philosophers and Neo-Platonists had considered the ancient philosophies of the East. But they no less represented a cultural tradition that had long been willing to accommodate itself to new modes of thought, and a credulous public whose curiosity had been awakened. In the following centuries which have been labeled the Renaissance and the Enlightenment, and which form the prelude to contemporary European and American thought, some fearful and a few amazing things were to be done by Europeans with the unfolding knowledge about Oriental peoples and their ways of life.

## III

After the voyages of Columbus and Vasco da Gama in 1492 and 1498, nearly a century and a half passed before Europeans organized anything like systematic study of the "rarities" of the Indies, which consisted chiefly of unknown flora and fauna, and of facts about foreign peoples, their traits, institutions, racial ideals, and religious beliefs. Astronomers, however, soon sailed with the mariners for the purpose of studying eclipses in distant regions, and scientists began to reconsider traditional European knowledge in the light of new facts. Aristotle's system of natural history, it was discovered, accommodated itself inadequately to new specimens of plants and animals found in other areas of the world and hitherto unknown to Europe. Clearly, the progress of Renaissance science was influenced by Eastern discovery.

This scientific interest soon crystallized into organized societies. As early as 1572 a Society of Antiquaries was formed in London and continued until it was dissolved by James I. A Royal Academy was projected in 1616-17; and in 1645 a group of English intellectuals, weary of political and religious turmoil, began weekly meetings in Gresham College. From this informal group, called by Sir Robert Boyle the "invisible College," there eventually grew the Royal Society of London, which was chartered by the King on April 22, 1662. On the Continent similar societies sprang up. In 1666 the French Academy of Science was projected. The extant records of such societies show that their attention was not directed to European antiquities alone.

How systematic and far-reaching were the efforts of the English Royal Society to gather new knowledge regarding the overseas world and its inhabitants may be judged from the "Directions for Sea-men, bound for far Voyages," published in its *Philosophical Transactions* on January 8, 1666. In that document appears the following statement:

It being the Design of the *R. Society*, for the better attaining of the End of their Institution, to study *Nature* rather than *Books*, and from the Observations, made of the Phænomena and Effects she presents, to compose a History of Her, as may hereafter serve to build a solid and Useful Philosophy upon; They have from time to time given order to several of their Members to draw up both *Inquiries* of things Observable in forrain Countries, and *Directions* for the Particulars, they desire chiefly to be informed about . . . and set down some *Directions for Sea-men* going into the *East & West Indies*, the better to capacitate them for making such observations abroad.

Seamen were instructed "to keep an exact Diary, delivering at their return a fair Copy thereof to the *Lord High Admiral*," another to the Duke of York, and a third to the Royal Society itself. The seamen were also to prepare careful accounts "of the Inhabitants themselves, both *Natives* and *Strangers*," and to enquire "about *Traditions* concerning all particular things, relating to that Country" and "regarding *Learning* or *Skill* in the *Answerer*." The Society asserted that the instructions were "thought fit to be publisht, that the Inquisitive and Curious, might, by such Assistance be invited not to delay their searches of matters, that are so highly conducive to the improvement of *True Philosophy*, and the well fare of *Mankind*."

As late as 1704, in Churchill's *Collection of Voyages* appeared an "Introductory Discourse" in which the writer "set down some general Rules which may concern all Travellers to observe." The suggestions clearly reveal the wealth of material which those who conscientiously observed the rules were to bring home for study:

> They are in the first place to consider, that they do not go into other Countries to pass through them, and divert themselves with the present sight of such Curiosities as they meet with. . . . If they will make an advantage of their Trouble and Cost, they must not pass through a Country as if they carried an Express, but make a reasonable stay at all places where there are Antiquities, or any Rarities to be observed; and not to think that because others have writ on that 'Subject, there is no more to be said. . . . Let them

therefore always have a Table-Book at hand to set down every thing worth remembering, and then at night more methodically transcribe the Notes they have taken in the day. The principal Heads by which to regulate their Observations are these, Climate, Government, Power, Places of Strength, Cities of note, Religion, Language, Coins, Trade, Manufactures, Wealth, Universities, Antiquities, Libraries, Collections of Rarities, Arts and Artists, Publick Structures, Roads, Bridges, Woods, Mountains, Customs, Habits, Laws, Privileges, strange Adventures, surprising Accidents, Rarities both natural and artificial, the Soil, Plants, Animals, and whatsoever may be curious, diverting, or Profitable.

These deliberate efforts to secure scientific data regarding foreign countries and peoples had, however, in a way been anticipated by the first independent compilers of cosmographies and universal histories. In 1544 Sebastian Munster published at Basel his *Cosmographia Universalis,* in which he surprised later cartographers by his desire to secure the latest knowledge on the history, ethnography, and geography of the world. Richard Eden's English translation of this book appeared in 1553. More than two decades earlier a Dutchman, Joannes Boemus, published in Latin, presumably at Antwerp in 1520, *The Fardle of Facions* which was translated by William Watreman for London publication in 1555 and contained "the aunciente maners, customes, and Lawes, of the peoples enhabiting the two partes of the earth, called Affricke and Asie." This work is described by Edward Godfrey Cox in his copious *Reference Guide to the Literature of Travel* as "the first scientific approach to ethnology." Several hundred titles are included in Cox's two-volume compilation of cosmographies and travel books. Hakluyt and Purchas were but two of a tribe of compilers who continued their work well into the eighteenth century, collecting the journals of travelers overseas and publishing them as "curious and entertaining" for an avid public. From these works other compilers set about the task of producing early encyclopedias with such titles as *The World Displayed, The Present State of the Universe,* and *The Travellour's Guide and Historian's Faithful Companion.*

In the light of these facts it is not historically presumptuous to consider anew the amazing revival of utopian literature. The long interval between Plato's *Republic* and St. Augustine's *City of God* is marked by an amazing dearth of utopian literature. The period following the appearance of the Latin version of More's *Utopia* in 1516, on the other hand, is a distinct contrast. Johann Valentin Andreae produced his *Christianopolis* in 1619; Francis Bacon the *New Atlantis* in 1627, Tomasso Campanella the *City of the Sun* in 1637, and James Harrington the *Oceania* in 1656. Many explanations may be offered for the shift in man's longing from the heavenly utopia of the Middle Ages to the earthly paradise of the Renaissance and the Enlightenment. To find one explanation in the startling discoveries of contrasts between European society and that of overseas peoples, with their differing scales of value and modes of thought, is not to overreach the evidence.

From the beginning of the European's direct contact with civilized Orientals there grew within him a contrasting sense of his own poverty, and even of his social needs and inadequacies. Astonished by the amazing new facts constantly presented by returning voyagers, European thinkers sensed their own provincialism and the artificiality of their society. In the New World were the Amerindians who apparently lived in freedom, without extreme restrictions of law, blessed with nature's bounties, often disdainful of gold for its own sake, in Edenic conditions conjectured to be original with man's first life on earth. In the Orient were highly civilized peoples who restricted Europeans to a few trading posts on the coastal fringes of their countries and constantly demonstrated amazing powers of cultural resistance, apparently preferring their own ways of life and thought to those of the white visitors.

It would be preposterous to assert that significant "orientalism" is to be found in More's *Utopia* and Bacon's *New Atlantis*. But it is historically accurate to place them in the intellectual context of a time when an exotic dream had seized the European imagination. Few utopian writers of the Renaissance had any scientifically accurate information about the life of Oriental peoples. On the other hand, consider the unequivocal opening sentence of the *New Atlantis:* "We sailed from Peru, where we had continued for the space of one whole year, for China and Japan, by the

13

South Sea, taking with us victuals for twelve months; and had good winds from the east, though soft and weak, for five months space and more." Researchers have suggested Bacon's probable debt to William Adams's letters and reports from Japan to the English East India Company, and have argued that a considerable part of the narrative in Bacon's book is based on actual travel records. More's *Utopia*, furthermore, had in its character Raphael Hythloday a sunburned sailor-philosopher who had sailed the seas and seen for himself the life of foreign lands. Of More's debt to Vespucci's Journals there is scant doubt.

The chief themes of the utopian books were of course basically European: the tyranny of princes, the problems of private property, social equality, class distinctions, education, and the advancement of science. But many of the themes were studied in the light of social systems prevailing abroad. The significance of the island "utopias" of the Renaissance is that they marked the first stage, both in their setting in Oceania and in their intellectual outlook, of the progressive tendency of Europeans to think of their own institutions and traditional modes of thought and life in a world context.

Utopian literature was heavily didactic and was not widely read. It was therefore inevitable that from the excitement of the times there should also come another *genre* of literature, somewhat similar in purpose but wider in appeal. The popularity of authentic travel books inevitably suggested to stay-at-home Londoners and Parisians the writing of "imaginary" voyages, of which Swift's *Gulliver* is a classic example. "Philosophic" voyages, distinguished from the imaginary type chiefly in academic terms, also appeared. Armchair travelers have for centuries delighted to inform their contemporaries about the maladjustments of the times and the superior ways in which the business of life is conducted abroad. Thus, like the greater utopian writers, many lesser scribblers sought to sugar-coat panaceas for social ills by offering their work in the guise of a popular travel book. Such literature may be likened to the "problem" novels of modern propaganda. They were intended for instruction and as such represented a sophisticated literature, at their worst merely imaginative potboilers, at their best a new medium of social satire. The expository and historical studies of the literature which have come from the pens of scholars like William A. Eddy, Geoffrey Atkinson, and Philip Babcock Gove will offer the interested reader amazing facts regarding the far-reaching excursions of the "imaginary" voyagers. The significance of their work lies in the revalation of the gradual diffusion of knowledge, the suggestion of place of the Orient in the popular consciousness, and indication of the extent to which writers exploited the current interest.

The opinion of a trustworthy observer of the time may suggest both the popularity of travel literature and its influence. Anthony Ashley Cooper, the third Earl of Shaftesbury, published in 1711 his *Characteristicks of Men, Manners, Opinions, Times,* an illuminating survey of the taste and fashions of his generation. He noted the audience for which travelers wrote and editors compiled: "Our relish or taste must of necessity grow barbarous, whilst barbarian customs, savage manners, Indian wars, and wonders of terra incognita, employ our leisure hours and are the chief materials to furnish out a library." He added, not too sympathetically: "These are in our present days what books of chivalry were in those of our forefathers. I know not what faith our ancestors may have had in the stories of their giants, their dragons, and St. Georges. But for our faith indeed, as well as our taste in this other way of reading, I must confess I cannot consider it without astonishment." Shaftesbury also indicated that the theosophies and Orient-inspired cults of contemporary Europe and America began more than two centuries ago. "It must certainly be something else than incredulity," wrote the amazed and observant Earl, "which fashions the taste and judgment of many gentlemen whom we hear censured as atheists, for attempting to philosophize after a newer manner than any known of late. . . . I can produce many anathematized authors who, if they want a true Israelitish faith, can make amends by a Chinese or Indian one. If they are short in Syria or the Palestine, they have their full measure in America or Japan. . . . Though Christian miracles may not so well satisfy them, they dwell with the highest contentment on the prodigies of Moorish and Pagan countries."

Shaftesbury's strictures on the taste of his contemporaries must be considered in the light of the current democratization of knowledge and the heady effects of stimulating ideas and suggestions from abroad. The scholasticism of earlier generations had created a learned caste and largely limited the intellectual life of Europe to an aristocracy. But after 1500 the world with all its wonders was slowly unfolded before every mentally awake man, however scant his education. Experimental science, as represented by the Royal Society, which had sought the aid of uneducated mariners who knew no Latin and made their reports in the vernacular, was no longer restricted to the ancient seats of learning. Once the topics and modes of speculation and contemplation had been removed from everyday subjects. Now the gradual extension of geographical knowledge compelled a shift to other objects of thought. It is not surprising that the common man of Shaftesbury's day had not the poise and balanced knowledge which would deter him from philosophizing "after a newer manner than any known of late."

It is from the books read by such men, no less than in the records of scientific societies devoted to the gathering of accurate and useful knowledge, that the beginnings of Oriental-Occidental cultural relations must be traced. Two questions dominated the thought of the Renaissance and the Enlightenment. The first was the true character of man and the secret of social felicity. The second involved the relation between traditional modes of thought and the new scientific temper. Both were deeply affected by the exploratory spirit of the times. Neither religion nor social dogma had immunity against change. To the medieval records and systems of thought there had been added an immeasurably extended store of useful knowledge by observers who, while not unwilling to embroider a tale in the telling, had much to gain by being accurate. The "virtuosi" of the Renaissance were laying the foundations of methodical investigation and of all branches of modern comparative studies.

# IV

The idealization of China was the first outstanding result of the impact of the Orient upon the European imagination. There had been previous Oriental "vogues" in the minor arts, in personal costume, and even in architecture. Samuel C. Chew's illuminating study, *The Crescent and the Rose*, an historical exposition of the relations between Islam and England during the Renaissance,

Architectural Chinoiserie. *From Paul Decker, Chinese Architecture, Civil and Ornamental, London, 1759.*

17

clearly indicates that even though Mohammed was widely considered an impostor and the centuries-old struggle with the infidel had not been forgotten, osmosis had long been active between Moorish and Christian civilizations when they met. But none of its consequences compares in import with the results of the "discovery" of Confucius and China.

The reason may not be far to seek. There has always been a close relation between the dominant mood of a time, the themes of its literature, and the trends of its speculative thought. No fact stands out more clearly before the reader of travel-utopian literature and the writings of Europeans viewing mankind "from China to Peru" than the growing concept of the Noble Savage. Rousseau formulated the idea of the unspoiled child of nature. In the forests of the New World and on the islands of Oceania, explorers discovered this child of nature, living by instincts uncorrupted by arbitrary social codes, presumably expressing in his songs Edenic sentiments and in his religion a morality untouched by knavish priests. He became a stock idea of poets who had never seen an Amerindian. The concept of the Noble Sage, with Confucius as a model, while not so widely discussed was no less impressive, however.

Whether the Noble Sage or the Noble Savage is the more important concept in the literary and intellectual history of the eighteenth century is an unprofitable issue to discuss. The fact is that both concepts existed—and were complementary. If the Noble Savage had more songs inscribed in his honor by poets, the Noble Sage was more exhaustively studied, dignified by debate, and idealized by thoughtful men. The reason can be readily stated. China had a great literature which was gradually being made known; the primitive natives of Oceania and America had no books. China had one of the oldest civilizations of the world, founded upon an ethic and a political philosophy which could be studied both in its textual precedents and in its current operation. The noble savages were simply children of nature offering in comparison meager materials for study save to the European poet whose romantic sentimentalism was awakened by dreams of uninhibited love and freedom from social restraint. Confucius was to become the idol of philosophers who seriously pondered

18

a social order founded upon the Deistic concepts of natural goodness, natural morality, and natural religion.

The neo-classical dictum that "Nature is everywhere the same" had led to the basic assumption that Reason is identical in all men and that in all parts of the world are to be found the truths by which mankind should live. As early as 1594 Bishop Hooker had written in his *Ecclesiastical Polity:* "The general and perpetual voice of men is as the sentence of God himself. For that which all men have at all times learned, Nature herself must needs have taught; and God being the author of Nature, her voice is but his instrument." This proposition was widely accepted both by scholastic philosophers and by the more rationalistic orthodox divines. Some agreed that all men shared the light that lighteth everyman coming into the world, but insisted that the light of Nature needed in addition the Gospel for a candlestick. Despite shadings of difference in the interpretations of Hooker's principle, however, it was widely agreed that the true principles of morality are throughout human nature the same in kind, though different in degree, according to the organization of various minds which had been perverted by prejudice and false associations. By the right analysis of human records the world over, particularly of those standards of taste and conduct which at all times revealed the uncorrupted feelings of men, it was assumed there would be discovered a universal and true principle for the conduct of life. There thus developed during the Enlightenment an appeal to the "Consensus Gentium" in addition to the appeal to Reason.

Charles Blount's *Oracles of Reason,* 1693, may be taken as an epitome of Deistic thought, although there were differences and shadings of opinion among its professors. The fundamental tenet of the system appears to have been that: "Natural Religion is the Belief we have of an eternal intellectual Being, and of the duty which we owe him, manifested to us by our Reason, without Revelation or positive Law." Crucial in the controversies of the Deists with the orthodox divines was the question of the adequacy of natural religion to save the heathen who are ignorant of the Christian revelation and who merely "live up to the height of their natural Reason or Religion." Upon such questions Blount wrote: "I answer; This is to dive too far in God's secrets, to conclude them all damned in all Ages, to whom that revealed Light

19

came not. The Apostle says, *They shall be judged by the Law of Nature. . . ."* In sum, the Deists insisted that God had struck the idea of himself upon the human mind in all times and places. Morality certainly, even religion itself some argued, could become a positive science if men would give their effort to ascertaining its universal manifestations.

The geographical range and the purpose of deistic speculation are suggested in a pamphlet published by Thomas Chubb in 1732 which reveals enough of the argument in its full-length title:

> The Sufficiency of Reason in Matters of Religion, farther Considered. Wherein is Shewn, That *Reason,* when carefully used and followed, is to everyman, who is answerable to God for his actions, under any or all the most disadvantageous circumstances he can possibly fall into, whether he resides in *China,* or at the *Cape of Good Hope,* a sufficient guide in matters of religion; that is, it is sufficient to guide him to God's favor, and the happiness of another World.

There was ample opposition to Deism; and among its professors there were limitations to the use actually made of available knowledge about a "religio generis humani." Dean Swift, for example, said that the system contained "nothing which could not presently be comprehended by the weakest noodle."

Despite their claim to universal views, the Deists were clearly creatures of their own age in their agreement that "Enthusiasm" was a temper of mind in which the imagination had got the better of judgment. Boswell's account of Doctor Johnson's observations on the "inner light" to which "some methodists pretended" illuminates the common attitude. The possibility of private revelations, said Johnson, was "a principle utterly incompatible with social and civil security," for if a man lays claim to channels of insight and pretends to a principle of action unknown to other men, "how can I tell what that person may be prompted to do? When a person professes to be governed by a written ascertained law, I can then know where to find him."

The majority of the Deists shared this view, which explains why they quite consistently ignored the religions of India. That they were not entirely ignorant of Vedantic thought may be as-

20

sumed, since opportunities for studying the religions and social life of India were no less available than for exploring the ethical foundations of Chinese society. Even Swift mentioned Yoga when in 1710 he published his essay on *The Mechanical Operation of the Spirit*. He noted that "the *Jauguis*, or enlightened Saints of *India*, see all their Visions, by help of an acquired straining and pressure of the Eyes." The Deists consistently opposed priests and all ecclesiastical systems based on "mysteries." They argued that the way to redeem civilization and to promote the moral life of mankind was to strip society of all its social vanities and religions of the accretions of time and prejudice. Thus they ignored the transcendental in the world's religions. Spiritual disciplines, especially, seemed to them unnecessary and, if directed to idealistic ends, distinctly dangerous. Yoga was but another manifestation of Enthusiasm and was completely irrational.

Thus the practical, social-minded Confucius became the Noble Sage of the Rationalists of the Enlightenment. Like them, he eschewed the mysteries of religion and transcendental speculation, devoting himself instead to an understanding of man's moral nature and the study of precedents. Confucianism recognized chiefly the guidance of reason and of carefully laid moral traditions. Herein lay its affinity with the current temper. The Deists and their contemporaries, as Professor Arthur O. Lovejoy has pointed out, found in the words *Natura* and *Natio* profoundly antithetic connotations, feeling that men should emancipate themselves from tribal partialities if they are to be true to nature in matters both of religion and of artistic taste. They also attempted, with the scientific temper of the time, to study the world's religions in the light of newly acquired intelligence and needs. Thus they did much to raise the level of European thinking about foreign peoples. Despite their prejudices, they made the eighteenth century perhaps the most sincerely cosmopolitan in European history.

Various writers soon turned to China and the Confucian texts for material to support their arguments, whether moral, political, or religious. Voltaire was perhaps the most outspoken of all European admirers of China—with Confucius as its ethical preceptor and the Emperor as its philosopher-king. In his article "De la Chine" in the *Dictionnaire philosophique* he answered skeptics who pointed out Chinese ignorance of Western science. The Chinese, he argued, were superior to Europeans in more important things, for they stressed the ethical values upon which the State should be built. "One may be a very poor physicist and an excellent moralist," Voltaire wrote. "Thus it is in morals, in political economy, in agriculture, that the Chinese have perfected themselves. We have taught them all the rest; but in these matters we ought to be their disciples. . . . The Constitution of their empire is in truth the best that there is in the world." He recognized the superstition of the lower classes, which travelers had not failed to note, protesting meanwhile "the fact remains that four thousand years ago, when we did not know how to read, they knew everything useful of which we boast today." Voltaire insisted that the pure religion of Nature, which the civilized peoples of Europe had lost, was to be found uncorrupted in China. And he exclaimed lyrically, "Worship God and practise justice—this is the sole religion of the Chinese literati. . . . O Thomas Aquinas, Scotus, Bonaventure, Francis, Dominic, Luther, Calvin, canons of Westminster, have you anything better? For four thousand years this religion so simple and so noble, has endured in absolute integrity; and it is probable that it may be much more ancient."

Such rhapsodies may appear little more than expressions of admiration which have no social implications. But among the Physiocrats and Encyclopedists of France there was also widespread interest in Confucian ethics and the Chinese theory of government. Numerous *philosophes* sought, as Adolf Reichwein has shown in his *China and Europe* and G. F. Hudson in *Europe and China*, for an enlightened theory which would justify political absolutism. Travel books and Jesuit missionary reports from abroad, the latter published serially for nearly half a century beginning in 1717 as *Lettres édifiantes et curieuses*, were their chief sources of information. Men like Quesnay, called by his disciples "the Confucius of Europe," valued Chinese philosophy above the Greek and sought a foundation for the human order in a divine order, a way whereby the Tao of the world or the cosmic realities of Natural Law might be used in France to establish the relations between the people and the monarchy. In the face of growing democratic unrest during the decades preceding the French Revolution, there arose a sincere desire to discover for France a moral foundation for a revitalized and proper sense of the relation between the citizenry and the monarchy. The Chinese conception of the relation between the masses and the Emperor contributed much to Quesnay's physiocratic doctrines. He announced that "China is a state founded on science and natural law, whose concrete development it represents." So live indeed was French interest, and so attractive the Chinese concept of government, that Louis XIV was actually induced to follow the example of the Chinese Emperors, solemnly guiding a plow at a public ceremony opening the Spring tilling.

Enthusiasm for the Chinese theory of the State seems to have been no less great in Germany. Leibnitz had earlier revealed his own interest in Confucian ethics, especially in the *De Novissima Sinica* which had appeared in 1697. The utterances of Christian Wolff, however, reveal the current view that the Chinese Emperor represented the Greek ideal of the philosopher-king actually institutionalized among men—and the dangers which proponents of the divine right of kings saw in the concept. In an oration entitled *De Sinarum Philosophia Practica*, delivered June 12, 1721 before the University of Halle on the occasion of his resignation from the Prorectorship, Wolff aroused a storm of protest. His remarks seem innocuous enough to modern minds: "What the Love of Truth, which *Philosophy* itself inspires, can effect in *Rulers*, the *Chinese* Emperors Yao and Xun are pregnant Instances, who when they would bring the Empire, founded by their Predecessors, to a Pitch of greater Perfection, and yet attempt nothing rashly, passing over their own Sons, they chose for Successors, and made Partners of the Empire those they judged equal to so great a Task. . . . Xun was so great a Lover of Truth, that distrusting his own abilities, he would know the Opinions of others both about himself and his Actions. . . . Here you see the Effect of *Philosophy* in philosophical Rulers, and that the same holds in a *ruling* Philosopher; Confucius the great *Chinese* Philosopher shews by his own Example." Wolff was branded a dangerous, pernicious character and ordered by the King of Prussia under pain of immediate death to quit the University of Halle in twenty-four hours, and the kingdom in forty-eight.

In England there were many echoes of the Continental enthusiasm for Confucian ethics and the Chinese system of government.

If the emphases differed slightly it was because England was blessed to a greater degree with parliamentary government. Nevertheless writers found other reasons for admiring the Chinese and for imitating them in the conduct of life. Eustace Budgell, whose *Letter to Cleomenes King of Sparta* appeared in 1731, said: "I have observed, that in *China* no man is a *Gentleman* by his *Birth*, but that the Mandarines, or Gentlemen, become such by their own *Parts* and *Learning*. These Mandarines, by a fundamental Law of the *Chinese* Empire, are allowed to tell the Emperor, in respectful, yet in plain terms, whatever they think is amiss in in his Conduct; and we are assured, that whenever they think the *Honour* of their Prince, or the *Good* of their *Country*, makes it necessary, they never fail to make use of their Privilege."

The Deistic heresy was dignified by receiving the attention of the Church itself. In 1727 appeared *The Bishop of London's First Pastoral Letter to the People of His Diocese . . . Occasioned by Some Late Writings in Favor of Infidelity*. It was the work of Edmund Gibson, then the presiding bishop of the English capital, and was followed by two other letters a few months later. Public interest was so great that several large editions appeared in the space of two years. In 1732 the three documents were printed collectively, and in 1831 were also published, with additions, in New York. The bishop's letters are full of pastoral concern for a continuing belief in an exclusive Christian revelation. The modern reader will find in them an impressive marshaling of facts culled from travel reports stressing heathen idolatry and all forms of social immorality which would discredit both the Noble Savage and the Noble Sage—and their "natural" goodness. "These and the like instances of corruption in worship, doctrine, and practice, which have prevailed, and do still prevail, in several parts of the Heathen world, may further show the insufficiency of *natural reason* to be a guide in religion, and into what monstrous opinions and practices whole nations may be led where that is their guide, without any help from *revelation*," wrote the bishop in his second pastoral letter. Notes accompanying the text refer to religious practices in China, Japan, Formosa, Ceylon, and India.

Gibson's letters did not remain unanswered. Curious is the fact, however, that debate was conducted not upon the merits of the various Oriental systems of belief, but upon the right of free thought in England. For example, in 1729 Matthew Tindal, arch-deist of his time, responded in a printed *Address to the Inhabitants . . . of London and Westminster:* "If Men in *Great Britain* no more than Japan," he argued, owe their religion to chance and education, they are mutually and equally obliged to examine what may be said on all sides. Referring to the Bishop of London he chided: "One wou'd have thought, that a *Protestant* recommending Sincerity in the Choice of Religion, shou'd not have us'd such Arguments, as any *Papist* might have urg'd at the Dawn of the Reformation, to hinder its Increase."

Another curious work, published in London in 1740, was the anonymous *An Irregular Dissertation Occasioned by the Reading of Father Du Halde's History of China.* Its manifest purpose was to ridicule the current idealization of China. Brief extracts will suggest the general character of the English Sinophilism—or Sino-mania, if that word is preferred. Proceeding "in the Road of Fooling," with ill-concealed contempt for the Jesuits, the Deists, and the Chinese, the writer recorded: "I have often heard it made a matter of Wonder, that this wide Empire should have subsisted so very long without any considerable Alteration of Maxims, Customs, Religion, Language, or Habit." The Jesuits he held suspect because they had "sworn allegiance to the *Lama of Italy*" and had failed to make clear "the Administration of *China* to be a little subject to Juggle." As for the social equalities and felicity of Chinese society, he noted pityingly the "poor *Chinese,* who being unable to provide for their *Infants,* are forced to leave them in the Streets, as Preys to the first Dog that lights on them." The book offered many pages of such familiar banalities in European accounts of Oriental life. When, however, the writer turned to what was currently known and regarded as admirable in Chinese ethics, his pages become most enlightening. A serious fault in the Chinese social constitution, he noted, was that Confucian philosophers laid "Weight only on the filial Duty, to the unavoidable neglect of every other." Indeed "they have no Parochial Clergy; but it is the Office of the Mandarin of the Place [merely] to convocate his Charge at stated Times, and there to preach their Duty to them." This was of course the very trait that men like Voltaire and contemporary priest-baiters found most laudable about the Chinese. But the climax of the book is the disclosure that the Chinese "Emperor is the sole priest in his Dominions, a Pope of this Deism." The conclusion can be readily surmised. European Deists had indeed come to a sorry pass when they could do no better than make the heathen Confucius the high priest, if not the Pope, of their own religion!

In 1786 appeared Ely Bates's *A Chinese Fragment, Containing an Enquiry into the Present State of Religion in England,* wherein the author posed as an "intellectual spy" who unceremoniously entered English homes, churches, and Parliament in search of proof that "he that wantonly stabs the *morals* of his country is a villain." Probably none of the writers who rose in protest against the current idealization of China was better informed than Bates; certainly few wrote from a background of more extensive reading or were more interesting. The *Chinese Fragment* appeared three-quarters of a century after Shaftsbury's *Characteristicks.* As Bates surveyed the state of England in his time, he found much reason for alarm, and like Shaftsbury he was most impressed by the advance of infidelity. "A *free thinker,*" he wrote, "can easily assume all shapes; which is not surprizing, if we reflect that a man who holds to nothing is best able to *act* everything; as stage-players who personate all characters are said to have none themselves. He is sometimes seen in the guise of a Chinese, talking notably of Confucius: Anon he is a Turk, and lavishing his praises on Mohammed: Next, perhaps he is a Magian, and then you hear wonderful things of Zoroaster: And thus by turns you may find him a Gymnosophist, a Talapoin, a layman or a priest, a Jew, or even a Christian: His business is to play the opinions of mankind upon one another with an eye to their common destruction, and to erect upon their ruins a monument to *Universal Scepticism. . . .*"

There was doubtless warrant for Bates's strictures against the colorless religionists of his day who assumed all shapes and consequently had no character of their own. C. Delisle Burns recently has wisely pointed out in *The Horizon of Experience* a fallacy which lay at the heart of not only the Deistic view of religion but also all subsequent efforts to arrive at some sort of universal faith: "To reduce Christianity and Buddhism to some 'pure religion' which is neither, would be as fantastic as to grow a flower which was neither a rose nor a lily, but just a flower." The

Deists's dream of a universal religion was therefore unrealistic. All religions and cultures have roots, though the seeds from which they spring may come from far on the wind; and these roots strike deep into the spiritual needs of a people, their traditional ways of thought, and their social milieu. Doubtless the playing of the opinions of mankind upon one another had unsettling effects. Heterodoxy was inevitable in an age of expanding intellectual horizons, when the outlooks of other peoples were being compared with the European, and new admirations were added to all that convention had institutionalized. But there was also much thoughtless tongue-in-cheek affectation of exotic religious belief, largely uninformed. It would be difficult to determine just where to draw the line between a vague catholicity of view which stemmed from an expanding world consciousness, and actual belief in the essential tenets held by "Gymnosophists" and "Talapoins." Genuine objectivity in evaluating religions had not appeared.

Time and a slow maturation of insight into the life, social institutions, and religious beliefs of Orientals were to be required before many Europeans could actually imitate or judiciously live by them. Nevertheless the movements and expressions of opinion that have been noted are not without historical significance. They mark the beginnings of our modern temper. Most important of all, they were the result of attraction, a voluntary turning of many Occidentals to the Orient for an ideal of conduct and life which somehow seemed wanting in their own heritage. In many instances we may find the reason for this turning Eastward in quixotism and the capricious human tendency to affect the bizarre or the sensational. But there is even greater warrant for seeing in it a desire by sincere Occidentals to profit by the experience of maturer cultures, to learn how others handle the business of life, and to appropriate from the race's cultural capital. Men set out to be citizens of the world, not of their native parishes alone. The first steps may have been awkward but they were definitely set in the road which many in subsequent generations were to take.

# V

The general literature of the Renaissance and the eighteenth century, no less than the literature of religious controversy, reflected the impact of the Orient upon the European imagination. Figures of speech based on the East India trade and quotations drawn from Oriental scripture or mythology are evidence of a slowly accumulating body of literary allusion, ornamentation, and reference. In the literature of the Ancients-Moderns controversy, a quarrel which involved the application of modern scientific critical principles to the study of the classics of Greece and Rome, the Orient played no insignificant part.

"Who were the ancients to those who are ancients to us?" was a question Sir William Temple raised in rhetorical defense of the cyclical view of history. If the principle of the cyclical theory was granted, the conclusion seemed obvious: the ancients to the Greeks were the philosophers of India and China. No reader of Temple's essays can fail to be impressed by his wide search for evidence to prove his thesis. William Wotton, Temple's opponent in the English phase of the quarrel which began in France, was no less willing to lay under debt the records of travelers who had visited the Orient.

The so-called literature of Primitivism was another reflection of the uses to which Europeans put increasing knowledge of the Orient in the support of a theory. Another subject worthy of study is the literature of chronology. Nearly a century before Lord Monboddo published in 1773 *Of the Origin and Progress of Language*, Matthew Hale had revealed in his *Primitive Origination of Mankind*, in 1677, how European chronologers had been staggered by reports which implied the apparent discovery, in the dynastic histories of China and mythology of India, of evidence suggesting that man had flourished in the East long before the creation of Adam. If this proved true, the entire Mosaic chronology, the authority of the Bible itself, and the foundations of the Christian faith would be undermined.

Similarly the discovery of unknown languages led to wild speculations. What was the original language of the world? Modern scholarship is no longer concerned with Pre-Adamites, or the theory that the ark of Noah eventually rested on mountains bordering China, that country being subsequently populated by descendants of Noah who were not at the building of Babel. The conclusion that the Chinese language was therefore the primitive and uncorrupted language of the race was seriously argued. Fantastic as such theories may seem, they suggest the extent to which Europeans were driven by new discoveries to a reconsideration of their historic relation to other branches of the human family.

In popular literature the extension of the "comparative" outlook is represented by such classics as Goldsmith's *Citizen of the World* and Montesquieu's *Persian Letters*. The travel observations of Europeans had for more than a century offered to their readers critical comments on Oriental institutions and life. Beginning in France about 1684 with Marana's *Letters of a Turkish Spy*, European writers turned the tables and anticipated the Orientals of our own day who point out Western fallibility. Assuming the role of skeptics, they created fictional observers who, presumably visiting London or Paris for the first time, affected a disconcerting naïveté, offered apparently innocent but fundamentally caustic comments on European civilization, and raised troublesome questions which cast doubts upon the perfection of its institutions and modes of thought. No literature of the time offers a better reflection of the kind of knowledge about the Orient which had become most challenging to the average Westerner.

The device of the mock-spy also offered matchless opportunities for irony and satire in the hands of men seeking to eradicate absolutist concepts, bad taste sanctioned by the "rules" of the Ancients, intellectual error entrenched in ecclesiastical institutions, and social customs or foibles. Much of Goldsmith's *Citizen of the World* may be trivia; but the careful reader will discover that he admired Confucius and Mencius and put some of their best passages to effective use. In the hands of Voltaire, the mock-spy sketch was devastating. At its best, the *genre* marks the beginning of an effort to balance sagaciously the social customs and philosophies of the East and West, to point out that concepts of morals and beauty are infinitely diversified in different times and places, that truth is relative and not to be ascertained through mere logic. An historian has appropriately observed that the human ant-hill of Europe was at last viewed as merely another ant-hill of the world. Essayists who used Persian,

Turkish, Chinese, and Armenian "spies" as their spokesmen, by a mixture of flippancy and sagacity demonstrated the unimportance of many domestic deities, ridiculed hollow platitudes, suggested that some conventions had no more value than pasteboard, and hinted that all European traditions did not correspond in every detail with universal values.

The mock-spy sketch as a mirror of European self-discovery and of the contrast between cultures cannot be better illustrated than by G. Lowes Dickinson's *Letters from A Chinese Official*. The book appeared anonymously in 1903 with the subtitle "Being An Eastern View of Western Civilization." A Cambridge don who for years had devoted himself to Greek studies, Dickinson through wide reading acquired an admiration for Chinese civilization that matched Voltaire's. His letters were clearly written in imitation of the mock-spy sketch which had persisted through two centuries. Their attack on conventional Christianity, on the economic foundations of European civilization, and on its moral and aesthetic outlooks was regarded by readers familiar with the traditional form in which it appeared as the work of a poet blessed with a richly stored mind and a mellow, kindly spirit. Not so by William Jennings Bryan, who had made little more than a tourist's visit to China where he was doubtless feted as a great American statesman, impressed by the trade of the treaty ports, and convinced of the justice of extraterritoriality. Having read Dickinson's book and been completely fooled by the author's pose, Bryan assumed the role of champion of European civilization and defender of its faiths. In 1906 his defense appeared under the title *Letters To A Chinese Official, Being a Western View of Eastern Civilization*. "Never having visited China and never having acquainted myself with Chinese philosophy," wrote Bryan in his preface, "the absurdity of his [Dickinson's] contrast between American life and Chinese life was not apparent. Now that I have had an opportunity to test his description by personal observation, I feel that a reply is due to him as well as required from us. . . ." The Dickinson-Bryan "debate" is a classic illustration of the differences between the appeal of the Orient to a disciplined mind, capable of sensing the inner spirit of a culture, and the impact of that culture upon an uninformed observer obsessed with materialistic Occidental achievements. But it should be regarded more as the climax of a body of revealing literature than as an example of Bryan's gullibility or the insensitivity of diplomatic officialdom.

No survey of "orientalism" in the popular literature of the eighteenth century would be complete which neglects mention of the *Arabian Nights* and the many imitations which it inspired, following the English translation of Galland's French rendering in 1704. The perennial appeal of the book is well suggested by Wordsworth:

> The tales that charm away the wakeful night
> In Araby, romances; legends penned
> For solace by dim light of monkish lamps;
> Fictions, for ladies of their love, devised
> By youthful squires; adventures endless.

Wordsworth's enthusiasm, when he discovered as a boy that the volume he had dearly purchased "was but a block hewn from a mighty quarry," was clearly anticipated by an earlier generation.

Martha P. Conant's *Oriental Tale in England*, though incomplete and occasionally exaggerating the known facts, contains an argument that is worthy of note. The chief elements of narrative art, plot, character, and background, are found in varying degrees in all literature. But not until the wide circulation of the *Arabian Nights* in England were they effectively combined by writers of English fiction. In the second decade of the eighteenth century, periodical essayists flourished and works like the "Sir Roger de Coverley" sketches were widely read, but men of letters offered their readers almost no plot. As literature, such writings satisfied the cultivated taste of the time; but they could hardly be called adequate fare for the imagination, fancy, and emotions. Later, Samuel Richardson published *Pamela* in 1741 and *Clarissa Harlowe* in 1747-48. Henry Fielding's *Joseph Andrews* appeared in 1742, and *Tom Jones* in 1749. Tobias Smollett and Lawrence Sterne are also prominent in the history of the English novel. But the slow-moving "epistolary" style was not designed for readers who liked swiftly moving plot, rapidly changing scenes, and the excitement of pages in which fantastically wealthy sultans, beautiful princesses, and disconsolate heroes worked out their destinies with magic and intrigue. Old heroic romances and tales of chivalry, to be sure, could be read for thrilling feats of arms and lovers' escapes in a charming world of medievalism; but it was not the world of the *Arabian Nights*. An interest in narrative action which stems from the enthusiasm aroused by that book, Miss Conant argues, is among the contributions of the Orient to Occidental literature.

One needs only to be reminded of the Spanish picaresque novel, to realize the dangers of observing too partially the influence of the Oriental tale. On the other hand, the career of Thomas Simon Gueulette, perhaps the most prolific of all imitators, who flourished between 1683 and 1766 and produced collections with such titles as *Chinese Tales, Mogul Tales,* and *Peruvian Tales,* is an indication of the popularity of the pseudo-Oriental in both France and England. Many other adapters who followed cared little whether their stories were spurious or farfetched, so long as the market flourished. Their work as a whole is hardly of genuine literary merit. But from this subsoil some of the great classics of Western literature grew. Samuel Johnson, financially embarrassed, knew what he was about when in 1759 he produced his *Rasselas*. Joseph Addison, himself an innovator, wrote his famous *Vision of Mirza* for the *Spectator*. Oliver Goldsmith wrote *Asem, an Eastern Tale: or a Vindication of the Wisdom of Providence in the Moral Government of the World*. William Beckford produced *Vathek*, one of the best oriental-gothic thrillers of the century. On the Continent Voltaire elevated the *genre* with such classics as *Zadig* and *The Good Brahmin*.

The uses of the Oriental tale in American literature may be illustrated by Benjamin Franklin's little story, *An Arabian Tale*, which at first glance appears one of the most inconsequential of his writings. But closer examination reveals that it was an expression of Franklin's spiritual experience, his misgivings about the existence of evil, his inability to justify the ways of God to man, and his honest confession that "the Dispensations of Providence in this World puzzle my weak Reason." The story is simply that of the magician Albumazar, who having renounced the society of men retired in old age to the mountain of Calabut. Living alone, he was nightly visited by genii and spirits who became his instructors. On one occasion his guest was a great genie named

32

Belubel. Albumazár began by confessing that, despite his love and respect for the wisdom and beneficence of God, he could not comprehend how the Most High permitted the existence of evil. Belubel chided Albumazar for attacking such problems with the puny weapons of Reason and advised him to contemplate "the scale of beings, from an elephant down to an oyster." Then followed an exposition of the "great chain of being" concept. The plan of the world is one in which "There is no gap, but the gradation is complete. Men in general do not know, but thou knowest, that in ascending from an elephant to the infinitely Great, Good, and Wise, there is also a long gradation of beings, who possess powers and faculties of which thou canst yet have no conception." Thus man may be comforted, for though the gradations of nature may not be apparent, there is warrant for the faith that ultimately they reach an entity whose faculties are infinite. The idea is to be found in Greek thought, and it persisted through the eighteenth century. Franklin's acquaintance with the concept may be assumed. Its development in *An Arabian Tale* is an illustration of the manner in which many writers put Western ideas into foreign forms of literary expression. The serious-minded found the Oriental apologue continuously useful.

The browser in the periodical literature of the eighteenth century will not be long in recognizing the varied purposes to which writers on both sides of the Atlantic put the pseudo-Oriental tale. It became also a vehicle for social and political satire, and in its more imaginative forms was blended with the fairy tale. Tales of adventure of course needed no apology; they were their own excuse for being. But the moral uses of the *genre* were widely defended. A couplet in the *Rambler* suggests the values as Doctor Johnson himself saw them;

> The cheerful sage, when solemn dictates fail,
> Conceals the moral counsel in the tale.

In the title page of the 1736 English edition of Gueulette's *Mogul Tales* the same suggestion appears:

> In pleasing Tales, the artful Sage can give
> Rules, how in Happiness and Ease to live:
> Can show that Good should most attract the Mind,

And how our Woes we from our Vices find;
Delighting, yet instructing thus our Youth,
Who catch at Fable—How to gather Truth.

Obviously no literature so freighted with preachment could long retain its popularity. The exotic tale flourished best when its function was chiefly a fictional device for presenting the platitudes of the Johnsonian and Addisonian essay.

To dismiss the pseudo-Oriental tale as inconsequential may be justified if it is compared with other contemporary literature. But such tales served a purpose which the social historian cannot ignore. The "Discourse on the Usefulness of Romances" in the *Mogul Tales* by Gueulette contains an apologia that is illuminating:

> The *late Humour of reading Oriental* Romances, such as the Arabian, Persian, *and* Turkish Tales, tho' I will not contend, *it has much better'd our Morals, has however extended our Notions, and made the Customs of the East more familiar to us than they were before, or probably ever would have been, had they not been communicated to us by this indirect, and pleasant Way. Now these are certainly very great Advantages, and very valuable Acquirements, even to Men, and many giddy young Fellows have been, by amusing themselves with Trifles, taught to conceive clearly, and to converse properly, in relation to Things which otherwise they would have known nothing about.*

The tales did convey useful knowledge to the European public. Fact was often mixed with fiction, and the pseudo-Oriental vocabulary is clear warrant for doubting the authenticity of many details. But many writers also sought widely for information which would give verisimilitude to their work and enable readers to live imaginatively in worlds which later writers like Rudyard Kipling and Pierre Mille, Richard Burton and Pierre Loti were to exploit. The intent and methods of such writers have changed. Moderns like Sax Rohmer and Ernest Brahma, Lin Yutang and Pearl Buck, continue to represent either fantastic and imaginative or idealistic themes, adapting them to various levels of public

34

taste. Ultimately all are engaged in creating a world of mystery and adventure or in revealing the essential traits of humble folk in distant lands. Whether fiction dealing with the Orient is finally to be analyzed for its objective sociological truth, or for all the shades of insight and of taste which it contains, is a task which historians and critics must ultimately determine. Of its influence on Western attitudes toward non-European peoples, and its usefulness in conveying information about them, there can be no doubt.

Fiction was not the only literary form in which the Oriental interests of eighteenth-century men of letters found expression. In the opera and ballet, no less than in drama, the influence can be traced. A competent study by T. Blake Clark entitled *Oriental England*, published in 1939 in Shanghai, is an impressive exposition of the influence on drama, which indicates that the Mikados and Madame Butterflies and the exotic vaudeville extravaganzas of the modern stage were also anticipated more than two centuries ago. "Writers of heroic drama," Clark noted after arduous research in widely scattered British and American libraries housing rare plays and manuscripts, "were not interested so much in learning from Oriental culture as in ransacking it. They chose Turkish, Persian, Egyptian, and Chinese heroes because Eastern monarchs suited the heroic tradition, which required of a ruler arrogance, boasting, and omnipotence. Audiences, however, grown tired of stale heroics, were attracted to the new scenery, costume, and atmosphere. These new interests had an effect on the plays." Thus, while the Oriental influences on English dramatic technique were negligible, the interest in character and setting was pronounced. Paul Whitehead's prologue to Arthur Murphy's *Orphan of China*, published in 1759 and based on Voltaire's earlier work which in turn had been derived from a version in the Jesuit Du Halde's writings, nevertheless suggests that playwrights sought to present Oriental thought to their audiences while they entertained them with exotic costumes and settings.

> Enough of Greece and Rome: Th' exhausted store
> Of either nation now can charm no more . . .
> On eagle wings the poet of to-night
> Soars for fresh virtues to the source of light;

> To China's eastern realms: and boldly bears
> Confucius' morals to Britannia's ears.

Poetry also reflected the current taste. The outstanding figure who, before the flourishing of the Romantic Movement, turned his attention to Oriental verse was Bishop Thomas Percy, famed for his *Reliques of Ancient English Poetry*. Historians intent on his "gothic" researches rarely have noted that the eminent compiler of the English *Reliques* did not restrict his antiquarian researches to the British Isles. In 1762 Percy published *Miscellaneous Pieces Relating to the Chinese*, which contained several essays on Chinese drama, poetry, and kindred arts. It was followed in 1775 by *Ancient Songs Chiefly on Moorish Subjects*. Scores of other Primitivists made studies in the "originals" of human expression, ignoring the fact that they necessarily devoted themselves to the secondhand versions made available to them by Jesuit scholars and educated travelers.

Among the pre-Romantic poets of England who extended the poetic use of Oriental materials were William Collins, Thomas Chatterton, John Scott, and Eyles Irwin. Their "Oriental Eclogues" may seem tame or wooden to the modern reader, and there is scant evidence that they took pains to discover the prosodic forms or the essential character of the great Oriental literatures. It is true that Sir William Jones, one of England's first great Orientalists and a poet in his own right, had presented the results of years of painstaking study to the public; and John Scott, inspired as a consequence, had written an apostrophe to Jones of which the following lines are representative:

> The Asian Muse, a stranger fair!
> Becomes at length Britannia's care;
> And Hafiz' lays, and Sadi's strains,
> Resound along our Thames's plains.

Sir William Jones may be regarded as the first outstanding example in English literature of the happy combination of erudition and literary skill, for he was both linguist and poet. But the work of Chatterton and Collins was distinctly different. Theirs was the self-appointed task, not of translating Oriental tongues into English, but of pouring into timeworn molds new knowledge about

Oriental peoples and their folkways. The artificial pastoral, long kept alive by the mighty names of Virgil, Spenser, Milton, and Pope, had fallen into the hands of a new generation which retained its conventional form but insisted on adapting it to new subject matter. The substitution of Orientals for the conventional rude swains and shepherdesses of the pastoral of classical tradition seems startling, almost grotesque. But with a shift in setting to some exotic place, a few descriptive details lifted from a recent history or travel book, a borrowed story of courtship between lovers of feuding Oriental tribes, the poet had no difficulty in producing work which satisfied both the current neo-classical sense of form and the romantic love of the strange.

Thus there were few departments of European intellectual and cultural life which, before 1800, did not to some extent feel the impact of overseas discovery.

## VI

To understand the "orientalism" of the nineteenth century we must comprehend the Romantic temper, which included more than mere poetic interest in something "far away and long ago." It was the expression of a state of mind rather than a literary movement. Hoxie N. Fairchild in *The Romantic Quest* defined the temper as "the endeavor, in the face of growing obstacles, to achieve, to retain, or to justify that illusioned view of the universe and of human life which is produced by an imaginative fusion of the familiar and the strange, the known and the unknown, the real and the ideal, the material and the spiritual, the natural and the supernatural." It is obvious, if this definition is accepted, that Romanticism may reflect exotic sentimentalism, or an "inspired muddleheadedness" or a search for either an earthly paradise or some City of God. It also touches many chords of human emotion and is inherent in many types of speculation. In its more popular forms, some romantics often substituted dissipation in naturalistic dreams for intellectual or moral discipline, and inevitably many in time discovered little more than surfeit of the emotions. The critical literature of Romanticism is consequently filled with discussion of the fate of minds which sought salvation by grace of nature rather than by grace of God. Rarely is com-

37

plete objectivity to be found in the critical literature of such work, and in few fields is there more lively controversy.

In the nineteenth century, it should first be noted, almost all the literary manifestations of the cultural discovery of the Orient are romantic. They can be understood, even if they may not be admired. Several basic facts explain the change in temper and the shift of interest from China to India and the Near East. Europeans with a taste for foreign expressions of human experience and speculation after 1800 were no longer restricted to the secondhand reports of travelers and to inadequate translations. Through learned Oriental Societies, the philosophical literature of the world gradually came into all the major languages, and Europeans had unfolded before them the greatest books of foreign peoples. From these they were free to select themes to be developed and ideas to be pondered.

The second factor was the rise of Anthropology and Darwinism. Superstitions fell like autumn leaves and religion became less identified with creedal or national traditions. The futility of fixed doctrinal positions dawned in the minds of generations compelled to adjust their thought to Evolution. There grew simultaneously the realization that the spiritual needs from which religions arise assert themselves in all parts of the world.

The third factor was the Industrial Revolution. The ugliness of smoky industrialism and the deplorable conditions of labor encouraged the "escapist" tendencies dormant in all men. The world-weary sought imaginatively for Arcadia or spiritually for some vague Nirvana.

Metaphysicians and mystics meanwhile created a new mythology of the "supernatural" and sought anew to understand physical phenomena or to secure kinship with the life in living things. During the Renaissance and the Enlightenment, the intellectual horizons of Europeans had been broadened. With the progress of the nineteenth century the natural order of human experience followed: after the discovery of new facts, new peoples, and new realms of thought and human experience, came the inevitable deepening of insights and understanding. The processes of discovery continued geographically and outwardly with the exploration of the hearts of continents; but they also became increasingly inward, as each new translation of great Oriental works revealed the dimensions of the mystical and intellectual worlds in which other peoples lived. The guiding principle of European cultural appropriation from the Orient continued to be *laissez faire*. Like the winds that blow as they list, often unpredictable in origin and indeterminate in direction, the drift of "orientalism" continued in startling ways in a different and newer age.

The list of great writers who reflected in varying degrees an interest in or a debt to the Orient increased: Rueckert, Goethe, Heine, and others in Germany; Gautier and Leconte de Lisle in France; Byron, Southey, Moore, and Landor in England; Emerson, Thoreau, Melville, and Whitman in America. All did not write with the same purpose, and they varied in their emphases and in the materials laid under debt. Some merely borrowed from the foreign literatures a metaphysical or symbolical apparatus, and had no intention of exalting the East above the West. Others were sensitive exoticists with a morbidly refined sense of values who nursed their grievances against the workaday world and sought escape from the dullness of Europe in a pseudo-Orient of opium, hashish, or voluptuousness where life, it was imagined, was freer and more abundant. The various worlds sought, depending upon the temperament of the writer, ranged from earthly Arcadias to the transcendental Over-Soul, from the Oriental equivalent of the Blue Flower to the world east of Suez where, as Kipling said, a man can raise a thirst.

The nadir of Romantic exoticism is found in the annual "gift book" anthologies published on both sides of the Atlantic. Most of the poems appear to have been the work of poetasters who followed a recipe guaranteed to produce sure-fire best-sellers. The English *Keepsake* of 1828, for example, suggests the desired hero, essentially Byronic in character:

> Next a hero with an air,
> Half a brigand—half Corsair.

His vocabulary was pseudo-Oriental and consisted of references to gazelles, bulbuls, peepul trees, Arab tents, and even Chinese bamboo bungalows. Little more was needed than a pale, melancholy heroine waiting for her Byronic lover. The final touch, contributed by the poet, completed the formula:

39

> And I give you, mix'd with western sentimentalism,
> Some samples of the finest Orientalism.

Much of the doggerel is of no literary value—save to those who like pretty sentiments dressed up in rhyme, or to the highly imaginative who indulge in dreams of being modern Don Juans kissing Burma maidens before the idol of the great god Buddha, or who like the less adventurous lines of the American poet Clinton Scollard:

> Before our eyes will gleam and glance
> The woven threads of old romance,—
> Those fabrics fair that never fade,
> Spun by the brave Scheherezade.
> And we will list the trancëd tales
> Of plaintive Shiraz nightingales,
> Bemoaning love around the tomb
> Where Hafiz sleeps in scented gloom.
>
> .    .    .    .
>
> No vintage-draught soe'er, compressed
> From the broad bosom of the West,
> Can yield the keen delight of this
> Enthralling, roseate cup of bliss.

From such sub-literature, however, flowered later some of the most representative works of the better-known Romantic poets. If only as literary humus, therefore, it has significance. When Byron and some of his friends studied the public taste and literary market of their day, they were not long in realizing the financial profits to be reaped by catering to the vogue. Thus in 1813 Byron wrote in a letter to a friend: "Stick to the East; the oracle, Stael, told me it was the only poetical policy. The North, South, and West have all been exhausted. . . ." Walter Savage Landor had anticipated the advice and in 1798 produced the *Gebir;* as had also Robert Southey when in 1801 he published *Thalaba,* which purported to be an "Epic of Islam," and in 1810 *The Curse of Kehama,* a verse romance based on Hindu materials. Thomas Moore's *Lalla Rookh,* an Oriental tale having much in common with the prose versions of the preceding century, was perhaps in one sense the outstanding work of its type. Written in easy-flowing verse ornamented with richly exotic imagery, the poem appeared in 1817 and became instantly popular. It went through six editions in its first year and is said to have commanded the highest price ever paid in England for a copyright—3,000 guineas.

Byron was both a mediator between the eighteenth- and nineteenth-century uses of the Oriental tale and an outstanding purveyor of exotic sentimentalism to his public. Even a casual glance through his poetry offers ample evidence; a careful reading of his letters indicates how persistent were his Oriental interests and how frequently he referred to them. His familiar *Giaour* carried the subtitle "A Fragment of a Turkish Tale"; and the "Advertisement" states that the "story . . . contained the adventures of a female slave, who was thrown, in the Mussulman manner, into the sea for infidelity, and avenged by a young Venetian, her lover. . . ." *The Bride of Abydos* also had the subtitle "A Turkish Tale." But Byron's position is more than that of a poet who saved the vogue from complete mawkishness. His chief significance in the history of literary "orientalism" is that his work marked the point at which slowly diverging streams eventually separated. Rasselas and Don Juan would have been strange bedfellows.

Preaching disappeared in the handling of the Oriental tale by Byron and his school, but exotic moralism did not pass out of fashion. The Occidental tendency to regard the Orient as the home of profound wisdom persisted and reappeared in work best typified by Leigh Hunt's "Abou Ben Adhem," a poem long known to schoolboys, which pleased readers who frowned on Byronic corsairs and houris. "Abou Ben Adhem, may his tribe increase!" Hunt's prayer was abundantly answered. Many readers have found the good sheik's literary descendants more platitudinous than profound. Others may regard the "tribe" as "tripe." But the growth of the new form was in no way fortuitous.

The best explanation is perhaps to be found in the essays of Theodore Watts-Dunton, who flourished from 1832 to 1914 and represented the average levels of Victorian taste. His *Poetry and the Renascence of Wonder*, posthumously published in 1916, reflected the tendency of the average Victorian to be sentimentally mystical rather than metaphysical, and to extend the explorations of the occult into the Vedantic and Sufistic literature which scholars and popularisers had made accessible. Watts-Dunton's essay on "Ethical Poetry," arguing that the greatest ethical literature of the world was not Hellenic but Buddhistic, is a revealing statement of the trend. His review of Browning's *Ferishtah's Fancies* in the *Athenæum* in 1884 offers the clearest apologia for the pseudo-Oriental moralistic poem. Browning's work was a sample of parable-poetry, suggested Watts-Dunton, a type which had long been popular in the East and which could profitably be used as epitomes of philosophies of life. The task of such poetry was "to set self-conscious philosophy singing and dancing . . . to the tune of a waterfall . . . and the preacher strumming a gypsy's tambourine." No critic, except with tongue in cheek, could seriously consider Watts-Dunton's essay as a contribution to critical literature. But it is a useful explanation of the popularity on both sides of the Atlantic of such poems as Browning's "Ben Karshook's Wisdom" and the better known "Rabbi Ben Ezra." The Anglo-American poets who wrote such poems are to be numbered by scores, if not hundreds.

In the popularity of pseudo-Oriental verse may also be found a partial explanation of the amazing reception given in England and America to two of the most widely read poems of the Victorian era—Edward Fitzgerald's rendering of the *Rubaiyat* of Omar Khayyam and Edwin Arnold's *Light of Asia*, an epic based on the life of Buddha. It would be difficult to find a more essentially incompatible pair than Omar and Buddha: the former a hedonist, the latter the founder of a religion based on complete renunciation. But the two poems represent the many-faceted attraction of the East for the West and the manner in which contradictory outlooks on life may exist side by side in a generation.

The dubious question of Sufistic symbolism in the *Rubaiyat* manifestly could not have concerned the general reader. Its popularity is explained by the fact that it expressed for a baffled generation some of the problems which occupied men like Thomas Hardy: man's fate in an inexplicable universe, the moral implications of Darwinism, and the great social issues posed by the Industrial Revolution. Matthew Arnold's "Sohrab and Rustum," outwardly an adaptation from the Persian *Shah Nameh* of Firdausi, was more than an episode from a great epic: like "Dover Beach," it epitomized a world wherein father and son, and ignorant armies, clashed by night, and in which little certitude and help for pain were found. Fitzgerald, through an Oriental, expressed the persisting human longing for release through the bowl and exotic delights. His art made the poem something more than the banal work of preceding poetasters who had mixed sentimentalism and orientalism for an insatiable public.

Edwin Arnold's *Light of Asia*, published in 1879 and reported to have gone into sixty editions in England and eighty in America, aroused the animosity of many Christian pulpits. But clerics whose theology offered release from life's troubles only in a heaven achieved after death could not divert readers who longed for a vague Nirvana. Furthermore, Arnold's sonorous blank verse included Oriental luxuriance and deft Tennysonian heightening of effects. A sympathetic portrayal of the life and teachings of a noble-spirited Indian prince who had solved the problem of evil, the poem contained a theosophy without the fantastic cosmology of Madame Blavatsky. Its message was clearly for minds staggered by Darwinism and the realization that nature was red in tooth and claw.

One reason for the popularity of the *Light of Asia* in America was doubtless the fact that its readers represented a generation of New Englanders who had lost faith in both its hope and ancestral traditions. Unitarianism had become a "sucked eggshell"; its positive content had been lost. Restless striving seemed purposeless, without direction; life had been emptied of spiritual meaning. "As I see the entire world today," wrote Henry Adams in a letter to his brother, "it has already reached its lowest level, and is likely to stay there. . . . It can't get much flatter. . . . Artists of course disappeared long ago as social forces. So did the church." For men like William Sturgis Bigelow, Percival Lowell, John La Farge, Henry Adams, the Spanish-Yankee of Salem, Ernest Fenollosa, and the cosmopolitan Lafcadio Hearn, Japan and Buddhism offered quiet, solace, and escape. Such men gravitated to Japan or China for various reasons, as art collectors or as mere travelers, but all sought for a true spiritual home where the whirlwinds of life are calmed and absolute truth might be found. Only a minority of Americans, to be sure, sympathized with their quest. In 1886 Henry Adams and John La Farge, en route to Japan, were interviewed by a reporter in Nebraska. Ad-

43

ams wrote in a letter to his friend John Hay: "At Omaha a young reporter got the better of us; for when in reply to his inquiry as to our purpose in visiting Japan, La Farge beamed through his spectacles the answer that we were in search of Nirvana, the youth looked up like a meteor, and rejoined: 'It's out of season!'" When later La Farge published *An Artist's Letters from Japan*, he dedicated the book to Adams and concluded with this melancholy note: "If only we had found Nirvana—but he was right who warned us that we were late in this season of the world."

The significant fact is that representative Americans of the nineties thought in these terms. The Nirvana which the disillusioned of New England sought is best defined in the Ingersoll Lecture which Bigelow gave at Harvard in 1908 on *Buddhism and Immortality*. That book, with La Farge's *An Artist's Letters from Japan*, Percival Lowell's *The Soul of the Far East*, Lafcadio Hearn's pages of spiritual autobiography, and the less historical passages of Fenollosa's *Epochs of Chinese and Japanese Art*, express the mood of the generation for whom the Western spiritual tradition had lost its force. It was not, however, merely a passing temper which was to leave no mark on American art and literature.

When La Farge visited Japan with Adams, he had been commissioned to paint the mural above the altar of the Church of the Ascension in New York. His letters to the art critic, Royal Cortissoz, in part printed in the latter's biography *John La Farge*, suggest one of the practical purposes of the journey. La Farge sought as a background for the figure of the ascending Christ a mountainous place where rocks and clouds would readily suggest the miraculous. He had a vague belief that in Japan he would find "certain conditions of line in the mountains which might help me. Of course the Judean mountains were entirely out of question, all the more that they implied a given space." In Japan, furthermore, was an atmosphere, both natural and spiritual, in which the appearance and disappearances of Buddhist saints could be sensed as normal events—and the ascension of Christ could be conceived as perfectly fitting, because the natural and the supernatural were never dissociated. Having found the site which satisfied him, La Farge made his background experiments and returned to New York to work. As he painted, his friend Okakura talked with him, he wrote to Cortissoz, "about spiritual manifestations and all that beautiful wonderland" which the Japanese cherished and "where spiritual bodies take form and disappear again and the edges of the real and the imaginary melt." La Farge apparently met only one serious objection. It came from a lady "who was troubled by certain news she had heard," namely, that "I made these studies of clouds in a pagan country." His comment was: "A true Episcopalian would make them, I suppose, in England."

The mural in the Church of the Ascension was not, however, the only result of La Farge's Oriental interests. He was later commissioned to paint panels to be placed in the Court House at Baltimore. Confucius was the subject of one. He was asked also to undertake four paintings for the Supreme Court Room in the State Capitol of Minnesota, and for "The Recording of the Precedents" he again used as the central figure Confucius busy with his pupils in the collation and transcription of ancient documents. Cortissoz wrote: "The figures were true types of Eastern intellectuality and spirituality." Reference to such works as these by La Farge suggests the moot question of the significance of the work of a host of lesser artists who have turned to the Orient for subjects and background. The results have never been systematically studied by specialists, and consequently no historian is in a position to damn with faint praise or to state with enthusiasm that in such American art there has appeared a happy meeting of the East and West. But the problem awaits the study of judicious critics. The famous monument which Henry Adams commissioned Saint-Gaudens to execute for his wife's grave at Rock Creek Cemetery in Washington is another landmark in the spiritual quest of one of the most sensitive spirits ever to appear in America. Goaded by sorrow at the loss of his wife, Adams often called the statue Nirvana, and others have vaguely suggested that it was inspired by the Chinese Goddess of Mercy. Obviously the influence of the Orient upon our artists who work with brush and chisel cannot be ignored.

The work of Ernest Fenollosa in the preservation of ancient art in Japan itself, and in encouraging its collection and study in America, is also worthy of note. He played no small part in making Boston and its famous museum one of the richest centers in the world. Fenollosa was also an influence in encouraging the study of Oriental literature. His work on the Noh drama of Japan was revised and published after his death by Ezra Pound under the title *Certain Noble Plays of Japan.* Of even greater significance was Fenollosa's essay on *The Chinese Written Character as a Medium of Poetry*, an "ars poetica" written in conscious realization that modern man "not only turns a new page in the book of the world, but opens another and a startling chapter" which will involve "world-embracing cultures half-weaned from Europe" and "undreamed responsibilities for nations and races." Few books threw clearer light on the essential interests of the Imagists who later turned to the Orient for inspiration and method.

It is not only in what Van Wyck Brooks has called the "Indian Summer" of New England culture that our representative men turned to the Orient for spiritual or intellectual support. The earlier period of the "flowering" of New England is significant for many reasons. One is that the temper of Emersonian Concord was positive, not negative. Another is that some of its most characteristic thought was the result of Yankee roots striking into Oriental humus and deriving therefrom rich nutriment. (In *The Orient in American Transcendentalism* I have offered an exposition of the outstanding manifestations.)

The grammarian Donatus once cried: "Damn those who said what we mean, before us!" But such men as Emerson and Thoreau, instead of feeling despair at discovering that great seers of the past had expressed their thoughts before them, were delighted. They trusted their own intuitions and fell back upon experience which, to use Emerson's phrase, affirmed the existence of the *One Bottom* in the universe. Their chief Oriental interest was in the Vedanta and they were led to the Hindus for proof of the fact that the "eminent men of each church" in both hemispheres "think and say the same thing." There can be little doubt of the reasons behind Emerson's orientalism, when one reads such words from his pen as: "In the history of intellect no more important fact than the Hindu theology, teaching that the beatitude or supreme good is to be attained through science: namely, by the perception of the real and the unreal, setting aside matter, and qualities and affections or emotions and persons, as Maias or illusions, and thus arriving at the contemplation of the one eternal

46

Life and Cause, and a perpetual approach and assimilation to Him. . . ."

The Transcendentalists were not system makers. They were men who sought an ethic and therapeutically useful religious philosophy at a time when European thinkers were wrestling with rationalistic Sensationalism and romantic Idealism. Both the Deists and the Transcendentalists sought a universal substrate for religion and ethics; but each started with totally different premises. In terms of their Oriental leanings they are differentiated by all that distinguishes social China from mystic India. The search of the Transcendentalists was for glimpses of the Over-Soul, of mystic insights and illumination which like glints of gold in a lump of ore shone through the plethora of the world about them and in man's beliefs.

This is the explanation of the numerous Oriental "lustres" or quotations which fill many pages of Emerson's and Thoreau's writings, as well as *The Dial*, official organ of the communion published from 1840 to 1844. The proverbs of strange peoples, pithy sayings which reveal the sharp-edged observations and universal insights of men into the nature of the world and the moral conduct of life, were valued for their undulled freshness and distilled proofs of the moral sentiment in man. Above all, when they were most orphic, proverbs revealed the universality of moral law and proved that the natural interest of man is in the ideal. Thus, Emerson and his followers welcomed with joy the evidence that the Over-Soul had spoken through men in divers times and places. Throughout their lives they sought the echoes.

If the contemporaries of the Concordians found their thought iconoclastic, it was because of their catholicity and not because of any negation of essential Christianity. This can be amply demonstrated in the writings of Thoreau. In his unpublished commonplace book entitled *Paragraphs Mostly Original* appears a note which clearly suggests his attitude toward the world's religions: "If the Roman—the Greek—and the Jew have a character in history, so has the Hindoo. He may help to balance Asia which is still too one-sided with its Palestine." Thoreau was not essentially anti-Christian. On April 3, 1850, he disclosed in a letter to his friend Blake the result of his reading of the Christian scriptures and his thoughts as he viewed the world: "I lived in Judæa

47

eighteen hundred years ago, but I never knew there was such a one as Christ among my contemporaries!" On another occasion he wrote in the *Week:* "What are time and space to Christianity, eighteen hundred years, and a new world?—that the humble life of a Jewish peasant should have force to make a New York bishop so bigoted." If such sentiments are anti-Christian, Thoreau might have shouted, let the world make the most of them! A mind like his had no interest in the purely temporal; it lived in worlds wherein the great-hearted were always welcomed and could feel at home. "I know, for instance," he wrote in his *Journal* of 1852, "that Sadi entertained once identically the same thought that I do, and thereafter I can find no essential difference between Sadi and myself. He is not Persian, he is not ancient, he is not strange to me. By the identity of his thoughts with mine he still survives." In the light of such passages must be interpreted the often-quoted confession of Thoreau to his literary executor, Harrison Blake: "Depend upon it that, rude and careless as I am, I would fain practice the *yoga* faithfully. . . . To some extent, and at rare intervals, even I am a *yogi.*" Manifestly such words from the pen of a Yankee jack-of-all-trades cannot be taken literally. To think of Thoreau contemplating his navel is preposterous. His real interest can best be suggested by other phrases from his writings: To live a "balanced life, acceptable to nature and to God"; to breathe a "divine perfume" and in serenity of mind and spirit to "enjoy our inheritance"; to make way "with our petty selves, wish no ill to anything. Apprehend no ill, cease to be but as the crystal which reflects the ray"—that was his conception of Yoga. "There is a kindred principle at the bottom of all affinities," he wrote in his *Journal* in 1840, half a decade before his retreat to Walden; and afterwards he recorded that while in solitude he "dwelt nearer to those parts of the universe and to those eras in history which had most attracted me." The reasons for the orientalism of the American Transcendentalists are to be found in these words. It was not the result of a desire to escape anything. Theirs was an intellectual quest, a search for historical evidence and experience to vindicate the fundamental principles of their thought. The most luminous pages of Emerson and Thoreau are filled with proof that in the great Oriental scriptures they discovered their affinities. To distinguish their mood from that of Henry Adams

48

and his contemporaries, it is necessary only to note that their favorite Bible was the *Bhagavadgita* and not the books of the Buddhists.

Kipling's assertion that the East and the West will never meet is the easy conclusion of an imperialist. He was the dean of Anglo-Indian fiction writers and the composer of Tommy Atkins' barrack-room songs. His interest was never in the realms Thoreau occupied, or in the Arcadia of the world-weary, or in the theosophies which today are offered as a solution for all religious contradictions. Clearly, at the end of the nineteenth century and continuing into our own day, the Occidental imagination created for itself two worlds which are romantically "oriental." One was a world of untrammeled nature, exotic mystery, and unchecked passions. The other consisted of the mysticism of the Sufis, Buddha, the Upanishadic seers, and Lao-tzü. It remained for the Neo-Humanists of the twentieth century, particularly Irving Babbitt and Paul Elmer More, to point out that the popular imagination of the West could not consistently live in both worlds. "If the temple bells are calling the British private to 'raise a thirst,' " wrote Babbitt in an essay on "Buddha and the Occident" published together with his translation of *The Dhammapada*, "to what, one may enquire, are they calling the native Burman?" Babbitt answers: "Certainly not to be 'lazy' and irresponsible . . . a central admonition of Buddha may be summed up in the phrase: Do not raise a thirst!"

Whatever may be said about Neo-Humanism, its amorphous character, and the emphases which differ with its various exponents, the writings of Babbitt and More clearly indicate a debt to the Orient. As a conservative literary movement, it was characterized by an intense hatred of Rousseauism and both literary 'naturalism' and exoticism. Modern fiction, said More, consisted chiefly of explosions in cesspools. The majority of the Neo-Humanist communion sought in the "wisdom of the past" for an "inner-check" to curb contemporary interest in sex and natural passion. As a religion, if Babbitt's works may be taken as representative, Neo-Humanism was Puritanism superimposed upon a Buddhistic sense of the worthlessness and impermanence of human attachments, and a search for moral disciplines, a higher will and

49

imagination to balance the natural will, the senses and their appetites, and the lower imagination.

For the historian interested in the values discovered by Occidentals in the Orient, the Neo-Humanism of Babbitt and More is a rewarding study. In their work there appeared, at last, an "orientalism" based on sound scholarship and an acquaintance with Sanskrit and Pali. Trained at Harvard under eminent philologians, for long years thereafter continuing to study Oriental languages with a view to translating and publishing their representative classics for the public at large, and eventually bent on the formulation of a social ethic if not a new religion for their generation, these high priests of the movement released their criticism of contemporary life through the most respectable journals of their day. Their quarrels during the 1920's with literary critics resulted in manifestoes and symposia like *Humanism and America*, edited by Norman Foerster for the communion, and *The Critique of Humanism*, edited by C. Hartley Grattan. Younger critics probably would have raised no voice in protest if the Neo-Humanists had been satisfied with the role of antiquarians crying "Mahabharata" from rooftops. But they rose in defense of modernism against the erudite attacks of the academicians and characterized their utterances as "Mahabracadabra." Outwardly the controversy seemed to many observers a tempest in a teapot. Seen in perspective, however, and studied in the light of the complete writings of Babbitt and More, it can with justice be regarded as the clash between an essentially Hindu sense of human values and a civilization hell-bent for the economic debacle of 1929.

# VII

The lessons which may be drawn from a brief survey of the past in Oriental-Occidental cultural relations are many and varied. Few of the giants of European and American intellectual history have thus far devoted themselves to a consideration of Oriental cultures per se. Yet the Orient has increasingly colored their intellectual and cultural milieu. This is the first fact to be noted in conclusion.

It is in the popular literature of Europe and America that the impact of the Orient upon our traditional thought may most effectively be traced. Popular literature is a weathercock which points the direction of all the winds of opinion that blow. This is its significance. It is the expression in words of the intellectual complex of an age, the summation of its culture in terms of ideas, activities, and impulses to action, and the revealer of the cultural dialects which paradoxically may appear side by side in the minds of representative men in any generation. Without benefit of the professoriat, average Occidentals have in varying ways been "orientalized" since the beginnings of contacts between the peoples of the East and the West.

To many this fact is the cause of alarm, and of a foreboding that our culture may lose its integrity. It was not so for Bolingbroke, who realized before Wordsworth that human nature's daily food is infinitely varied and that there are both physical and spiritual hungers. Bolingbroke's *Letters on the Study and Use of History*, published in 1752 at a time when the Orient was unfolding before a generation priding itself on its cosmopolitan outlook, contains a rational observation which should be considered by all who would encourage cultural exchange between peoples or who, contrariwise, would preserve the "purity" of their cultural heritage. "The study of history will prepare us for action and observation," Bolingbroke wrote. "History is the ancient author: experience is the modern language. We form our taste on the first; we translate the sense and reason, we transfuse the spirit and force: but we imitate only the particular graces of the original; *we imitate them according to the idiom of our own tongue*, that is, we substitute often equivalents in lieu of them, and are far from affecting to copy them servilely." Time has demonstrated the truth of Bolingbroke's observation.

A second fact is that there are more things in heaven and earth than merchants dream of. "What have death, and the cholera, and the immortal destiny of man, to do with the shipping interests?" asked Thoreau on one occasion, and his question suggests problems too frequently ignored. In contrast to his view it may be noted that in the September, 1933, *Pacific Affairs* a Dutch economist wrote: "I am unwilling to allow any artificial separation of the cultural factor from other factors, and am even convinced that I am right in posing the thesis that the relations between Eastern and Western peoples are primarily economic and that

51

cultural activities are only an *appendage*." For such forthright honesty there can be nothing but admiration, although one may doubt the writer's knowledge of cultural history and his sense of the relative importance and permanence of the forces loose in the world today.

The dangerous tendency of the typical Occidental to self-glorification and pride is abetted by many compelling facts which divert attention from his own debt to the Orient. It is necessary only to mention the influence of modern science, education, forms of government, and industrialism upon Asiatic life to realize what the white man has done to his neighbors. In India and China factories now belch smoke as black as any in Pittsburgh and Manchester; labor unions provoke strikes hitherto unknown in the so-called brooding East; the imported cinema has subverted native modes of life and sense of values. Obviously nothing comparable can be found for the influence of the Orient on the Occident. Commercial relations appear dominant, and the cultural traffic seems mainly bound in one direction. But such facts blind the Westerner as he faces the dawn of a new age in which ideas, philosophies, and theories of art will embark upon conquests of their own, and settle colonies without the aid of economic processes.

Certainly few of the Occidental thinkers and writers who have been challenged by the Orient have had the remotest interest in trade. They have overleaped geographical and racial frontiers chiefly because they discovered artistic, intellectual, spiritual values which they admired. Whether the resulting manifestations of "orientalism" in European culture are to be deplored or considered trivial is an academic question. That they are prophetic cannot be doubted. The process of appropriation cannot be thwarted by those who fear that it will neutralize the essential genius of a culture. If the materialistic civilization of the world will continue to be enriched and the physical life of all peoples made more comfortable, as the physical resources of continents, from *materia medica* to raw materials, are widely distributed, it is to be expected that men everywhere will similarly appropriate from the world's store other values which may make their lives more beautiful or give it depth.

A third fact is suggested by Doctor Johnson's observation that "the good and evil of eternity are too ponderous for the wings of wit." This is demonstrated in any popular literature which reflects an Oriental influence. Much ignorance and misuse of Oriental thought prevails, and some fearful and amusing facts are to be found in the record. For example, an American insurance company recently advertised: "Buddha, who was born a prince, gave up his name, succession, and heritage to attain serenity. But we do not need to give up the world; we have only to see a life-insurance agent who can sell us serenity for the future, the most direct step to peace of mind." Such words might suggest that America is the land of the half-educated. Only those with limited imaginations, however, will think of them as a reflection of credulity or ignorance alone. They indicate, rather, a want of stability. As men sense the artificiality and limitations of their lives today, feeling like trees with thin rootage in a high wind, they grope for sound footing and hunger for certitude. "Freud has unfortunately overlooked the fact," wrote Jung in *Modern Man in Search of a Soul*, "that man has never yet been able single-handed to hold his own against the powers of darkness—that is, of the unconscious. Man has always stood in need of the spiritual help which each individual's own religion held out to him. . . . It is this which lifts him out of his distress."

The Christian clergy may profitably consider the reasons behind the flourishing of Orient-inspired cults in Europe and America. Apparently in their parishes are hungry sheep who look up and are not fed; and many find in the exotic gospels of swamis some therapeutic value which they miss in their own religious heritage. The Thoreauvian insistence that the world is round, not lopsided, and that the Orient has both a character in history and a contribution to make, is a challenge to all who would be healers of souls that find no comfort in logic or Christian apologetics or tradition, whose spiritual problems are untouched by social gospels, and who desire above all else to believe that the enterprise of life is a worthwhile process and that in the end man will not dissolve like snowflakes in the stream of materialism. Underlying our contemporary faith in the curative powers of the psychoanalyst is the persisting desire to believe that man's spirit is continuous with a larger spirituality from whose universality are to be derived confidence, courage, and cosmic security.

Men who feel so find that the psychiatric therapies directed toward the adjustment of the outward business of life are also often superficial and inadequate. The intelligentsia may scorn them; but they are legion. They are those who in the truest sense live in a culture, and it is in their minds that the most significant meeting of the East and the West is taking place.

A fourth fact is that among other sincere, thoughtful, and educated Occidentals there has also grown the belief that the world's great religions are not hostile systems but are revealers of fundamental psychological needs and universal moral laws. Some consequently seek to reconcile contradictions in the world's faiths. Others find satisfaction in their great separate affirmations, believing that the best in the universe is the revelation of the deepest or most beautiful in it. A hymn by George Matheson, sung in many liberal churches of Protestant Christendom, serves as an illustration:

> Thine is the mystic life great India craves;
> Thine is the Parsee's sin-destroying beam;
> Thine is the Buddhist's rest from tossing waves;
> Thine is the empire of vast China's dream.

> Thine is the Roman's strength without his pride;
> Thine is the Greek's glad world without its graves;
> Thine is Judea's law with love beside,
> The truth that censures and the grace that saves.

Such lines suggest no careless heterodoxy, and the Oriental allusions clearly represent much more than mere poetic ornamentation. Indeed they were written in 1890 by the poet who gave to his fellow-believers the better-known hymn, "O Love That Will Not Let Me Go." There are increasingly deeper levels of experience which the ordinary folk of our workaday world must face. Duplicating in their own lives the varied experience of the race, it is inevitable that they should also discover, as knowledge of the great Oriental cultures increases, essential insights and values in all departments of human endeavor which they will make their own. The vaunted modernity of the present generation consists more in what it does than in what it believes. To future generations, as to our own, the records of the past are clearly a source of something more significant than amusing reading for an idle summer's day.

So long as we can imagine, there will be recurrent turning to the Orient for the material satisfactions of this world, for literary themes and artistic design, for the foundations of utopias, and for passports to the cities of God. As mankind struggles for the brotherhood of men, the trend will be toward the integration of the individual in the unity of the world's experience.

The sense of the past is therefore plain. The task of international democracy is to underwrite its dream with a world-wide political organization. Any structure it might raise, however, will be but a house of cards if it is not cemented with knowledge of the interdependence of peoples and their contributions to the common heritage of mankind. The spiritual foundations upon which the world society of the future is to be built must consist of a knowledge of all the affinities which exist between peoples and the ways in which they may complement each other. The history of the cultural discovery of the Orient by the West is simply the story of a search for values which will give life flavor, zest, and completeness. It contains much that is silly and absurd, but that is inevitable in any record that began with man's ignorance about his fellows and reaches from spices to God.

*Curt Sachs*

# THE ORIENT AND WESTERN MUSIC

## I

AT THE beginning of our era, the Greek geographer Strabo stated: "Those writers who have consecrated the whole of Asia, as far as India, to Dionysus, derive the greater part of music from there. And one writer says, 'striking the Asiatic cithara'; another calls flutes 'Berecynthian' and 'Phrygian'; and some of the instruments have been called by barbarian names, 'nablas,' 'sambykê,' 'barbitos,' 'magadis,' and several others." [1]

This is the earliest acknowledgment of Western indebtedness to Asiatic music.

Strabo could have added: that the two main tonalities and modes after the Dorian were called Phrygian and Lydian; that not "some," but all Greek instruments had Asiatic names, including the two leading lyres *kithara* and *lyra;* that the "national" Dorian mode itself was a filled-in enharmonic mode, as they called it, with two major thirds and two semitones in the scale of seven notes, and that this enharmonic mode still exists in Mongolia, India, Java, Bali, and, above all, as the "national" mode of Japan; and many other details.

Strabo also should have mentioned the peculiar ideology of Greek music from the later fifth century on, with the theory of *ethos* as the climax. It teaches that music must not be looked at as an indifferent matter of entertainment. It is intimately connected with the Universe and acts on man's character, either stimulating and exciting, or soothing and even enfeebling. More specifically, it gives courage and mental vigor or inspires religious devotion, or lasciviousness, or effeminacy, according to the tonalities, rhythms, and instruments used. Therefore the nation is in-

56

terested in an educational system that gives music the first place, but, while it stresses desirable qualities, eliminates those types likely to damage morale. However, exactly the same ideas had existed in China long before, and Confucius, who lived a hundred years before Plato, .expressed them nearly in the words that the great Hellenic philosopher used. Plato himself, who probably did not know how much he owed to Chinese thinking, referred to the priests of Egypt as his teachers in music as a problem of education and *res publica*.[2]

## II

Doubtless, Asiatic elements have contributed to the music of prehistoric Europe long before Greek and Roman times. Unfortunately, most problems of prehistoric relations between the two continents have not yet been solved; however, anthropology and history are agreed on several migrations westward. There is, for example, the so-called birch-bark civilization (to which the alphorn belongs), shared by certain peoples of Siberia and those of the European Alps, and also the remarkable migration that brought the horse and religious horse rituals to Europe. It is hardly possible that such vast movements, in which objects of everyday life and beliefs with their ceremonials were included, should not have carried the songs of worship and dance from the old to the new homes in the West.

Recently, the author was indeed able to show that the typical style of old-European melody, preserved in ten thousands of medieval notations and folksongs of our days all over the continent, from Iceland and Scandinavia to Spain and the Balkans, follows the same principle of chains of thirds, alternately major and minor, on which the music of the Ugro-Finnish peoples and other North Asiatic groups are based.[3,4] That these chains of thirds reappear among North American Indians, who likewise derive from archaic North Asia, is a valuable confirmation. Some years before my research in prehistoric thirds, I had outlined a method of musical chronology in ancient Europe.[5] Work in this direction would be one of the most fascinating tasks of musical archaeology.

Another question of prehistory is whether there has been a formative influence from Asia on Mediterranean music long before the times of Greece and Arabia. The author often heard vintage songs in Anacapri above Capri, which were quite un-European both in style and in the way in which they were sung; and one should keep in mind that Anacapri in its building style still shows the traces of Phoenician colonization. The same is true of Balearic songs, of which Catalan scientific missions have made an impressive number of records (preserved in the phonographic archives at Barcelona); they, too, have nothing to do with European music and hardly anything with Moorish music. Thus, the tentative suggestion of an extremely old, say, Phoenician style might at least be acceptable as a working hypothesis. A careful investigation on all Mediterranean isles should be made as soon as possible after the war before it is too late; the results would be as important for the history of mankind as any archaeological excavation.

# III

The earliest foothold for a discussion of post-Grecian influence from the East is the liturgical music of both the Byzantine and the Roman Churches. Neglecting the Christian music of Byzantium, which has been much less important in the history of Western music, we turn to the melodies of the Roman Church.

The cantillation of the Catholic Church has been called the Gregorian chant or chorale, in honor of Pope Gregory I the Great (590-604) who is credited with unifying and codifying the musical liturgy. The melodies and the singing style that the pope had written down in a definite and obligatory form had come from various stocks: Italian and Greek folksongs, but, above all, the Jewish synagogue. Some melodies of the latter stock must have existed in the Palestinian homeland before 600 B.C., since the late Abraham Z. Idelsohn, Professor at the Hebrew Union College in Cincinnati, found the exact counterparts of several Gregorian melodies in the isolated Jewish congregations of Yemen in Arabia, Babylonia, and Persia, which had been separated from Palestine and the further development of Jewish ceremonial music after the destruction of the First Temple and the abduction of the Jews into the Babylonian Exile (597 B.C.).

The Oriental elements of the Gregorian chant clashed with the quite different traditions and potentialities of Western music

58

with its chains of thirds, its syllabic nature, and its ever-growing tendency toward harmony and polyphony. They had to tolerate the infiltration of third melodies; they had to accept the dissection of the most fluid coloraturas into syllabic configurations with additional texts, because, as Roman church singers in Charlemagne's time complained, the Franconians with an artless, barbaric, bestial voice crushed the melodies in their throats; and nine hundred years ago, the tradition of Gregorian rhythm was lost for good when part singing began to undermine the free melodic style of Eastern cantillation.

Yet, the ascendancy of Gregorian music was tremendous. With the fourth as an essential interval, the church modes gave a new structural principle that the West had little known before and that became helpful when the native chains of thirds were slowly twisted into octaves of major or minor character. Gregorian chant also preserved its innate independence from metric patterns and the fetters of beaten time, its freer forms, and its even and yet dynamic flow. This kind of singing and shaping, with which medieval men were familiar from early childhood on, has probably had a decisive influence on the secular solo music of Europe. The art of the *troubadours*, *trouvères*, and *minnesänger*, that musicologists of our time have mistakenly interpreted as running in an eternal limping triple time, is in the most important treatise of the thirteenth century expressly characterized as *non ita praecise mensurata* ('not so precisely measured'), that is, just as free in rhythm as the Gregorian chorale. This explains why all the secular songs of that time were written down in the same rhythmically non-committal notation that the chant has used, though the composers had a 'mensural' notation at hand.

This notation, too, had been devised in the western Orient and was only later adapted to the specific needs of European music. Temple musicians of the Eastern worlds between the Mediterranean and the Indian Ocean had developed various notations in order to secure an unadulterated and unadulterable singing of the holy texts in times of crisis, when oral tradition was in danger of being lost. They were different in their symbols, but similar in principle. Most of them ignored the single, isolated note (*c* or *d* or *e*), but provided signs for short, ever-recurring 'melodicles' or basic turns out of which the melody was composed in the way a mosaic is put together—a second, or third, or fourth, upward or downward, empty or with fillers, straight or bent, plain or trilled. To put it philosophically, the ancient Oriental composers felt that melody, as a sounding movement, was composed of movements, not of stops. Best known of the symbols are the little hooks, dashes, and angles, called *nginot* or masoretic accents of Palestinian-Jewish cantillation, which still are printed above or below the corresponding syllables of the text in all Hebrew Bibles.

The *neumes* that European monks used for many centuries in the holy books of Christian service were an outgrowth of the old accents. There was the *pes* or *podatus*, a step upward; the *clivis*, a step downward; the *scandicus*, an ascending triplet; the *climacus*, a descending triplet; the *climacus resupinus flexus*, a quintuplet of a particular form; and a score of other combinations of dots and vertical and oblique dashes to be written above the texts. Neither did they express the pitches, nor the exact distances and intervals, or the relative time values of the individual notes; the direction of the melodic movement was paramount.

Still, there were certain difficulties in imposing such notation on the West, even on Western church music. Here again, the syllabic tradition of most European countries was often imperative enough to chop the easy flow of Gregorian melodies into units of a more stationary character, and these in turn required suitable means of writing and memorizing. For notation, a way out was found in the eleventh century when the *neumes* were written on staves, which would be modern had they not had four lines only (as still in today's antiphonaries, hymnals, and missals): every *neume* is split into two or more stationary notes the exact pitches of which had to be strictly observed in singing.

Assistance in memorizing was particularly necessary because from note to note there could be the distance now of a whole tone, now of a semitone; because the place of the semitone among whole tones differed in the eight church modes, and sometimes even within the same mode; and because any mistake would destroy the tonality of the mode. As a remedy, so we learn, Guido of Arezzo (d. *ca.* 1050) invented solmization: the choir boys memorized the melodies by singing them, not with their texts, but on the since well-known syllables *ut re mi fa sol la,* which had to

PLATE I "Vue du Kiosque de Rembouillet," a typical and charming example of the very widespread use of Chinoiserie in garden architecture.

PLATE 2 "Old Battersea Bridge," lithograph by James A. McNeill Whistler. *Courtesy, Brooklyn Museum.*

PLATE 3 "Twilight Moon at Ryogoku," wood-block color print by Utagawa Hiroshige. *Courtesy, Brooklyn Museum.*

PLATE 4 "Morning Glories in Flowers and Buds," wood-block color print by Katsushika Hokusai. *Courtesy, Brooklyn Museum.*

PLATE 5 "Les Grenouilles," woodcut by Charles Houdard. *Courtesy, Brooklyn Museum.*

be alined so that any semitone fell upon the step *mi-fa*. The word "invented," however, is inadequate. Not only had practically all Oriental nations known some kind of solmization (although on different syllables); not only did it play an outstanding role in the musical education of Greece. Abbot Odo of Cluny, who died in 942—more than a hundred years before Guido of Arezzo—had in his *Tonarius* mentioned certain queer names of notes, and among them *re, scembs, caemar, caphe, asel,* which, though slightly disfigured by the Latin-writing author, are easily recognizable as Semitic words—particularly *scembs,* the Arabic word for 'sun' being *shams* or *shems,* and the Hebrew word, *shemesh.* Thus, European monks knew Oriental solmization before 1000; and this fact becomes even more remarkable as the only three-letter syllable in Guido's solmization, *sol,* means 'sun' in Latin.

Guido also is generally credited with having devised the famous 'hand,' a method used far into modern times to facilitate solmization in melodies of a more elaborate character. This is the method: every note throughout the whole range had a fixed place on one of the various joints of the fingers; so the pupils, touching them with a finger of the other hand while they sang, were prevented from going astray. However, this method, too, had precedents in the Orient. The Chinese have used the hand to memorize the four types of tonal inflection in their language and, consequently, their music: they touch the third phalange of the forefinger to indicate the level tone; the tip of the same finger for the rising tone; the tip of the ring finger for the falling tone; and the third phalange of the same finger for the dialectal (and musically meaningless) shortening of any of the foregoing movements. One of the Hindu methods of memorizing the cantillation of the holy Vedas was even more similar to Guido's hand; with the right index, the singers touched a certain place on the left hand where the note to be sung was situated. There were five such places: the small finger, for the lowest note; the lower end of the forefinger, for the following note; then the ring finger; and finally the index again for both the fourth and fifth notes.

A paragraph on the Oriental sources of the Gregorian chant, its performance, and its auxiliary means, would not be complete without discussing antiphony. Hebrew and other West-Oriental poems were conceived in a peculiar parallelism—*parallelismus memborum* is the scientific term—every half verse being answered by another half verse which expressed either an intensification of the first idea or else an antinomy, not exactly in the same poetic meters, but in similar words. The beginning of the well-known psalm Nineteenth, for example, reads:

> The heavens declare the glory of God,
> And the firmament showeth His handiwork,
>
> Day unto day uttereth speech,
> And night unto night revealeth knowledge.

Such parallel lines were sung either by two alternating half choruses or by a soloist and an answering chorus. In both forms, alternation passed to the Christian Church, as *antiphony* and as *response*. Antiphony played so important a role in the Oriental church that one of the Church Fathers, St. Basil, who lived in the fourth century, defended the singing of the psalms both antiphonally and responsorially, as did "the Egyptians, Libyans, Thebans, Palestinians, Phoenicians, Syrians, and the dwellers by the Euphrates"—that is, all congregations in the Western Orient. In the same century, Pope Damasus (366-384) introduced antiphony into the Roman liturgy. The Church had kept it for about eleven hundred years when the famous Flemish director of music at St. Mark's in Venice, Adriaen Willaert (d. 1562), adapted the old Oriental-Gregorian antiphony to extra-liturgical works written in the polyphonic style of the Palestrina age: two half choruses were stationed in the two organ lofts, which, in St. Mark's, face each other, and sang, now alternately, now together, in sharp contrasts and in mystic *chiaroscuro*. This innovation met the stylistic needs of the later sixteenth century so well that Venetian and Roman composers did not hesitate to follow Willaert's example and to use the polychoral style both in religious and secular music. Often, the choruses were of different pitches, one clearer, without basses, one darker, without sopranos; or else, one was entirely or partially vocal, and the other instrumental; if both were instrumental, one of them would be composed of brass instruments, that is, cornets and trombones, and one of bowed strings. However, the grandiosity and love for color and shades after the Renaissance and particularly in the Baroque did not rest satisfied with two choruses. Three and four choruses became frequent, and many times even four did not suffice; indeed, Queen Elizabeth's court organist, Thomas Tallis (d. 1585) wrote a motet, *Spem in aliam nunquam habui*, for no less than forty voice parts in eight choruses. The polychoral climax seems to have been reached sometime in the first half of the eighteenth century with a composition for forty-eight voices by Giuseppe Ottavio Pitoni (d. 1743), *maestro di cappella* at St. Peter's and the Lateran. It certainly must have been embarrassing to give adequate places to so many choruses; but, making a virtue of necessity, the composers added to the effect by fully utilizing all advantages that the architecture of churches and palaces granted. Thus, Virgilio Mazzocchi (d. 1628) wrote a much admired, impressive *musicone* for St. Peter's in Rome and placed its twelve or sixteen choruses, partly on the ground floor under the dome, partly on the gallery on the level of the roof, and partly in the dizzying height of the lantern above the dome.

But this was a long, long way from the simple antiphony that the Bible describes: "And the women sang one to another in their play, and said: 'Saul has slain his thousands, and David his ten thousands.'"

Two relics of Oriental trends in church music in the first thousand years A.D. are the organ and bell chimes, such as the one on the tower of Riverside Church at New York. The organ seems to have been created in the second century B.C. in Egypt; small specimens reached Western Europe as gifts from Eastern rulers about a thousand years later in the times of Pipin and Charlemagne. Bell chimes came to Europe about the same time and were often depicted in the miniatures of psalters to illustrate the last psalm—*Laudate Eum cum cymbalis*—the (not quite appropriate) name *cymbala* being the one that the monks gave to the bell chime.

The arrival of the organ and the bell chime were important, indeed decisive, as they were the first instruments with fixed pitches in the West, able, and actually used, to introduce fixed standard pitches and intervals where players of fretless stringed instruments and singers had been blindly groping from note to note. Organs made constant retuning imperative, and both organs and bell chimes were at an ever-faster rate copied and reproduced to meet the increasing demand of monasteries and churches. This implied recipes, experiments, and mathematical calculation. In other words, medieval Europe had for the first time to face the grave problem how to establish music on fixed ratios instead of caprice and anarchy. To appreciate the vital importance of the two instruments, one must have seen how many among the treatises on music written throughout the Middle Ages deal with this problem.

# IV

The following tide of Oriental influence came from the civilization of Islam, from nations speaking Arabic and Persian, and it lasted during the almost eight hundred years of Moorish and Arabian domination in Spain (711-1492), in which Oriental culture was not only combated, but also eagerly imitated and absorbed.

All the instruments that we have used in modern times once came from Asia, some via Byzantium, some as a consequence of the crusades, but most of them through the Iberian gateway: flutes, oboes, and clarinets; bagpipes, trumpets, and kettledrums; the violin, the mandolin, and the guitar; cymbals, xylophones, and *glockenspiele*. Even the harpsichord and the piano, apparently so fully European, are Western only as far as keyboards and actions are concerned; the instruments themselves on which these devices have been grafted are the psaltery and the dulcimer of the Middle East. The poetic literature of the fourteenth century is full of Arabic names of instruments: *canon, enmorache, naquaires, atambores, guitarra morisca, rabé morisco, exabeva, albogón, añafiles, atabales, cors sarrazinois,* and many others. The lute still bears an Arabic name (*al'ūd*); the word *tambour* is Persian; *pandora* and *bandurria* can be traced back to Sumerian terms.

Europe's achievement has been the variation and improvement of Asiatic instruments—either by altering and fusing Oriental types, as with the bassoon, the saxophone, and the hybrid brasses of the cornet and the tuba families; or by perfecting their technical contrivances, ranges, and sonorities. However, these fusions and perfections set in at a comparatively late time, at the end of the Middle Ages, when the musical situation had posed problems to European instrument makers that their Oriental predecessors

64

had not known—particularly the extension of the musical range and the ever-growing polyphonic and harmonic tendencies.

Long after that time of de-Orientalization, Europe still had the old Oriental bipartition into *musica alta* and *musica bassa*—outdoor and indoor music. Clamorous, indeed deafening was the outdoor music of shrill oboes, brasses, and stick-beaten drums; the indoor music of strings and flutes was soft, restrained, limpid, yet more trenchant than modern Western music is. The poets of the fourteenth century keep them carefully apart, and so do the painters: on the Sienese Lippo Memmi's little "Coronation of the Virgin" in the museum at Munich, the indoor music is strictly separated from the outdoor band.

I just dared to characterize the indoor ensemble as soft and yet slightly more trenchant than modern Western music. Indeed, the similarity of such ensembles, recorded by either poets or painters, with groups that we hear today in North Africa, Syria, or Iraq is so close that we are able to compare the timbres of medieval European and modern Arabian music.

Even vocal music must have had the Oriental character: the angels forming chorus on van Eyck's famous altarpiece at St. Bavo's in Ghent (*ca.* 1425), obviously modeled after the choir singers of Flemish cathedrals at the beginning of the fifteenth century, betray the nasaling style of the East in the wrinkles around their noses and mouths (a trait that commercial photographs of the painting rarely show).

It has generally been claimed that a wandering instrument carries its music along, in other words, that instruments transplanted into new climates were prone to retain the customary styles that they had possessed in their home lands. But all attempts at finding direct traces of Oriental melodies, forms, or styles in Europe proper have failed, including the latest ones by Henry George Farmer. The reason is evident. Most Oriental instruments were detained many decades, and often centuries, in the Iberian quarantine before they were allowed to cross the Pyrenees and had all the time necessary to acclimate themselves and to conform to the style of Europe.

At the time the instruments were absorbed, Europe had definitely shifted from unaccompanied to accompanied melody, and this process had necessarily destroyed the characteristic features

65

of melody in its proper sense. It was then that organs, mono-chords, and psalteries were given keyboards, and that Persian lutes lost the quill plectra with which they had been plucked, since either transformation facilitated chordal and polyphonic playing. Under such conditions, Arabian melody could hardly influence the music of the West.

There might be one curious exception in the thirteenth and fourteenth centuries, particularly in France and, of all things, in polyphony. The phenomenon itself has a decent Greek name: *isometry*. It means that a certain melody follows two different cyclic laws. The melody itself or, better, the set of notes that form the melody might be, say, ten measures long and then be re-peated as often as the text requires. But there also is a certain rhythmical pattern—a peculiar arrangement of, say, half notes, dotted quarter notes and regular quarter notes, which in a similar way is repeated over and over again to the end of the piece. The rhythmical period does not necessarily coincide with the melodic period—it would be twelve or sixteen measures long and therefore start its repetition when the melody is already in its third or sev-enth measure; and its second repetition would begin still later in the second repetition of the melody. Thus the two periods over-lap each time in a different way and the notes of the melody ap-pear each time in a different rhythmical arrangement.

Rhythmical patterns have never been a trait of European music; but they are of basic importance in the Islamic Orient, and particularly in India, where all pieces are headed by the indi-cation of both their melodic pattern or *rāga* and their rhythmical pattern or *tāla*. Moreover, the medieval musicians, writing in Latin, called the rhythmical period *talea*, a word non-Latin, in-deed un-Latin, but closely reminiscent of the correct Sanskrit name, *tāla*. The melodic pattern was given a true Latin name, *color*; but the Sanskrit term, *rāga*, also meant 'color.' This is so striking a coincidence that a connection between the Indian and the European conceptions can hardly be doubted.

# V

There was hardly a trace of Oriental influence in the follow-ing four or five hundred years. However, European self-sufficiency changed with the exotic fashions of the eighteenth and nineteenth centuries, which concentrated on themes Chinese and Turkish. At about 1700, when Turkish armies no longer threatened the peace of Europe, the armies of the West began to imitate the Turkish bands, the intoxication of which they had experienced in more than two hundred years of warfare in Eastern Europe. The newly organized 'Turkish' or 'Janissaries' music of European regiments provided a first stronghold to noisy percussion, such as bass drums, cymbals, triangles, and jingling crescents, which before had been used only as a *musica irregularis* for masquerades and similar occasions.

Slowly, military percussion made its way to the regular orchestra. Cymbals had already appeared in Nicolaus Adam Strungk's opera *Esther* (Hamburg 1680); and triangles were used in 1710 in the Hamburg opera and 1717 in the court orchestra at Dresden. At first, they merely provided local color for subjects taken from the Orient, which from the eighteenth century on have so much attracted the composers of operas, and particularly of comic operas—Gluck's *Cadi dupé* (1761) and *La Rencontre imprévue* (1764), Mozart's *Seraglio* (1781), Weber's *Abu Hassan* (1811) and *Oberon* (1825), Peter Cornelius' *Barber of Bagdad* (1858), Puccini's *Madame Butterfly* (1904) and *Turandot* (1924), Henry Rabaud's *Marouf* (1914), and hundreds more of 'Oriental' operas and ballets.

The Romantic period, eager to add new shades to its musical palette, did not hesitate to give permanent seats to the guests from Asia, even when no Oriental theme was in need of exotic colors. From the first quarter of the nineteenth century on, the Turkish music is dissolved in its components and has merged with the orchestra.

The same is true of the symphonic orchestra. In Joseph Haydn's *Military Symphony* (1794), the Turkish music was still a merely characterizing factor; in the last movement of Beethoven's *Ninth*, it was no longer military, but in a more general way suggestive of enthusiasm and resolute energy; the Romantic symphony, like the Romantic opera, embodied it wholeheartedly as a coloristic agent.

It is obvious that the composers of Oriental operas and symphonies did not rest satisfied with Turkish music, but also tried to orientalize their melodies—in the eighteenth century, as they thought Oriental melody might be, and in the nineteenth and twentieth centuries, as they knew it was. But from the point of view of our survey, it is entirely meaningless that Weber wrote his *Turandot* overture on a genuine Chinese melody taken from some book on China; that Cornelius indulged in the augmented seconds of the Arabian maqām *Higāz;* or that Puccini's *Madame Butterfly* sings in the major thirds of Japanese pentatonism. They drew from Oriental music without transforming the music of the West.

# VI

But the general trends in Western music around 1900 became different, at first in France. The world's fairs at Paris from 1889 to 1900 presented excellent examples of Oriental music from all parts of North Africa and Asia. Certainly not for the first time. But European music had entered a critical stage in which sensitivity and receptivity were extraordinarily increased. On the one hand, Wagner's *Tristan* had irrevocably dissolved the narrow-limited dualism of major and minor; on the other hand, the young Frenchmen tended away from the opaque grandiloquence of the German school and from both Classicism and Romanticism; the fundaments of the nineteenth century were shaken, and the world was waiting for something new to be born. Oriental music was no longer listened to with the supercilious self-satisfaction of the *arrivé*, but with the humbler eagerness of the unprejudiced open mind. As a little-known pioneer, Louis-Albert Bourgault-Ducoudray in Paris published Greek and Oriental melodies in the 1870's, "hoping to extend the horizon among the musicians of Europe." Some twenty years later, Claude Debussy (1862-1918) is said to have taken his famous whole tone scale from a Javanese orchestra at the world's fair, which is probably true with the restriction that the Javanese *salendro* scale (which must be the one that inspired the French master) consisted of five more or less equal six-fifths of tones, while Debussy's scale comprised six whole tones. But the true Oriental experience might have been different.

Faced with Oriental music, the world of 1900 began to realize the limitations of Western music. Maybe for the first time, it dawned upon the European musician and critic that the great achievement in harmony, polyphony, and orchestration had meant sacrifices in other fields; that the unbelievable riches of modes which the Orient still possessed had burnt down to major and minor; that under the straitjacket of harmonic function melody proper had become a poor connecting line between related chords; that rhythm had become an all too simple time-beating.

It was a wholesome shock to realize that our music was not the only real thing in the middle of what we had thought to be the primitive babble of less advanced nations. And it seems that the shock has even been stronger in this country than in Europe; America's estrangement from chordal music is more radical. Her predilection for modern Russian and Negro music hints to the Orient, though only indirectly: both the Russians and the African Negroes have in thousands of years absorbed Oriental influences, and both have brought us a restoration of innate motor impulse and melodic freedom. We will not be foolish enough to imitate Oriental music or to forget the glorious traditions of our own world. But we are trying to widen our scope and re-win grounds lost and forgotten—lost and forgotten in the lands of the West, but alive and faithfully kept in the East.

*Laurance P. Roberts*

# THE ORIENT AND WESTERN ART

## CHINA

RELATIONS between Europe and China have a long but broken history, dating back to the third century before Christ with the Han dynasty. In the beginning Chinese silk, carried overland across Central Asia and distributed to the Mediterranean world by the Parthians, was the medium of exchange. This silk, quite literally worth its weight in gold, was, until the outbreak of present hostilities in the Pacific, one of the major exports of the East to the Occident.

Wars and civil unrest and the resulting unsettled conditions closed this overland trade at different times, though it was thriving in the T'ang dynasty (618-906) and again under the Yuan or Mongol dynasty (1260-1368). But with the coming of the Ming Emperors of China, who did not rule over Central Asia as the Mongols had done, the overland trade route was once more closed and it was left to the Arabs to carry on a combined land and sea trade through the Near East and the Indian Ocean. The Portuguese as a result of their exploratory voyage in the late sixteenth century were the first European nation to open direct seaborne trade via the Cape of Good Hope to Canton. The English, French, and Dutch soon followed with their East India Companies founded, respectively, in 1600, 1664, and 1602, with the English eventually getting the largest share of the business. The United States entered the trade in the early nineteenth century. Its clipper ships, which were faster than the English East Indiamen, made the American flag famous in the Far East and soon flooded the Eastern seaboard states with a variety of Chinese goods.

Finds of Han textiles on the overland trade routes and fourteenth century Chinese silk stuffs still in European church treasuries bear witness to the continuing importance of silk as the primary export from China to the West. But the influence of Chinese silk was much greater on the economic life of the Occident than on the artistic. Even in the Renaissance the designs found on Western silks are those of the Near East.

Next in importance to silk as an export commodity were the porcelains and ceramics. The presence of T'ang ceramics at Samarra near Bagdad, a capital of the Abbasid Khalifs from 838 to 883 A.D., shows an early regard for the superior Chinese ware. Under the Ming dynasty (1368-1644), porcelain began to rival silk as an export commodity since its weight and bulk were not the problem to the new sea traffic that they had been to overland caravans. During the last forty years, examples of Ming celadon ware have been found in the Philippines, in India, on the West coast of Africa, and on the narrowest part of the Malay peninsula over which they were transshipped from the Gulf of Siam to the Bay of Bengal. The famous Wareham bowl in England, dated *ca.* 1530 by its English silver mount, is of celadon, and in the National Museum in Constantinople is a famous collection of blue and white ware, begun by the Sultans of Turkey during the late sixteenth and early seventeenth centuries. In the eighteenth century, Augustus the Strong of Saxony, a contemporary of K'ang Hsi in China, made a large collection of famille verte, and Mme. de Pompadour, as befitted one of the biggest stockholders in the French East India Company, did her best to popularize Chinese Porcelains. Eventually in the late seventeenth and early eighteenth century blue and white became so popular that the manufacturers of Delft ware in Holland quickly copied it to save part of the home market for themselves. It was Johann F. Böttger's discovery in 1709 of the method of making porcelain that saved the European ceramic industry from the overwhelming Chinese competition. A number of the more popular shapes and designs continued to be Chinese, and Chinese porcelain remained in great demand.

The cargo ships in the late eighteenth and early nineteenth

centuries were laden with dinner sets, mantel garnitures, punch bowls, and a variety of other household porcelains as well as with lacquered furniture, wallpaper, silks, and ivory trinkets. It was these household wares which, in the eighteenth century, most affected European taste and finally produced a fanciful but wholly charming "style chinoise" in all forms of decorative art. This "Chinoiserie," with overtones of present political significance, has but lately been revived, and the familiar design of the small Chinese figures against a background of pagodas and willows is once again seen in fabrics, wall coverings, prints, and porcelains. Although these are Occidental interpretations of the Orient with no real understanding of the aesthetics or philosophy behind them, they have much that is truly delightful. Thus by the end of the great days of the China Trade in the mid-nineteenth century, supercargoes on the clipper ships and the Chinese merchants in Canton had spread Chinese goods, even though in many cases deliberately manufactured to standards of European taste and for the European market, to the homes of Europe and America.

Despite all this trade the importers had not dealt in fine porcelains made for the Chinese taste, old bronzes, paintings, or samples of calligraphy. It is probable that no Chinese *objet d'art* was ever brought home as a curio by a New England captain, for such objects were not for export, even if the captain had had the taste to appreciate them. It remained for the art dealer, both Occidental and Oriental, to take advantage of the distressed economic conditions in China from the last years of the nineteenth century until the present war and to bring these things to the growing group of collectors and museums interested in Chinese art. This group, however, was and remains but a minute fraction of the Occidental population that since the eighteenth century has used the Chinese exports made for the Western trade. Connoisseurs today know more of Chinese art and taste than ever before, but the effect of this knowledge on the artistic life of the West is almost negligible.

The influence of Japan on recent Western art has been greater than that of any other Far Eastern country. But the results of this influence are restricted almost entirely to the French art of the last three decades of the nineteenth century. Since 1909, with the exception of minor interest in the fields of architecture, interior decoration, garden planning, and flower arrangements, the artists of Europe have not turned to Japan for inspiration. Inasmuch as the Japanese color print was the medium for the influence of Japanese on French art, it might be well to relate briefly the history of Japanese print collecting in the West, with specific examples of just what elements of this art the French artists of the late nineteenth century adopted.

Until its failure in 1797, the Dutch East India Company had for two centuries traded with the Japanese at the island of Deshima in the harbor of Nagasaki. The goods exported from Japan were primarily lacquers and Imari ware porcelains, both decorated with elaborate patterns calculated to please the European taste. Paintings, sculpture, prints, and textiles were unknown to this trade and although, on the death in 1814 of Isaac Titsingh, former chief of the Dutch East India Company at Deshima, nine Japanese prints were found among his belongings, in general the Dutch trade did not handle paintings, sculptures, prints, and textiles. Prints, in particular, remained unknown to collectors and artists until after Perry's expedition to Japan in 1853 had opened the way to modern trading methods.

The London Exposition of 1862 boasted a Japanese court and it was here that prints were first shown publicly. Later in the same year these prints were sent to Paris where an art shop kept by one Houseil in the Rue de Rivoli seems to have been the French outlet for them. Almost at once they were noticed by Alfred Stevens, Whistler, Diaz, Fortuny, and Legros. Manet, Fantin-Latour, Degas, and Monet as well as the engravers Bracquemont and Jacquemart also came under their spell. Japanese art became better known to the public at the Paris Exposition of 1867. In the same year the "Jongleur," a society of artists, began weekly meetings at the home of M. Solon, the director of the ceramic factory at Sèvres, to study this new art. Although the great paintings and sculptures of Japan were still unknown to the most eager French collectors and students, the prints became their all-absorbing passion. The story of those great collecting years, especially those of the eighties and nineties, has been charmingly told by the late M. Raymond Koechlin. His pages are filled with the excitement of the discovery of this hitherto unsuspected and rich art world.

The movement grew rapidly and in 1873 there was a Universal Exposition in Vienna which spread the knowledge of Japanese prints still further. In the Paris fair of 1878 there was a Japanese section organized by a Japanese dealer, Wakai, and in 1888 the Burlington Fine Arts Club in London had a Japanese print show followed two years later in Paris by a special show. By then the roster of collectors contained the names of men important in all fields of artistic endeavor: Louis Gonse, Charles Edward Haviland, A. Rouart, Galimard, Koechlin, Isaac de Camondo, Guimet, de Goncourt, Champfleury, Zola, and Villot. Another Japanese dealer, Hayashi, was in charge of the Exposition in Paris in 1900, for which the Japanese government lent really good sculptures and paintings. Although these rare examples of the real Japanese art returned to Japan at the end of the exhibition, they opened another new vista to those interested in the Orient. This fervid admiration for Japanese art is reflected in the tenuous and wavy style of Aubrey Beardsley's drawings. It also found expression in the so-called "Style Nouveau" of interior decoration. This style adapted to wrought iron and other decorative materials the same Japanese influence that was expressed in the art of Beardsley. The art dealer, S. Bing, decorated his shop in this style and a room at the Invalides of about 1900 also represents it. But it was a sterile form and, within a few years, a dead one.

The first important sale of Japanese art was that of the Goncourt collection in 1897. In 1902 and 1903 Hayashi offered his collection at auction and in 1904 Villot followed suit. The Bing sale in 1906 brought to an end the great period of Japanese art in France. Buyers from other countries built up their collections from these sales. Charles Freer of Detroit, Otto Kummel of the Far Eastern Museum at Berlin, Moslé at Leipzig, and Olden at Dusseldorf entered the Oriental field. From 1909-1914 there was a series of six print shows at the Pavillion de Marsan for which Charles Vignier and Hogitaro Inada did the catalogues. These exhibitions also included lacquers, potteries, and sculptures, and nearly all the private collectors lent for the occasion. These famous shows reviewed twenty-five years of collecting, and although there were no paintings, since these were kept in Japan, it was clear that Paris was the center for Occidental knowledge of Japanese minor arts. It was these minor arts in truth that had the greatest influence on European design, an influence which is still felt in the fields of the graphic arts and in textile and ceramic design. With the retirement of Bing and Hayashi, the domination of the Oriental art field by Japan was at an end and the new dealers and new collectors turned to ancient China. Hayashi indeed had had a few Chinese bronzes, but the pieces came too high for the Paris collectors and eventually went to Gonse at Freiburg. A few others of the old Japanese group, among whom were Alexis Rouart and Isaac de Camondo, admitted Chinese objects to their collections, but in general France remained the center for Japanese collectors while Chinese collecting became international.

The first name that comes to most minds when the subject of the influence of Japanese prints on European art is under discussion is probably that of James Whistler, the American painter who worked in England. The results of his contact with this new art form were twofold: a new subject matter in his paintings and a stylistic influence in his prints. "La Princesse de le Pays de Porcelain," done in 1864 and now hanging in the Freer Gallery in Washington, is an example of his introduction of Japanese accessories into a painting that is primarily European in style, while his series of prints of the Thames are close in feeling and technique to the best of the Japanese print-makers.

If one compares such a print as "Old Battersea Bridge" (*Pl. 2*) to the Hiroshige "Twilight Moon at Ryogoku" (*Pl. 3*) this derivation is at once apparent, for the similarity not only in subject matter but in the treatment of the component parts is clear. There are even such particular details as the "butterfly signature" placed under the left of the bridge in the Whistler to compare to the calligraphic signature in the upper right of the Hiroshige.

There were other artists who very strongly felt the impact of this new art with its bold design and strong, clear colors. The

Impressionists, officially launched in 1863 with Monet as their sponsor, had been struggling with the problems of pure color and light. They now added to their findings the new and fascinating angular composition which they discovered in Japanese prints. Clear examples of their borrowing are Monet's "Waterloo Bridge," now in the Adolph Lewisohn collection, and any one of Degas' ballet compositions.

Startling evidence of European borrowing of subject matter and style from the Japanese is to be found by comparison of the three illustrations of prints in Plates 4, 5, and 6. Plate 4 is a print by the great Japanese artist Hokusai. Here we have the continuation of realism and flat areas of pattern which are so characteristic of all Japanese work. In Plate 5, a woodcut done in 1894 by Charles Houdard and called "Les Grenouilles," we find in the artist's rendering of the iris and water a deliberate borrowing of stylistic treatment, and although the frogs are more naturalistic in the use of light and shade than the one in the Hokusai, the general effect is so similar as to give the feeling that the artist was deliberately working in a foreign style. There is even the detail of the artist's initials, rendered calligraphically and placed in a cartouche in the upper right-hand corner.

The resemblance is, perhaps, even more striking when we study the lithograph of Henri Rachou dated 1892 (*Pl. 6*); for the areas of flat color with no cast shadows, the use of a calligraphic line, and even such a trick as the inverted signature in the cartouche are, when combined with the subject matter, a direct borrowing from the Japanese. Or take such an example as the Utamaro reproduced in Plate 7 and compare it with the Mary Cassatt in Plate 8. Here we have the same broad treatment of the figures, the same diagonal design, and almost the same flat colors.

Another French artist working under this influence was Paul Gauguin, and although his late works done in the South Seas have a palette produced by that environment, his early Breton work has not only the general pattern but the subdued coloring of the Japanese work.

But the artist who made the Japanese contribution most particularly his own was Toulouse-Lautrec. There is almost no print of his which does not owe something to the basic Japanese

PLATE 6 "Panneau Décoratif," color lithograph by Henri
Rachou. *Courtesy, Brooklyn Museum.*

PLATE 7 "Kaiyoikomachi," wood-block color print by Kitagawa Utamaro. *Courtesy, Brooklyn Museum.*

PLATE 8　"The Fitting," drypoint by Mary Cassatt. *Courtesy, Brooklyn Museum.*

PLATE 9 "Au Moulin Rouge," color lithograph by Henri de Toulouse-Lautrec. *Courtesy, Brooklyn Museum.*

concept of large, flat areas of pure color, no shadows, and an ingenuity of design that is found in such print-makers as Sharaku and Bunsho.

In addition to those outward resemblances Toulouse-Lautrec was also greatly influenced by the technical genius of the Japanese print-makers. In the lithograph reproduced in Plate 8 there is a brilliant example of the omission of what in a Japanese woodblock print would be the key block. This can be seen in the passage of the woman's hand against her waist and in the outline of the neck of the dress. Such tricks as those were, of course, the ultimate refinements of an incredibly complicated process. In a late Japanese print sometimes as many as fifty different blocks are used, one for each color or shade, and the technical skill responsible for the perfection of printing has only recently been matched in the Western world by the development of highly complicated printing machines.

Toulouse-Lautrec, more than any of the contemporary French artists, understood the brilliance of this new influence and its adaptability to what was then, in Europe, the new art of the poster. Inasmuch as many of the Japanese prints had been originally designed as advertisements for individual actors or the more famous Geisha it was not too extraordinary that Lautrec's series on Jean Avril and Loie Fuller, to mention only two, should have come into being.

It is, moreover, from this original source, distilled through French taste and training, that the best of our contemporary poster work derives.

Several attempts have been made to graft Japanese architecture onto European design. Some have been more successful than others, the best being those where the architect has tried to make use of the principles of Japanese building rather than to reproduce the "quaint" or "charming" effect of a Japanese house.

These principles of Japanese architecture can be described in a somewhat oversimplified generalization as an approach to building by means of post and lintel, a type of structure in which there is the closest relation between exterior and interior; a type of residence in which, in a country where overpopulation and lack of dwelling space are two irreconcilable facts, the greatest

77

possible use is made of each square foot. The modern flat with its one-room combination of living-, bedroom, and sometimes kitchen too, is the European equivalent of the Japanese house in which screens are used to subdivide the one large area used as a communal living-room during the day, into the more or less requisite number of bedrooms, or more properly speaking sleeping quarters, at night. It is, of course, a truism that the lack of furniture simplifies the Japanese problem. As a corollary to the use of this basic type of building, we have the fact that the principle distinction between the home of the very rich noble and that of the very humble farmer is one of quality of materials and size of dwelling; the architectural style remains the same. The exceptions are the results of the attempts on the part of the wealthy to imitate European period or modern architectural designs with almost universally disastrous results.

The book by the German architect Bruno Taut, *Houses and People of Japan* (London, Gifford, 1938), is the most comprehensive study by a European of Japanese methods of construction and the way in which the Japanese house fits the Japanese life and climate. It is true that the ideal climate for such building is found in the south or tropical zones, but several houses have been built in Southern California in the last few years making excellent use of the Japanese principle of relating the house to the gardens in order to derive the greatest benefit from both.

Among the elements of Japanese architecture of which European and American designers have made use the most important adaptations seem to me to be: the window running from ceiling to floor which can be either lowered or moved to one side to open up one or more sides of a room to the lawn or garden; the experimentation with texture and design in the building materials and decorating fabrics; and, in some cases, the actual use of paper screens copied from the shoji. The next step may well be when the mural artist is called in as collaborator with the architect to decorate in seemly fashion these paper walls.

There is one great fallacy in this field which should perhaps be corrected at this time. The Imperial Hotel in Tokyo, on which rests much of Frank Lloyd Wright's fame, is, contrary to the accepted version, most decidedly not the result of any study of Japanese architecture. There are few dwellings less suitable to the regional climatic conditions or in which the problems of a hotel such as circulation and service have been less successfully solved. To be sure, it stood through the great earthquake of 1923, but it sagged badly as a result, and it should be mentioned that a block of 1890 red brick houses adjoining the hotel and the Tokyo station of the same period not too far away, stood intact while many buildings of purely Japanese design suffered no damage whatever.

It is, obviously, impossible for the West to adopt completely a style of architecture which gives no thought to central heating and plumbing, but the basic Japanese elements of simplicity, appropriateness, and quality of materials may well be important contributions to our present somewhat muddled and eclectic architectural styles.

The minor arts of Japan, such as lacquer, basketry, landscape gardening, and flower arrangement, have had some influence on European living, though the Japanese forms have, in many cases, been lifted bodily from their native habitat and set down without understanding or real appreciation in a foreign environment. The Japanese garden, so permanently symbolized by the small arrangement in a flat dish of mirrors, pebbles, rocks, moss, and arched red wooden bridges with sometimes a Tori and small figures, has only recently come into prominence as the ideal solution for the minute plot of ground of a city dwelling. The West has, however, a long way to go before it reaches the Japanese freedom from non-essential elements whether in its homes, its paintings, or its flower arrangement.

The art of flower arrangement, about which so much has been written and said and so little comprehended, has in Japan strong religious overtones and is often tied to the canons of Buddhism, which demand above all else simplicity and naturalness. Here again the American housewife, whether she spends several dollars for handsomely bound and illustrated books or a dime for a pamphlet on the art of flower arrangement, has yet to learn the fundamental rule of Japanese flower arrangement, which is that the flowers, except in the formal or ritualistic arrangements, must approach as closely as possible the natural appearance of those same flowers when actually growing.

The various Japanese styles of flower arrangement are far too complex and too subtle for an American, untrained in Japan and with a different type of home to decorate. Yet the Japanese emphasis on flower arrangement has spurred Americans to attempt something more in the way of interior decoration than the tight bunch of posies so popular in the Victorian era. Today every flower show has its flower-arrangement section, there is considerable literature on the subject, including many books on the Japanese style, and the field is a fertile one for lectures. Americans as a people are temperamentally unable to duplicate the economy and subtlety of the best Japanese work, as could be seen when American and Japanese work was exhibited side by side at Yamanaka's in New York in the early spring of 1941. But under the inspiration of Japan, our arrangements are achieving more variety and interest than before.

### INDIA

The early story of Indian artistic influence on the West parallels rather closely that of China. In the eighteenth century, when England had taken over most of the East Indian trade at the expense of Portugal and France, Indian cottons were in great demand and the incredibly fine textiles, like the Dacca muslins, were rightly regarded as treasures of the East. The small all-over floral patterns with which the cottons were printed soon set the fashion and were copied in Europe on woolens, linens, and silks. In the nineteenth century, the infant American textile industry adopted the craze and did a thriving business with sprigged cottons of local manufacture as well as with plain white but incredibly sheer muslins made for Empire dresses but technically inspired by Indian weaves. At the same time, Kashmir shawls became fashionable, and the Scottish Paisley shawl business grew up to meet the demand for a similarly patterned but cheaper article.

Like the Chinese porcelains and Japanese lacquers, the Indian trade goods gained wide acceptance and inspired a host of imitators, but they had nothing to do with the great arts of Indian sculpture or painting. With the exception of the short-lived architectural style in Portugal, a relic of Portuguese maritime trade in the seventeenth century, Europe and America have known little of these Indian arts until modern times. Then, as in the case of China and Japan, the knowledge of the specialist grew side by side with the increase of the art collections, but little of this knowledge trickled through to the general public. One looks in vain for traces of Indian influence in contemporary fashion or art.

The story of Indian collections begins with the British Museum, which was an early nineteenth century repository for certain Indian sculptures, especially the superb reliefs from Amaravati. The Victoria and Albert Museum honors its Indian objects by housing them in a separate building. But until 1937 when the collection was happily regrouped, nineteenth-century presents to Queen Victoria were exhibited in preference to those pieces which better illustrated the true Indian taste. It remained for the Boston Museum under the curatorship of Dr. Ananda K. Coomaraswamy and with the support of Dr. Denman W. Ross to show Indian painting and sculpture most adequately to the Western world. The Boston collection, together with its published catalogues and other books by Dr. Coomaraswamy, affords an unrivaled survey to which every student of the subject must turn. The Metropolitan Museum also has an Indian collection, and there are fine Indian things in Philadelphia, Chicago, Kansas City, Brooklyn, and several other museums, but there are no great American or European private collectors in this field.

It is especially disappointing to find Indian art not more warmly appreciated in England. Perhaps the Anglo-Saxon temperament shrinks from the frankly sensual quality of Indian sculpture and is equally repelled by the jungle-like complexity of the multiple heads, arms, and symbols of many Hindu deities. At any rate, in a book like E. B. Havell's *Indian Sculpture* you find almost a hostility to the subject, which certainly does not help to interpret to the Western mind Indian sculpture and the Indian religious concepts which they embody. The English evidently have liked the Mughal miniature paintings, for there are good collections of them in the Victoria and Albert Museum and in private hands.* But this type of painting, a combination of Persian and European influences grafted on a native style and used to portray and glorify the Mughal emperors and their countries, is not truly Indian. In the West, it is only at the Boston Museum

* For instance, the superb group belonging to Sir Chester Beatty.

and in a few other collections on the eastern seaboard that one can see more than a scattering of the older Indian paintings from Nepal and the Jain monasteries, or the more recent and wholly charming paintings from Rajputana and the Hill States that illustrate Hindu mythology and poetry.

It is not too much to hope that the archaic strength of the earliest Indian sculpture or the sweetness and charm of the early nineteenth-century paintings from the Hill States may introduce the more interested public to an appreciation and understanding of the fine achievements of India's artists.

## SOUTH PACIFIC

The arts of the South Pacific islands have had absolutely no influence, to my knowledge, on contemporary Western artists, although the Western world has known of them for more than two centuries and now, thanks to museum collections, offers a better view of the South Pacific cultures than can be found *in situ*. Wood carvings, masks, painted shields, and textiles from these regions have been seen in England since the eighteenth-century voyages of Captain Cook, for the "curiosities" he collected were soon placed in the British Museum. American clipper-ship captains occasionally picked up South Sea things in their China trade. The cabinets in the houses of their New England descendants were full of them a generation ago, as shown by the fact that the larger part of the Brooklyn Museum's Melanesian material was purchased from Connecticut houses about 1906.

Serious collecting, chiefly in the field, has followed the growth of museums in the last forty years. At Leyden, the Dutch have superb textiles, masks, paintings, sculpture, and weapons from their East Indian Empire. The Germans, especially at Hanover, have collected with typical diligence. And the British Museum, perhaps as a result of the acquisitiveness of the early English explorers, has excellent material from the entire region. Indeed the value of these seventeenth- and eighteenth-century pieces cannot be overestimated, for they show the art forms of the islands completely untouched by the white man's trade goods or missionary principles.

The Bishop Museum in Honolulu, as befits its geographical

location, specializes completely in the Southern Pacific cultures. In the United States, the collections of the Field Museum are prominent, with those of the American Museum of Natural History in New York, the University Museum in Philadelphia, the Peabody at Cambridge, the Smithsonian in Washington, and the Brooklyn Museum following close behind. In many cases, however, these collections are treated as ethnology rather than as art, and are not accorded the same position or presentation as the products of India, Japan, or China. To the public they remain outlandish curiosities, with the same heathen tinge that they had for the clipper-ship captains. Perhaps some artist will discover the primitive force of Maori wood carving or the bold stylization of a painted New Guinea shield, and we shall have such a brief flurry in the painters' world as occurred when Picasso in the twenties took up African art; but the day has not yet come.

*Walter T. Swingle*

# OUR AGRICULTURAL DEBT
# TO ASIA

DO WE have an agricultural debt to Asia? Many people would answer no, since many, yes, most of the cultivated plants and domesticated animals which constitute the backbone of our agriculture came to us via Europe and had been utilized so long in Europe as to seem like native European plants and animals. Most of us do not realize that they are, almost all of them, of Asiatic origin.

As a matter of fact all of our cereals except maize, sorghum, and some forms of oats, originated in Asia. Almost all of our vegetable crops are likewise Asiatic plants. All of our common temperate-zone fruit trees, except the pecan and the native persimmon, came from Asia, and all citrus fruits too. Horses, donkeys, cattle, sheep, goats, hogs, and chickens are all Asiatic animals. Our debt to Asia is enormous. Without Asiatic plants and animals, our agriculture and that of the whole Western Hemisphere could not have developed properly, as we would have no domestic animals except the llama, an ill-tempered brute, and the turkey. We would have a few good food plants, potatoes, sweet potatoes, maize, lima and kidney beans, and the tomato, but no green vegetables, no important fruit trees except the subtropical avocado, and a few plums, grapes, and berries.

If we should suddenly be deprived by some malicious magic of all the Asiatic plants and animals we now use we would at first be amazed, then terrified, and soon starved unless we could at once mobilize all the transportation facilities of the world to bring us food, as well as wool for winter clothing, leather for shoes, and a host of near-necessities we use every day.

# CHINA, OUR CHIEF AGRICULTURAL CREDITOR

Few Americans realize that our chief agricultural creditor is China. We are indebted to the Chinese not only for the best varieties of oranges which we grow, but also for many other fruits and vegetables grown commercially in the United States. The soy bean (*Pl. 11a*), whose extraordinary food value is now at last beginning to be appreciated throughout this country, was one of the five sacred grains believed to have been given the Chinese people by the semimythical Emperor Shen-nung, "The Divine Husbandman," about the twenty-ninth century B.C. Rice (*Pl. 10*), wheat, proso (millet) (*Pl. 11b, c*), and barley, the other four of the five sacred "cereals," were grown in China many centuries before they were known in Europe; and the same can be said of many vegetables that we commonly regard as European.

From the beginning of American intercourse with China, ornamental plants such as the gardenia, the camellia, and the Cherokee rose were brought from China and grew well in our Southern states. A few handsome trees were also introduced such as the ginkgo and the camphor. As American merchants and missionaries gradually penetrated into China, they sent home more and more plants and trees. The Arnold Arboretum, organized and directed by the great tree expert, C. S. Sargent, financed extensive trips to the Orient to obtain botanical specimens and seeds of ornamental trees and shrubs as well as photographs of them as they grew in their native habitat. These trees and shrubs revolutionized the garden and park plantings of the northern parts of the United States. The illustrated, popular books of E. H. Wilson, who made many trips to the Orient for the Arnold Arboretum, helped to arouse interest in the very rich arboreal flora of China. The Arnold Arboretum also sponsored scientific technical works such as *Plantae Wilsonianae* and numerous botanical articles on the trees and shrubs of China.

The Plant Introduction Service of the U. S. Department of Agriculture was organized by David Fairchild in 1897; he did very extensive exploring for foreign economic and ornamental plants from 1898 on, and directed the Plant Introduction Service from 1907 to 1928. I was fortunate enough to be one of the first "agricultural explorers," as they are called, commissioned for foreign work in the new service, though my field at first lay in the Mediterranean regions and not in the Far East. Early in this century other agricultural explorers were already sending to Washington thousands of packages of seeds and hundreds of bales of living plants from China. Of these men Frank N. Meyer and P. H. Dorsett were outstanding, not only for the number and value of the plants they secured, but also for the detailed and accurate descriptions of every plant they sent to Washington.

P. H. Dorsett, some years later, in the early twenties, traveled widely in North China, taking many fine photographs of Chinese crop plants and writing descriptions of the culture, harvesting, and curing of each. On these trips he collected many varieties of soy beans (*Pl. 11a, 14*), largely through the utilization of a new and potent method of securing the willing co-operation of all educated Chinese people. A complete translation, prepared by Michael J. Hagerty under my direction in 1917, of the chapter on soy beans contained in a standard Chinese work on economic plants (the *Chih Wu Ming Shih T'u K'ao* by Wu Ch'i-chün) had been furnished the plant explorers looking for soy bean varieties. This translation, covering eighty-two pages, discussed several hundred varieties, telling where they were largely grown. In all cases the name of the variety and the name of the locality where it was grown were not only spelled out in English letters, but also written carefully in Chinese characters. An index made it easy to turn to any variety under discussion and see what was said about its culture.

This was a turning point in field explorations in China. Such indexed translations in the hands of foreign plant explorers insured the attention of all educated Chinese, who gladly directed the explorer to the nearest source of the various named varieties. I had learned this at first hand in 1915 when studying varieties of Citrus in southern China. Surprise and skepticism about the foreigner's knowledge of Chinese books gave way to astonishment and warm approbation. The detailed indices of these translations made it possible for the traveling American experts to ask intelligent questions and often to check the accuracy of the replies. Without such annotated lists of varieties and with no knowledge or appreciation of Chinese works of reference the agricultural explorer got very different treatment—polite reception accompanied with profound doubt of the foreigner's knowledge of the subject. He could buy seeds or plants actually on hand for sale, but no active effort was made to point out to him other, perhaps superior, varieties, which grew in other districts, even if these districts were near by. The peasants of China have always been profoundly influenced by the attitude of the gentry, and a foreigner who can get the respect and confidence of both the gentry and the peasants can go far, very far, in China.

China will probably continue to be the chief donor of new crop plants, of new foods, and of new dietetic uses of vegetable foods for the United States. The main reasons for this preferred position of China as a source of new and useful crops are:

(1) China has the largest array of crop plants of any temperate-zone country because it has by far the largest flora of any temperate-zone region of the whole world.

(2) Because of the essentially agricultural civilization of the Chinese, their long occupation of China, and their enormous population, every useful plant has been utilized to the full.

(3) Recurring famines, coupled with poor transportation over mountain barriers or flooded plains, have forced the Chinese to utilize for food every wild plant not actually poisonous.

(4) The great importance given to dietetics by the Chinese since ancient times—an importance probably equaling that given to medicine—has led to the very efficient use of innumerable food plants which grow wild or are cultivated in all parts of China.

(5) The climatic conditions prevailing in southeastern China are very similar to those of the east central and southeastern United States.

(6) The United States is the only country with a population of European origin having numerous widely distributed Chinese restaurants which already serve hundreds of thousands of American clients. These restaurants are eager to make use of the numerous Chinese food and flavoring plants. And this makes it easy for Americans to introduce these plants into their own kitchens as they are doing now, more every year.

The soy bean is a striking example of the introduction of a new crop. China has known the soy bean for fifty centuries (in ancient times it was called *shu*, or pulse; now it is known as *ta tou*, or "big bean"). Soy beans were sent from China to France as early as 1740, and from 1779 were grown in the famous Botanic Garden of Paris. Benjamin Franklin, who had been a member of the French Academy of Sciences since 1772, sent seeds back to the United States while he was the United States Ambassador to France, and urged that they be given a trial. But in spite of his plea, the soy bean remained merely a curiosity in this country for more than a century.

In the late eighties Prof. C. C. Georgeson brought soy bean seeds from Japan, where he had been teaching at the Agricultural College at Komaba, and planted them in a field on the campus of the Kansas State Agricultural College. I could see the stunted soy bean plants from the windows of the botanical laboratory where I was a teen-age research assistant. This variety, adapted to the perpetual spring climate of Komaba near Tokyo, did not do well on the bare Kansas hills, often swept by hot dry winds. And nothing happened. Soy beans did not arouse interest among Kansas farmers until many years after this failure.

In the third decade of the twentieth century Dorsett sent to Washington more than 800 named soy bean varieties from China, Manchuria and Japan. These, together with shipments secured by Dr. David Fairchild from his numerous correspondents in the Old World, especially in Asia, amounted by 1928 to a total of more than 2,800 packages of soy beans, almost all named varieties but many of them duplicated, some of them many times. Meantime tests made by W. J. Morse, in charge of soy bean culture for the Bureau of Plant Industry, showed that many varieties had a narrow range of adaptability. Accordingly, from 1929 to 1931, Morse joined Dorsett in the Orient and these two experts, with trained Chinese helpers, brought to this country the largest single collection of soy bean varieties ever assembled. As soon as Morse returned from studying soy beans in Asia and attacked the problem of finding which Asiatic varieties were adapted to the different regions and of selecting and breeding to make them fit various American soils and climates, a remarkable change occurred in soy bean culture. Yields went up and plantings increased year by year. In 1924, 1,782,000 acres were planted to soy beans in the United States and the average yield was 11 bushels per acre. In 1942 the acreage is estimated by Morse to have been 15,102,000 (this was more than 25 per cent increase over the 1941 acreage) and the part of the crop harvested for beans was worth over $200,000,000. About half of the total acreage was not harvested for beans (*Pl. 14*), but grazed or cut for hay. The yield per acre reached 18.7 bushels per acre, an increase of 847 per cent in acreage and 17 per cent in yield!

Soy bean culture for seed-crop production has, for the past few years, attained a relatively stable position as is indicated by the estimates published annually by the Soy Bean Association.

In 1943 the acreage was up 7 per cent above that of 1942 but the yield per acre was down about 6.6 per cent; in 1944 the acreage was up 1 per cent above 1943 but the yield per acre was 7.7 per cent less. Prices per bushel have shown only small variation. Mr. W. J. Morse's estimates show the price per bushel was up about 8.4 per cent in 1943 over 1942. The soy bean crop is now one of the seven or eight major crops of the United States. As our people learn to utilize more fully what the Chinese have discovered during the last 4,000 years about making delicious, nourishing, and easily digested food from soy beans, this crop may even rise to fifth or sixth place in our agriculture.

This growth of soy bean culture in the United States has been rendered possible by a rapidly expanding market for more and more soy bean products. Soy bean oil, which makes up about 18 per cent of the weight of the bean, is used on a very large scale for making shortening, oleomargarine, and other edible products. Such uses, even in 1935, absorbed 63,613,000 pounds, while 13,-003,000 pounds were used in the paint and varnish industry, 4,816,000 pounds in making linoleum, oilcloth and waterproof goods, including artificial leather, and finally 2,549,000 pounds for soap. Year by year much larger amounts are being used for these purposes.

One of the best-known industrial uses of soy bean proteins is for making a water-resistant glue. No less than 30,000 tons of soy bean glue were made in 1942 by a single firm and its licensees annually, most of it being used in the rapidly growing plywood industry. Soy bean proteins have been enthusiastically used by Henry Ford in his automobiles, being mixed with the more expensive phenolic resins, thereby reducing costs and also yielding a more plastic, freer-flowing mixture which takes dyes better.

Soy beans are also employed on a large scale as green manure

89

to build up the fertility of the soil. Unlike cotton, soy beans fix the free nitrogen of the air and, if the plants are plowed under, the soil is enriched. Hay fed to livestock is usually returned to the soil in the form of manure.

Soy bean products contain certain amino acids, essential for human nutrition, of the kinds usually found in meat and not occurring abundantly in vegetables other than soy beans. In fact the use of soy beans probably enables China to support twice as many people as would otherwise be possible. As N..Gist Gee, a well-known American naturalist, who spent many years in China, wrote of the Chinese in 1918: "They do not use milk and butter as we do, and it is very difficult indeed to supply meat for the entire population, even if they were all able to buy it. Yet in spite of these facts, they make up a splendid balanced ration at a most reasonable price by the large use of the bean."

Soy beans contain small amounts (2 to 3 per cent) of a valuable constituent, one of the phosphatids (a complex compound of phosphoric acid, an organic base choline and other substances) which is called lecithin. Lecithin has been found very useful in facilitating the mixing and preserving of foods such as margarine, chocolate and other candies and ice cream. It is said to help in conserving vitamin A along with the fat in which it is dissolved. Lecithin contains the organic base, choline, which poultry husbandmen have found to be almost indispensable in raising chickens, especially in enabling the hens to make good laying records. In a test made recently at the Florida Agricultural Experiment Station, at Gainesville, Florida, it was found that young hens well fed except for choline laid on the average only 5 eggs during the first 3 months of laying, while comparable hens given choline in small amounts laid 35 eggs (7 times as many) during the same period.

The soy bean proteins, which constitute 40 per cent of the weight of the beans, are used on a rapidly increasing scale for human food and for feed for hogs and poultry. Some 61,377,000 pounds of soy bean flour were supplied to the United Nations under the lend-lease and 5,000,000 pounds were distributed to schools eligible to receive school lunch commodities by the Agricultural Marketing Administration at Washington, during the year ending August, 1942. The Army is now using soy bean flour in the K ration as K biscuits, and also employs many soy beans in the Army pork link sausages because such use permits "stretching of available meat supplies, a saving in connection with fat release," and because "from a nutritional standpoint the product is improved and the cost to the Army lowered." Some 25 million pounds of soya flour and grits were sold in 1940, 110 million in 1942 and by 1943 no less than 290 million pounds were used. Very recent research by D. Breese Jones and J. P. Devine, of the Bureau of Chemistry and Agricultural Engineering, U. S. Department of Agriculture, has shown that the addition of as little as 10 per cent of soy bean flour to ordinary bread produces bread much like white bread in appearance but slightly firmer in texture and of better keeping qualities, and that such bread, fed to rats for six weeks, *gives almost four times as much growth as ordinary white bread.* If 15 per cent soy bean flour is used, five times the growth-promoting value of white bread is obtained. No doubt such bread will come rapidly into use in feeding the people of post-war Europe.

Soy bean milk is made cheaply and rapidly by grinding the beans between millstones with a small flow of water between them. The milk is boiled, coagulated, and the slightly yellowish curd is sold in cakes about three inches square and an inch thick. This *tofu* has the smooth texture of baked custard. It has a very mild flavor and is not only very nutritious but also easily digestible. It blends with soft meat dishes like calves' brains or stews. As long ago as 1917-1918 Dr. Yamei Kin set up under my general supervision for the United States Department of Agriculture a soy bean mill in New York City in the hope of supplying *tofu* to increase the bulk and food value of meat dishes served to soldiers in training at near-by camps. Dr. Kin succeeded in making excellent tofu. She even served to a group of army officers a meal composed entirely of soy bean dishes! However, it proved impossible to test tofu on a large scale at that time, since we could not get priorities for transporting of soy beans from North Carolina, then the nearest region where they were grown on any considerable scale.

One of the greatest discoveries made by the Chinese many centuries ago is the use of double or multiple fermentations in preparing soy bean or other food products. The first of these fermentations is accomplished by a special mold fungus which speedily invades the beans or *tofu*. This fermentation must be brought to an abrupt close at the proper time by immersing the molded soy beans in strong brine. During several months a ripening and mellowing of the product takes place in the brine under the influence of special fermentation bacteria. These complex processes require great skill and are held as guild secrets. Few foreigners indeed ever have the opportunity to see them.

A splendid example of double fermentation is the soy bean cheese called *nam yüe* by the Cantonese and *sufu* in North China. It is preferred even to the best Roquefort as a salad dressing constituent by those who have had the opportunity to try it. It is made by Chinese masters of the cheesemaker's art who believe that its fermentation is an insoluble mystery.

Shih Chi-yien, then working in the American University of Soochow, published in 1918 the first English account of the most important fermented bean foods. He traced the making of *tofu* from soy beans back to the Han dynasty (A.D. 22). Ten years later Wai Ngan-shou, one of the first scientifically-trained Chinese microbiologists and fermentation experts, was able to isolate and identify as a new species of Mucor the mold that makes possible the *nam yüe* fermentation. It is a curious fungus, *Mucor sufu*, distantly related to the miraculous *Penicillium notatum* whose marvelous curative action has only recently been discovered. A third fermentation expert, Shih You-kuang, studied another soy bean fermentation product, *meitauza*, made by another species of Mucor, and published an illustrated account of it in German in 1937. In his review of the literature of Mucor fermentations Shih You-kuang cites no fewer than thirty articles by eighteen authors all based on Chinese fermentations.

The best-known example of double fermentation is the very widely used soy sauce, which also furnishes the basis for many condiment sauces in Europe and America.

It is made on an enormous scale in China. The boiled soy beans are covered with wheat flour, fermented with a yellow Aspergillus mold for one to three weeks, put into strong brine (18 per cent), and cured for several months in the sun with occasional stirring. Miss Elizabeth Groff, under my direction in 1918, made a thorough study of the fermentation of soy sauce in the famous factories of Canton, China, and published the first detailed account of the process in the *Philippine Journal of Science* for 1919. With the rapid advance in the use and study of soy bean foods, this highly nutritive condiment sauce should soon be as well known here as it is in China.

## REPAYING OUR DEBT TO CHINA FOR THE SOY-BEAN

The people of the United States can now repay, at least in part, the debt which we owe to the Chinese who have willingly supplied us with thousands of sacks of seed of their best varieties of soy beans and thereby made possible the phenomenally rapid expansion and utilization of this new crop in the United States. Our plant breeders have been able to combine the good qualities of some of the best soy bean varieties and some of their new hybrids have shown marked superiority to the Chinese varieties in some parts of our country. We can now benefit also from the research discoveries of the Chinese experts, which I am told by Dr. Wen-Tsai Chang (of the University of Nanking at Chengtu in West China) have led to the discovery of disease-resistant soy beans able to give large yields in southwestern China where most north Chinese varieties (such as we have introduced into America) do not do well because of their susceptibility to virus disease. It will be mutually advantageous to exchange our hybrid soy bean varities for the south Chinese varieties resistant to virus.

Mung bean (*ch'ing tou*) sprouts are a favorite dish of the Chinese in the United States and are eaten by almost every American patron of the Chinese restaurants. These beans, *ch'ing tou*, after being soaked, are placed in a warm corner of the kitchen on a sieve or net a few inches above water standing in the bottom of a vessel, germinate rapidly, and in a few days the slender sprouts, one to two inches long, are blanched for a few minutes in scalding water (not cooked throughout but sterilized on the surface) and used in the Chinese dishes. Such sprouts of green beans can be used for salad instead of lettuce at a very much lower cost. These beans, widely grown in China and India, are now being grown on a commercial scale in Oklahoma. The sprouted beans are known to be a very good source of vitamin B, and an excellent

93

source of Vitamin C (of which they contain more than lettuce usually does). The Chinese method of scalding the sprouted beans would conserve almost all the vitamin C. Recent analyses show these sprouted beans to have a good content of riboflavin. Due to transportation priorities and labor conditions resulting from World War II, gram bean sprouts may assume an important role in the United States as a cheap source of necessary vitamins. They are now on sale to American customers in many grocery and meat stores in California. Recently, sprouted soy beans are being used in the same way.

Buddhist monks have lived for more than two thousand years on a purely vegetarian diet. In China they have perfected the most tasty, nutritious, and digestible substitutes for animal foods. The fermented soy bean cheeses and sauces have made possible this gastronomic miracle. Large as is our agricultural debt to the Chinese, it will become much greater when we learn from them their art of preparing delicious vegetarian dishes, rich in vitamins, easy to digest, and reasonable in cost, and secure from them the numerous savory vegetables they grow, most of which we do not yet grow in this country.

For several thousand years agriculture was almost a state religion in China. The Emperor Shen-nung, the semilegendary "Divine Husbandman" of about the twenty-ninth century B.C., to whom I referred above as the donor of the five sacred cereals—rice, wheat, proso (or millet), soy beans and barley—is supposed to have tasted innumerable plants and studied their medicinal virtues, as well as to have taught agriculture to the Chinese people. His son Chu was Minister of Husbandry. The great ceremony of the plowing of the soil and the sowing of the seeds of these five kinds of grain at the spring equinox by the Emperor himself was inaugurated at this early epoch, indeed at the very dawn of Chinese history, and persisted until the overthrow of the Manchu Dynasty in 1911.

Shen-nung's successor, the Emperor Huang Ti, is said to have compiled the Herbal, still extant, called the *Shen-nung Pên Ts'ao*, and through the centuries Chinese works on agriculture and its special branches, including economic plants, have been both numerous and valuable. As recently as the reign of Emperor Ch'ien Lung (1736-1796), a monumental work, *Yü Ti Mien Hua T'u,*

94

was issued by the Emperor with an introduction by his great ancestor, the Emperor K'ang Hsi, urging the culture of cotton in northern China where silk culture is difficult to carry on. The implication is plain that the Emperors as late as the eighteenth century felt almost personally responsible for the continuance and improvement of agriculture in China. The earliest existing works on Chinese agriculture are treatises on silk culture, after which the Imperial monumental work on cotton was modeled.

One of the oldest works on economic plants is the *Nan Fang Ts'ao Mu Chuang*, an account of about a hundred economic plants classed under herbs, fruit trees, forest trees, and bamboos, written by Chi Han, a Minister of State in the Western Chin Dynasty (290-307 A.D.). Chi Han had served as governor of Canton, so he had had an opportunity to study at first hand the plants of South China.

In discussing oranges, he said that if they have ants they are good, otherwise, not. This cryptic sentence was quoted in many Chinese encyclopedic works but never was explained and hence never understood until some twenty-five years ago when a group studying the citrus fruits in the vicinity of Canton for me, under the supervision of Professor George Weidman Groff, found a small village where the inhabitants said their principal business was "growing ants." Some of Professor Groff's Chinese student helpers from Lingnan University at Canton made fun of this claim, since they saw mulberry trees and silkworms in the village and thought silk was the true product. The villagers then said: "True, we have mulberry trees and do grow silkworms, but we feed them before they are full grown to the ants, which we sell to orange growers for a dollar a nest."

This ant, *Oecophylla smaragdina*, a well-known tropical or subtropical species, constructs silk nests on the trees, into which all the ants retire at night. The orange growers connect the orange trees with one another by means of bamboo poles, over which the ants travel to build nests in all the orange trees. The ants no longer eat silkworms but devour the insects which attack the orange trees or the fruits. The owner of a lychee tree in his home garden near Canton told me he had purchased a nest of ants (the nests are cut off the tree at night and tied in a tight bag) which had prevented all insect injury to his crop of lychees and were

95

particularly efficient in driving off a large insect, *Tessarotoma papillosa*, a pentatomid bug nearly an inch long.

These ants never attack the plants and never nest in the ground, so they are easily removed from a garden by cutting off the silken nests in which the colonies live at night. Probably they can some day be utilized in the United States to keep fruit orchards free from insect pests. They are now employed in Indo-China and New Guinea as well as in southern China, where Chi Han reported they were in use sixteen and a half centuries ago. Incidentally this is, so far as is known, the earliest record of the "biologic control" of insects, now used on an ever-increasing scale all over the world.

Among other ancient Chinese agricultural works is the *Li Chih P'u*, written in 1059 A.D. by Ts'ai Hsiang, a famous scholar, calligrapher, and engineer, who built the noted stone bridge, used to this day, over the estuary of the Min River in Fukien Province. Ts'ai Hsiang had an artist go with him to make paintings of all the best varieties of lychee. Unfortunately these paintings have been lost, but a painting of the variety considered by Ts'ai Hsiang to have the finest color, aroma, flavor, and to be the best of all, the Ch'ên family purple lychee (*Pl. 12*), was made by the Sung Emperor Hui Tsung about half a century later (1101-1126 A.D.). This painting is preserved in the Metropolitan Museum of Art in New York City. Professor G. W. Groff, whose volume *The Lychee and Lungan* gives a summary of the Chinese and Western literature on the lychee and describes all of the important varieties grown near Canton, is now living in Florida, where he encourages and helps all lychee growers (*Pl. 13*) by drawing on his long experience in China.

A great work on Chinese agriculture is *Nung Chêng Ch'üan Shu* by Hsü Kuang-ch'i, a distinguished Chinese scholar who was Minister of State during the reign of the Emperor Wan Li. He lived from 1562 to 1633 and warmly supported the scientific work of the Jesuit scholars at Peking and became himself a convert. This well-known work, which was published in 1640 by imperial command, covered the whole field of agriculture and includes an account of a method of separating and discarding light cotton seeds by rejecting those which float in water. "The seeds which are empty, old, fire-dried, oily, or rotten will float," the author says, "while those which are hard and solid will surely sink. Those seeds which sink may be planted." It was not until the first decade of the twentieth century that the practice of rejecting light seed and planting of heavy seed only was discovered and recommended in the United States as giving from eight to eleven per cent increase in yield.

Another beneficial treatment of cotton seed, by treating with scalding water, was advocated in 1765 by Fang Kuan-ch'êng in the Imperial Memorial on Cotton Culture (*Yü Ti Mien Hua T'u*), to which I have referred above. This volume includes twelve large plates, with a rhythmic prose introduction by the Emperor K'ang Hsi and descriptive and allegorical poems, one by the Emperor Ch'ien Lung, as well as brief instructions on cotton culture and use by the Viceroy of Chihli, Fang Kuan-ch'êng, opposite the plate to which they refer. Not until the second decade of the twentieth century did we discover by scientific tests made in the United States that such treatment destroys a fungous parasite which often kills the germinating cotton seedling.

These references and many others in this article indicate how many important things we could have learned from the Chinese if we had had Chinese books, say a century ago, and what is more important, capable scholars to translate them. It has been my privilege to assist in building up a great Chinese library in the Library of Congress, under the enlightened policy of Dr. Herbert Putnam, beginning in 1912. The Orientalia Division, headed by Dr. Arthur Hummel, is now the largest Chinese library outside of Asia and is probably larger than all the European libraries of Chinese books combined. It now contains, Dr. Hummel estimates, about 230,000 Chinese volumes (*Chüan*) and some 20,000 more will soon be added in the form of bibliofilm copies of very rare works from the Chinese National Library, sent to Washington for safekeeping.

The outbreak of citrus canker in the orange and grapefruit groves of Florida early in the second decade of this century reached such a crisis about 1914 that it was decided to make a thorough search in China for oranges and other citrus fruit trees possessing resistance to this bacterial disease to which all the standard varieties of oranges and grapefruit were subject.

97

I was sent to Japan, China, and the Philippines by the Bureau of Plant Industry in 1915 to search for canker-resistant varieties and soon saw that it would be necessary to make a methodical search for such resistant varieties in China, where many, doubtless several hundred, varieties were cultivated in all of the provinces south of the Yangtze River and also in Szechwan. It became evident that the numerous references to citrus fruits and their culture which crowd the pages of the Chinese encyclopedias should be read and translated into English. Fortunately, a talented translator of Chinese, Mr. Michael J. Hagerty, was working under my supervision, and he was able to proceed rapidly with such translations.

The largest single Chinese account of the citrus fruits is contained in the great Chinese Imperial Encyclopedia *Ch'in Ting Ku Chin T'u Shu Shi Ch'êng*, the largest encyclopedia ever printed in any country. It was compiled by order of the Manchu Emperor K'ang Hsi by Ch'êng Mêng-lei, but the work was not completed when K'ang Hsi died in January, 1723. His son and successor as Emperor, Yung Chêng, promptly dismissed Ch'en Mêng-lei, and appointed Chiang T'ing-hsi, a scholar and statesman of some distinction, under whose care the manuscript was printed in 1726. This giant work fills 5020 large volumes, each containing two books or chapters.

The chapter on citrus fruits translated by Mr. Hagerty consists of about 500 pages and the translation covers 529 typewritten pages, with an index of 39 pages and an introduction of 14 pages—a grand total of 582 pages. In addition to a general summary in brief form of what is known about each citrus fruit, there is given under the title *Hui K'ao* a great number of quotations from Chinese works of every description, so that practically every word, every paragraph of every form of discussion regarding citrus fruits is reprinted in full and arranged, as far as possible, chronologically. This would be comparable to an English work on grapes or roses where every poem and every essay concerning grapes or roses was quoted in full. Mr. Hagerty not only renders the literal sense of the poem or essay, but explains clearly the numerous literary, mythological, and historical allusions.

Another famous Chinese classic of agriculture is the first monograph on citrus fruits to appear in any country, the *Chü Lu,* written by Han Yen-chih, while he was magistrate in Wenchow in Chekiang Province. This work, published in 1178, described in some detail all the citrus fruits then cultivated in Wenchow, some twenty-seven varieties, with a discussion of remarkably up-to-date methods for picking and shipping oranges.

At this early date Han Yen-chih warned against injuring the skin of oranges in picking them or in careless handling. He insisted that the pedicel on which the fruit is borne should be cut off close to the fruit so that it could not scratch or perforate the skin of other fruits in the same container. Unfortunately this classic on the oranges of Wenchow had never been made available to the American orange growers and the citrus experts of this country until Hagerty's annotated translation of the *Chü Lu* appeared in 1923.

As a result of our ignorance of Han Yen-chih's sound advice, heavy losses were incurred early in this century in shipping California oranges to the eastern markets of the United States. The farmers blamed the inadequate refrigeration given the shipments by the railway companies, but the installation of better methods of refrigeration did not entirely stop the decay of the fruit. It was proved by elaborate research made under the direction of G. Harold Powell that some of the losses were due to scars or cuts in the peel of the fruits which were attacked by fungi or bacteria. More careful cutting of the fruit and more careful handling of it afterwards prevented this decay.

The best varieties of oranges which we grow all originated in China, as did many of the other citrus fruits grown commercially in the United States (all the citrus fruits are from Asia with the possible exception of the limes, which may have originated in some of the northern islands of the East Indian Archipelago). A study made for me by Mr. Kwok Wa-shau of the citrus fruits cultivated in the vicinity of Canton, China, resulted in a volume containing detailed descriptions and figures of close to one hundred distinct varieties. Indeed it is probable that there are now cultivated in China at least five hundred and possibly as many as one thousand distinct varieties of citrus! These varieties merit careful study because some of them are disease-resistant, some are hardy, and many have fruits of high quality. We have certainly not tested more than ten per cent of them—probably not more than five per cent. China still has great reserves of agricultural experience upon which we may draw.

Famine Herbals constitute an outstanding example of the thoroughness with which the possibilities of China's varied plant life were long ago explored. Because of frequent droughts and floods in densely populated parts of China, many people have often died of starvation, especially where mountains or flooded river valleys prevented the transportation of food to the stricken region. The starving people sometimes managed to keep alive until help arrived or a new catch crop matured by eating weeds and other wild plants. The books known as Famine Herbals described these plants and usually illustrated them and gave recipes. The most outstanding of such books is the *Chiu Huang Pên Ts'ao* or "Relieve Famine Herbal," by Chou Ting-wang, the fifth son of the first Ming Emperor, Hung Wu. From 1382 to 1400 this prince is said to have lived on his estates near Kaifengfu, in Honan province, where he obtained from farmers and hermits four hundred or more kinds of plants supposed to be suitable for food in time of famine. These he set out in a garden where he personally observed them, drew up descriptions, and had artists make drawings of them. He then arranged these plants in groups according to the edibility of their leaves, fruits, blossoms, roots, and so on, and published the work with a preface by his friend and helper, Pien T'ung, dated 1406. The illustrations in the Famine Herbal are large and, in spite of their primitive technique, of high artistic quality. As a result of the long-continued study given to this and similar works, many species first used for food only in time of famine finally became well-known food plants and were regularly cultivated.

Most of the Chinese works noted above were written by Chinese scholars, many of them holding high places in the Chinese civil service; several were compiled with the collaboration of Emperors or Imperial princes. This shows clearly the great importance given in China since remote antiquity to all problems concerning agriculture, food, or medicine.

For more than a thousand years (until 1911) the highest provincial and imperial posts were filled by civil-service examinations open to all Chinese, even the sons of small farmers. As nearly eighty per cent of China's huge population is engaged in some

PLATE 10    Rice (*Tao*), chief of the five sacred grains and one of China's greatest gifts to the world, sown ceremonially each year by the Emperor since the reign of Shen Nung, "the Father of Agriculture" of forty centuries ago. *From Wu Ch'i-chün's standard work on Chinese economic plants.*

PLATE 11   (a) The soy bean (*ta tou*, big bean), probably the most important crop of China. (b) Proso (*shu*, panicled millet), another of the five sacred grains, recently introduced into the United States. (c) Sorghum (*shu shu*, Szechwan panicled millet). (d) Loquat (*p'i pa*), grown in Florida and California.

陳紫荔子綉香囊

PLATE 12   The Chên Purple Lychee, considered by Ts'ai Hsiang in his monograph (1059 A.D.) to be the best. A painting attributed to the Sung Emperor Hui Tsung (1101-1126 A.D.). *Courtesy, Metropolitan Museum of Art.*

PLATE 13   A beautiful cluster of ripe lychees (2/5 natural size), produced in southern Florida. It was introduced from Fukien province by Rev. W. N. Brewster in 1907. *Courtesy, G. Weidman Groff.*

PLATE 14 A soy bean plantation in Iowa, one of the leading soy-bean-growing States, showing a remarkably uniform height of the plants, all of them healthy. *Courtesy, William J. Morse.*

PLATE 15 A giant mango tree growing near Bahia, Brazil. *Photograph by P. H. Dorsett, Bureau of Plant Industry.*

PLATE 16    A pure-blood two-year-old zebu bull of the Guzerat breed, Millungera, Queensland, Australia.

PLATE 17    Half-breed zebu-shorthorn hybrids, raised at Millungera during two very dry years when many shorthorn calves and some cows died. Photographs by Dr. R. B. Kelley, *courtesy, Australian Council of Scientific and Industrial Research.*

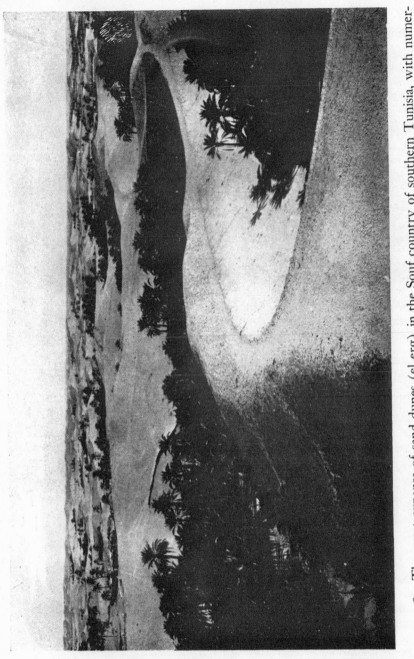

PLATE 18   The great expanse of sand dunes (el erg) in the Souf country of southern Tunisia, with numerous sunken date gardens. *Photograph by F. Bougault.*

PLATE 19   A ten-year-old Deglet Noor date garden at Indio, California. This variety, the one most largely grown in the United States, was first introduced into the New World in 1900 through the Plant Introduction Service of the U. S. Department of Agriculture. *Courtesy Avery Field.*

PLATE 20   An Arab mare. The photographer reports that nothing would induc[e]
this mare to stand still until the owner finally put on her Arab bernous an[d]
mounted her. "This," the photographer says, "acted like magic, for under its spe[ll]
the animal at once became quiet." *Photograph by T. Fall, from "Animals of t[he]
World," courtesy, Garden City Publishing Company.*

form of agriculture, the ·Chinese system of recruiting talented men to fill all important official positions led to the appointment of very many high officials of scholarly training who brought to their tasks a clear understanding of agricultural problems and an intense interest in them.

The gentry of China, much more influential than is supposed by most foreigners, was recruited and strengthened in its power by the continual accession of these well-trained scholars and their descendants. The children of high officials did not, *ipso facto*, follow in the footsteps of their fathers but had to earn their own places in the government hierarchy by passing the higher examinations. The potentially perpetual privileged hereditary aristocracy as developed in Europe was something unknown in China.

In many cases the Chinese medicinal plants are in effect supplementary foods as well as remedial medicines. The rare seasoning *lo han kuo* (*Momordica Grosvenori* Swingle) grown by a non-Chinese tribe (the Miao-tze) in a segregated district in the mountains of Kwangsi Province, is used as a prized condiment in soups, as well as a household remedy for throat and intestinal disturbances. Until the Japanese invasion of China cut us off from Hong Kong and Canton, this fruit was exported to the United States for use by Chinese to the value of several tens of thousands of dollars. Many other Chinese food plants are listed in the Chinese Materia Medica, which includes more than a thousand items.

Until recently, however, our debt to Chinese medicine was limited largely to rhubarb from the Tibetan foothills and West China—not our common rhubarb, which is also of Asiatic origin, but another species of *Rheum* which, although used in Europe and America for centuries, is still imported from China, since the Chinese drug is more potent than that grown in Europe.

Another drug plant, called *ma huang* by the Chinese, has been known and used for forty centuries in China. About three decades ago it was investigated in the American-founded and supported Peking Union Medical College and found to contain the very potent and valuable alkaloid ephedrin, much like adrenalin in its action but much easier to administer, very much easier to store, and also cheaper. Imports of *ma huang* to Europe and America took a big jump, and soon ephedrin became indispensable to throat and nose specialists and useful to other physicians as well.

The plant which furnishes *ma huang* in China proved to be a species new to science, named *Ephedra sinica* as late as 1924, by Stapf, a famous botanist of Kew Gardens, England. In 1926 I secured in China authentic seeds of this species, and soon we had brought together the largest collection of Old World species in the world at the Torrey Pines field station of the Bureau of Plant Industry, near San Diego, California. Two Chinese species and two Indian ones grew well in the United States and produced fair amounts of ephedrin. When the Japanese invasion of North China, beginning in 1937, closed our access to the *ma huang* of North China and Mongolia, it looked at first as if *Ephedra* would have to be grown on a large scale in our country. However, it proved possible to make ephedrin synthetically (something very unusual for a medicinal alkaloid) and now the synthetic product supplies the throat and nose specialists. Market quotations show, however, that the natural product extracted from the Chinese *ma huang* is rated higher than the synthetic drug. It may yet prove possible to produce natural ephedrin at a small profit on some of the Indian Reservations in Arizona, where Indian children could collect the plants.

Some idea of the extent of the European and American literature regarding the plants of the Chinese region, that is, Indo-China, China, Manchuria, Korea, and eastern Siberia, is shown by the fact that a recently published bibliography of Eastern Asiatic botany by E. D. Merrill and E. H. Walker contains about 73,-500 titles of books and articles on the plants of the Chinese region, all but about 250 in European languages.

A classified list of the articles in Chinese journals and bulletins regarding agriculture published from 1858 to 1931, completed by the Division of Agricultural History of the University of Nanking, contains about 27,150 articles in Chinese, from 357 journals or bulletins, and 6,232 articles in English from 60 journals and bulletins—a grand total of 33,382 articles, all indexed by subject. The supplement covering the years 1932-1934 contains about 12,900 articles in Chinese from 555 journals and bulletins, and 1,120 articles in English from 30 journals. The recent astonishing growth of agricultural literature is shown by the fact that the list for the three years, 1932-1934, contains 42 per cent of the number in the main volume covering the 74 years from 1858 to 1931. Also the average number of Chinese papers per annum in the 74-year period was 451, while just as the rape of Manchuria occurred and just preceding the all-out Japanese attack on China, they averaged 4,673 per annum, nearly 11 times as many! As the Chinese return to peaceful pursuits after the war, the world is certain to be surprised at the number and value of the scientific studies on Chinese economic plants which will be written by the people most interested and best informed about them, the Chinese themselves. North Americans will automatically play a very important part by collaborating with their Chinese colleagues in this work, often getting new light on old problems by studying these crop plants under different climatic, soil, and economic conditions from those of China.

## PERSIA THE HOME OF ORCHARDS

Persia, now called Iran, and the near-by lands of Afghanistan, Iraq, and Turkey, are the Garden of Eden of the fruits and nuts of the world. Here delicious peaches, apricots, plums, and table grapes without peer in the world and numerous vegetables grow in almost every garden. The choicest nuts of the world, pistachio, almond, and Persian walnut, are at home here. Many of these fruits and nuts were carried to other countries long ago and even reached the New World shortly after Columbus discovered America.

A tenth-century geographical treatise, the *Masalik al-Mamalik*, compiled by Ibn Haukal and translated by Sir William Ouseley in 1800, speaks repeatedly of Persian cities and towns famous for their orchards and gardens. For example, referring to Berdaa, or Berda', Ibn Haukal says, "For one day's journey the whole country is laid out in gardens and orchards. The fruits are excellent, their filberts are better than those of Samarcand, and their chestnuts superior to the chestnuts of Syria, and the figs of Berda' are more delicious than those of any other place."

It is probable that some of the citrus fruits originated in Iran or southern Arabia, but they have been cultivated so many centuries that it is impossible to determine certainly their native home. The citron was named by Linnaeus *Citrus Medica*, "apple of the Medes"—after the people who were so closely associated with the Persians in ancient times. The lemon has not been found growing wild in any country, but is undoubtedly of Asiatic origin. Perhaps it originated in the mountains of southern Arabia well inside the tropics.

Our debt to Iran for such delicious fruits and nuts is likely to become still greater, because every visit made to Iran by our agricultural explorers has resulted in bringing to this country some new fruit or vegetable. Dr. William E. Whitehouse of the U. S. Plant Exploration and Introduction Service, for example, on his last trip to Iran found many good varieties of pistache including some with giant nuts never seen outside of Iran, and, while studying them in the mountains of Iran, he obtained many other promising fruit trees.

## OUR DEBT TO INDIA

To India the whole tropical and subtropical world owes a great debt for the mango, probably the most noted and certainly the most beautiful and most delicious of any of the widely cultivated subtropical fruits. What Babur, the founder of the Mogul Empire, said of this fruit in his memoirs published in 1525 is still true—"Many are eaten but few are good, such mangoes as are good are excellent." In justification of Babur's dictum, it should be remarked that the best mangoes, when fully ripe, are beyond praise, but poor seedlings or even immature fruits of good varieties may be almost inedible. Fortunately the mango is now acclimatized and fruiting abundantly in south Florida and in most of the Central and South American countries and the islands of the West Indies, as well as in all the tropical regions of the East. Dr. David Fairchild, who organized the Plant Introduction Service of the U. S. Department of Agriculture, for many years sought out all the best mangoes of India, Indo-China, and the Dutch East Indies (*Pl. 15*).

We are likely to incur a large debt to India for the zebu, *Bos indicus* (*Pl. 16, 17*), a humped species of cattle of which many breeds are known. This species is certain to play a steadily increasing role in our Southern states in the production of zebu hybrids which can stand high temperatures much better than European breeds of cattle and are able to graze all day in bright sunshine. As there are a great number of breeds of zebu in India, some fast walkers, some good milk-yielders, it is highly probable that it will be necessary to introduce many of these breeds in order to find the best ones to use in hybridizing, both for beef and for dairy cattle for our Southern states. Zebus were introduced into Texas early in this century and by their use the Santa Gertrudis hybrid has been created and has shown itself able to endure hot weather which forces ordinary cattle to stop grazing and seek the shade.

Although the hybrids between zebu and European breeds of cattle are able to graze all day in the sun without showing distress, it has been found that zebu oxen doing heavy work are better than hybrid oxen, and light-colored zebu oxen, like the bull shown in *Pl. 16*, are able to do heavier work in hot climates than the dark-colored breeds. Zebus of the Guzerat breed are often very light colored (*Pl. 16*), and are used in the hotter regions of tropical Brazil for heavy work. Zebu hybrids are now common in Southern Florida and are widely used in Brazil, where much attention is given to breeding good pure-blood zebu bulls. Zebu hybrids have made a very good record in Queensland Australia, as is shown in Dr. R. B. Kelley's Bulletin 172, "Zebu-Cross Cattle in Northern Australia."

### THE ORIGINAL HOME OF GARDEN VEGETABLES

The great Hindu Kush region, which borders on a half-dozen different Asiatic countries, is apparently a storehouse of superior wild or semiwild strains of some of our most important cultivated crops. The carrot, for example, was until recently supposed to have originated by selection from the wild carrot (a roadside weed in Europe and America). It is now asserted by experts that this cannot be true and that the garden carrot is apparently derived from some Central Asiatic species still inadequately known. Recently a carrot was found growing in Persia which, when tested in the United States, showed high resistance to some of the worst carrot diseases.

The same thing was found true of the cantaloupe. About fifteen years ago the new and dangerous powdery mildew disease threatened to destroy the whole cantaloupe industry. Fortunately cantaloupe seeds were obtained from northern India and some of the seedlings showed very high resistance to the disease. After a few years the expert plant breeders of the Bureau of Plant Industry and of the University of California, in friendly co-operation, created new strains which enabled cantaloupe growing to remain one of the leading industries of California and Arizona. The plant breeders found no resistance to this disease in any of the many strains of cantaloupes secured from other parts of the world.

Hundreds of millions of dollars are invested in the American truck crop industries and several tens of millions of dollars in sales are made annually. The crops are, most of them, produced by annual plants and must be planted anew every year. As soon as a disease appears, every effort is made to breed new and disease-resistant varieties rather than face the almost impossible task of spraying the vast fields of truck crops. An onion with a tight-fitting ligule at the junction of the leaf which prevents thrips, one of the worst enemies of the onion, from gaining access to the sensitive stems was recently discovered by a plant explorer in a mountain village in Persia. This was so important that breeding work was at once inaugurated to give the onions grown by truck farmers protection from their worst enemy. In the Hindu Kush region and adjacent mountainous countries, wild relatives of our principal truck crop plants have won the fight against the fungi and bacteria as well as against adverse climatic conditions. Their good qualities can be transferred by skillful plant breeders to our choicest varieties of vegetables without any evident change in appearance or quality. Doubtless many other important plants with high resistance to disease and to extremes of temperatures will be found in the mountain valleys, foothill slopes, and plateaus in Iran, Afghanistan, India, Nepal, Tibet, Western China, Chinese Turkistan, and in Tajikistan and others of the Soviet states of southern Siberia.

## OUR DEBT TO SIBERIA

The hardy, high-yielding, hard wheat varieties which were introduced into the United States early in the twentieth century revolutionized wheat culture and extended profitable agriculture hundreds of miles westward in the Great Plains States, as well as far to the North both in the United States and Canada. Some of these new wheats were introduced from Russia, but doubtless all of them originally came from Siberia. Mark A. Carleton brought most of these wheat varieties to this country through the Plant Introduction Service of the Bureau of Plant Industry.

Both Carleton and N. E. Hansen of South Dakota (who made five extended trips to Siberia from 1898 to 1924—two for the Plant Introduction Service and three for the state of South Dakota) brought new and superior varieties of another cereal, proso or panicled millet, highly esteemed by the Chinese since remote antiquity. Hansen reports that he "found a white-seeded variety of proso at Semipalatinsk, Siberia, in 1913 among the Kirghiz Tartars who grew it extensively as a grain for themselves and their livestock. It is the cornerstone of their agriculture in this eight-inch rainfall climate, a sure crop in the driest years." Proso, Hansen says, matures a crop in sixty days. In eastern Tibet and western China it is grown at very high levels in the plateaus where ordinary crops cannot ripen. This new-old cereal has succeeded not only in South Dakota but also in other Great Plains states where a short-season crop is needed on account of scanty rainfall. It has been tested for many years at Akron, in eastern Colorado, at an altitude of about forty-six hundred feet, in the Field Station of the Division of Dry Land Agriculture of the Bureau of Plant Industry in co-operation with the Colorado Experiment Station. The Turghai variety sent from Western Siberia in 1906 by Hansen has given yields as high as 57 bushels per acre in favorable seasons.

Hansen also obtained hardy Siberian apples and crabapples, pears, and ornamental trees and shrubs as well as many varieties of alfalfa. Among them was one yellow-flowered alfalfa able to grow at Verkhoyansk, the "north pole of cold," the coldest point known in Asia, where a temperature as low as 91° below zero Fahrenheit has been recorded. In recent years the crested wheat grass and other forage grasses from Siberia have been very largely planted in the United States, especially in the Northern Great Plains and Montana. Thanks to the new and comprehensive *Flora of the U.S.S.R.* which has been in course of publication for several years, it will be easy to draw further on the rich flora of Siberia as well as of European Russia. Undoubtedly this will increase our indebtedness to the vast Asiatic territories of our brave ally.

## OUR DEBT TO THE ARABS

When the Plant Introduction Service of the U. S. Department of Agriculture was first organized, some forty-odd years ago, I began to send to Washington seeds and plants from the Mediterranean regions of Europe, Africa, and Asia Minor. These included the first offshoots of superior named varieties of date palms to be landed successfully in the New World and also for the first time the all-important *Blastophaga*, a tiny wasp which carries the pollen from the Capri fig (male tree) to the fertile flowers of the best fig varieties of the Smyrna type, which do not fruit unless the fig wasp pollinates them. These two fruit trees are among the finest which we owe to Asia.

Many Americans have never even thought of asking whether we owe any agricultural debt to the Arabs. Yet, we do owe them much, because we have many desert regions very like those of Arabia and North Africa, although our deserts are smaller and more easily watered from the neighboring mountains. Europe has no such deserts; and because we still think much like Europeans, we have failed to realize that the deserts in our Southwest are rapidly becoming the most productive regions in our whole country.

The Arabs showed conspicuous ability in agriculture at a very early date. Although they migrated into North Africa about the middle of the seventh century, their agricultural discoveries were all, or almost all, made in Asia and carried west into Tripoli, the Barbary states, and the Iberian peninsula.

By their skillful methods of culture and of selection of new varieties, the Arabs perfected the date palm, a crop plant which produces more well-mineralized, high-flavored, nutritious, and healthy human food per acre than is yielded by any other temperate-zone crop—as much as 8 or 9 tons of cured fruit per acre is sometimes harvested in Coachella Valley date gardens near Palm Springs, California.

The Arabs say "the date palm must have its feet in running water and its head in the fires of heaven." Often where American irrigation engineers would see no possibility of developing an adequate supply of water for irrigating the thirsty date palms, the Arabs can and do develop amazing irrigation systems. If an Arab digs a well and finds a water-bearing stratum yielding a few gallons of water a day, he at once digs another a few hundred yards away and if he finds the same water-bearing stratum, he excavates a tunnel connecting these two wells. If each well is 3 feet in diameter, then each will have cut the water stratum for a distance of 9.4 feet, or 18.8 for the two wells. If the wells are 100 yards apart, the connecting tunnel will cut 300 feet on each wall, or a total of 600 feet on the water-bearing stratum. Suppose the water stratum yields 3 gallons a day for each 10 feet of cut, then each well will yield about 1.9 gallons a day and the tunnel 180 gallons! If a mile long such a tunnel will yield more than 3,000 gallons a day. Often such tunnels run for miles with wells every few hundred yards and the flow at the end of the tunnels suffices to irrigate a large oasis planted to date palms, other fruit trees, and vegetables. These irrigation works are called *foggara* and are found from Morocco to the slopes around the Gobi in northwestern China, in all semiarid countries ever occupied by Arabs or by other Mohammedan peoples.

A few years ago while obtaining offshoots of a remarkable date variety, the Medjhool (still famous in Spain where it is called the Barbary date), I had occasion to study a date garden in the outskirts of the famous Tafilalt region of southern Morocco. This garden was watered from a canal bordered by date palms. In order to be sure that none of the palms had the *baioudh* (blanching) disease, which could contaminate the water, I inspected all of them until I came to the place where subterranean *foggara* supplied the water flowing in the canal. From this point I could see for miles across the barren desert, regularly spaced piles of dirt, which indicated the wells through which the accumulated silt in the *foggara* had from time to time been removed from the large, nearly horizontal tunnels connecting the series of wells. I brought offshoots from one of these healthy date palms back to the United States, and they were planted in southern Nevada with the help of Mr. Frank Thackery on July 4, 1927. These

Medjhool date palms grew very well in Nevada, but a few years later had to be transferred to the United States Experiment Date Garden at Indio, California, because of scarcity of water on the tiny Indian farm where they were so well started. This variety shows great promise in the Coachella Valley, the leading date-growing community in the United States.

Another equally striking method of irrigating is exemplified in the sunken date gardens of the Souf country in southern Tunisia (*Pl. 18*). In this barren region where almost nothing but sand can be seen in any direction, the Arab date growers discovered, apparently centuries ago, that by digging into the sand, moisture is found at a certain level. Extensive gardens were then excavated and date offshoots of the Deglet Noor and other choice date varieties were planted in this moist sand. At first sight there seems to be no water supply, and even if wells could be developed the dates could not have been made to grow on the sand hills without very frequent irrigation, since water sinks rapidly in loose sand and wastes away below the level of the roots. By planting the date palm just above a permanently moist layer of sand the costly labor of developing wells and irrigating is made unnecessary. But the sunken gardens must be protected from sandstorms by palm-leaf windbreaks built over the surrounding sand hills. When great sandstorms occur often, the windbreaks are unable to stop the blowing sand. Then the entire population of these oases of the Souf are called out to work day and night carrying the sand out of the gardens to prevent the famous old date palms from being smothered to death. Probably such sunken date gardens are made in Arab lands wherever a water-bearing layer of sand or gravel is underlain with a layer of gypsum or clay impervious to water. It may be that sunken gardens could be developed with profit in some parts of our Southwest.

Olives, almonds, pomegranates, oranges, and lemons, all of which are grown by the Arabs under the partial shade of the canopy of date fronds far above them, succeed better there than without such protection from the intense sunlight of desert regions. In the United States we have only begun to utilize such shaded orchards, which are found wherever Arabs have established themselves. Experts report on the average about one hundred and forty fruit trees grown per acre in the wonderful date gardens of Iraq. And underneath the deeper shade of these fruit trees, sheltered from the burning sun, grow flowers and vegetables, thus making the land support willingly three tiers of crops—first, the leafy palms high in the air, then the friendly fruit trees, having their laden branches within easy reach, and finally, below them, delicious vegetables and berries or lovely flowers.

The greatest single collection of date palm varieties in the whole world was assembled in the United States from Mesopotamia, Muscat, Iran, and Baluchistan, as well as from Egypt and the Barbary States of North Africa, during the first three decades of this century. This collection was started in 1900 when I introduced into the New World, for the first time, offshoots from choice Old World varieties. Thanks to a new system of packing, these offshoots grew as well as if they had been planted by the Arabs in an adjoining garden in the Sahara. Today the date gardens of southern California and southern Arizona are in many ways the best managed in the world and the most profitable. More than one hundred choice varieties have been tested there and half a dozen varieties are grown on a large scale, producing some 20,-000,000 pounds, about ⅓ of the dates consumed annually in the United States (*Pl. 19*). Through a vast region nearly half the size of Arabia flow perennially the waters of the great Colorado and Rio Grande rivers, and here we have perfected the art of irrigation as nowhere else in the world. Our knowledge of this art and of date growing will now return to help the Old World. King Ibn Saud recently sent American engineers on a ten thousand mile trip to study the sources of water available in the drier parts of Arabia. Thanks to the recent discovery of one of the largest oil fields in the world, this water can now be lifted from deep wells by using this cheap fuel, and literally make the barren desert bloom.

### THE ARABIAN HORSE

One of the greatest gifts of Asia to the world is the wonderful Arabian horse. It is easily domesticated, yet spirited and intelligent, very strong (able to stand galloping for hours over sand), and lives to a ripe old age (35 years or so). As the automobile and the tractor drive out the draft horse from common use, we are almost certain to return more and more to man's first use of the horse as the proudest, most beautiful, and most lovable riding animal man ever knew. In our Southwestern states, the climate favors the retention of the superlative qualities of the Arabs' chief contribution to our outdoor life—his unrivaled steed. For, tunately there are several good collections of Arabian horses in the United States, and one of these is now the property of the University of California, donated in perpetuity to the University by W. K. Kellogg, together with a great estate near Pomona, California, especially chosen and fully equipped to provide a proper home for these splendid animals. Carl R. Schmidt, who helped Clark build up the fine stud of Arabian horses in Indio, California, before its purchase by Kellogg, has published under his nom de plume Carl R. Raswan some small parts of his vo-luminous notes on the rules of breeding the breeds and strains of Arabian horses (*The Black Tents of Arabia: My Life among the Bedouins*, London, 1942).

The remarkable achievements of the Arabs in horse breeding have been summarized as follows by Victor A. Rice:

"The development of the Arabian horse by the Bedouins of the desert is generally recognized as the first great achievement in animal breeding of which there is any definite record. Because the Bedouins' safety often hinged upon the speed and endurance of their horses, these people surrounded their breeding operation with an air of superstition and mystery, much of which has per-sisted in certain quarters to the present day."

There are several breeds of Arab horses and numerous strains. the latest work which discusses this moot subject is Lady Went-worth's imposing work (*Thoroughbred Racing Stock and its Ancestors*, London, 1938).

Our first enlightening account of the Arab horse was that pub-lished about sixty-five years ago by Lady Anne Noel Blunt and her poet husband Wilfred Scawen Blunt (*A Pilgrimage to Nejd*, London, 1881).

According to Pycraft (Pycraft, W. P., in J. Walker McSpad-den et al, *Animals of the World*, 1941-1942) the British thor-oughbred was built up by an infusion of Arab blood into "the swiftest horse which the world has ever known." He also says the American trotting horse is a "Combination of barb and Arab on an English stock." The barb horse itself, a splendid animal at its best, seems to have been produced by the breeding of Arab horses with native North African stock. Many of the best horses of Spain and of Spanish America have an infusion of Arab blood. Pycraft gives a superb photograph of an Arab mare with its rider, Lady Wentworth herself (*Plate 20*).

Doubtless the crossbreeding of Arab horses, freed from the complicated conventions of the Arabs, and practiced by scientific experts, will lead to the creation of superior horses for every field left open to them in our automotive world of the future.

## FUTURE BORROWINGS FROM ASIA

American borrowing has by no means exhausted the plant resources of Asia. Hundreds, probably many hundreds, of new crop plants and new ornamental or drug plants are certain to be found either wild or under culture in Asia and many of them will some day be grown in the United States and other countries. In addition we must search out and import many more wild relatives of our cereals, garden vegetables, fruit trees, and drug plants. Our losses from recently introduced plant diseases, such as chestnut blight, citrus canker, and cantaloupe mildew (all of them unknown before 1900) have amounted to scores of millions of dollars. Citrus canker fortunately was eradicated, but if it had not been killed out in this country, it would have destroyed all orange and grapefruit groves in Florida, Louisiana, and Texas and it would have been necessary to spend many years breeding canker-resistant varieties of oranges and grapefruit by using Chinese and Siamese citrus varieties immune to canker. Cantaloupe mildew was conquered by using half-wild melons from northern India for crossbreeding with the susceptible varieties in this country. Blight-resistant chestnuts were found in China and Indo-China and the tree breeders have already made promising hybrids between them and our own chestnut now well on the way to extinction. But new plant diseases may make sudden inroads at any time.

World War II interrupted a very successful search by the Plant Introduction Service of the Bureau of Plant Industry, not only for new Asiatic plants but for wild relatives of the Asiatic crop plants we now grow. Perhaps in the future we can establish in several climatic regions of the United States permanent gardens planted to these wild relatives so they will be always on hand for use when needed and not have to be sought for hurriedly at very high cost after great damage to our own crop plants has already been done.

## REPAYMENT OF OUR DEBT TO ASIA

From 1915 to 1930 T. Ralph Robinson, Eugene May, and I worked out methods to permit the introduction of canker-resistant varieties of citrus mentioned above from China, Thailand, the Philippines, and Japan without danger of introducing insect pests or fungous and bacterial diseases. The plants from the Orient were held in screened and oil-moated quarantine greenhouses near Washington, D.C. Each plant was grown in a small screened cage inside the greenhouse until clean twigs developed which could be used for propagating. These twigs were then cut off, under aseptic precautions, and budded on clean citrus seedlings growing in another screened greenhouse. When these buds had made vigorous growth the original imported plants were destroyed completely—burnt in a furnace along with the soil in which they had grown. This system is now used by the Plant Introduction Service of the United States Department of Agriculture at Glenn Dale, Md. Now this aseptic plant propagation system can be reversed and disease- and pest-free strains of economic plants from other parts of the world can be sent to China and other Asiatic countries in exchange for the many valuable fruits, trees, grains, and medicinal and ornamental plants we have secured from them.

*Stephen B. L. Penrose, Jr., and Oliver J. Caldwell*

## TIES THAT BIND

AMERICAN contacts with Asia have been primarily of three types: commercial, governmental, and those which may be described as private and civilian. The authors of this chapter will discuss the nature and origin of certain popular ideas regarding the peoples who live in Asia and some of the institutional channels through which they have been derived. The main emphasis will thus be placed on social agencies which have acted as bonds between the populations of the East and West. Anglo-Saxon contacts, and in particular American relations since 1900, will be stressed. Limited space prohibits extensive historical discussion. It is obvious, however, that what has happened during the twentieth century in our relations with Asia has been for the most part a flowering of seed planted earlier. The confusion and knowledge which have long existed in the public mind, indeed most beliefs and misconceptions concerning Asiatics, are in the main a result of the work of social agencies and movements which have influenced the conduct of cultural relations between the hemispheres.

## I

When one seeks to analyze the impression which the so-called "average" American has of the Near East, as distinct from those who have deliberately sought information, one finds that it is apt to be a curious mélange of notions, images, feelings, and prejudices, the source of which is frequently obscure and the content of which is usually vague. Yet analysis will reveal that there is much that is actually specific in the general impression. Americans have far more information, much of it erroneous, about the

Near East than they are apt to believe possible on first thought. Leaving out of account events connected with the world wars, and all concern with anything but the non-European part of the area, it will be worth while to point out some of the ways in which the Near East has impinged on the American consciousness.

Consider the countries included in the area. Turkey, Syria and Lebanon, Iraq, Palestine, Transjordania, Egypt, Saudi Arabia, Persia, Ethiopia—though some of these are not in the strict sense part of Asia, they are all involved. Listing them separately breaks up the first general idea that the Near East is all sand and camels, and brings into view a series of rather definite stereotypes familiar to most of us. Observe them as they march before us.

Turkey: the Terrible Turk (a famous wrestler-strong-man of supposed brutality who appeared on the American scene in the early part of this century); hook nose, bulbous body in baggy pantaloons, red fez perched on small head, possibly a handle-bar mustache; the harem beauty: sloe-eyed, heavily veiled, and wearing little else but long pantaloons and turned-up slippers; sultans of unimaginable wealth living in tiled palaces, lolling on wide divans, smoking water pipes, drinking coffee served by obsequious slaves, amused by dancing girls very sparsely clothed, surrounded by a thousand wives. The men, sly, treacherous, cruel, deceitful, fond of torturing enemies and slaves; the women, mysterious, heavily guarded, beautiful, desirable, enchanting; the land filled with luxurious palaces and domed mosques with needle-like minarets.

The Arab countries (generally including everything except Turkey): sand and more sand, stately camels plodding slowly over the dunes, oases with palm trees, pyramids, sphinx; the men, tall, stately, handsome, eagle-eyed, hook-nosed, brave, wearing flowing robes and head cloths, given to wild riding of fiery horses with much rifle shooting; the women, seldom visible, heavily veiled, almost a minus quantity.

These are two examples of common stereotypes and it is rather easy to trace their origins. Primarily they come from highly imaginative motion pictures like *The Thief of Bagdad* and *The Sheik*, through which Rudolph Valentino captured the imagination of countless Americans and added a new word to adolescent vocabularies. They also derive from the *Arabian Nights* tales, often beautifully illustrated. They are made more specific by our familarity with Persian rugs, brassware, inlaid furniture. They have perhaps been confirmed by cartoonists who inevitably characterize nations in their drawings according to popular stereotypes of their citizens. This analysis is superficial, for each individual may have been subject to varying influences, but it will probably fit a considerable number of cases.

The unfortunate thing about these stereotypes is that they are hopelessly erratic. Many of their possessors will freely admit this fact, and when pressed for more detailed and accurate information will be able to produce it. For though it is typical for the majority of us to think in pictures, Americans have a surprisingly large number of personal connections with the Near East which can provide more accurate and circumstantial knowledge. These connections have a modern history extending well over a hundred years.

Moving across desert, mountain, and ocean, we come to India. The popular American conception of the people of India is apparently a composite of snake charmers, hideous idols, elephants, and mysterious ladies hidden behind veils. We know that there is great poverty as well as great wealth in India, and that the population is divided into unfriendly groups. What we do not generally realize is the richness of her culture, and the profundity of her philosophy, which is thousands of years older than Gandhi. Yet in spite of our ignorance, India and her problems are now matters of prime importance to every American, and the manner of the solution of these problems will affect the lives of millions of Americans as yet unborn.

Still farther east are the Indies, and there are few parts of the world concerning which the average American is more ignorant. Popular books and motion pictures have conspired to create an illusion of sensuous glamour about the East Indies and their people. Solid historical and geographical facts regarding this region have had little circulation in the public mind on our side of the Pacific. One reason for this is doubtless that European imperialism has dominated the islands of the East since the time of Columbus. Jealous Western powers have competed for control of these rich islands, and most of our contacts have been indirect and commercial. The average American has discovered the Indies only since the first World War, and has been intimately aware of their existence only since December 7, 1941.

Among all the peoples of Asia, the Chinese have traditionally been our best friends. Whereas the Japanese have been regarded for many years with increasing suspicion and distrust, our relations with the Chinese people have grown increasingly cordial. It is a remarkable fact that the Chinese, about whom the typical American actually knows very little, are regarded in general with a sentimental trust and admiration, an attitude not to be found in our relations with any other Oriental people.

Yet it was not always so; in the not distant past there were race riots against the Chinese on our Pacific coast. In 1900 the United States participated in an international military expedition against the Chinese Empire. There has long been a conflict between several popular concepts regarding the Chinese.

One was the Dr. Fu Manchu legend, which was created by the popular novels written by Sax Rohmer. According to this conception, the Chinese were a race of wily rogues with sparse, drooping mustaches, and an unholy appetite for opium and white ladies in distress. This picture competed with another, which depicted the average Chinese as a clever and taciturn follower of Confucius, so honest that he did not use written contracts, so thrifty that he was never in debt, wise and honorable in all his dealings, and a model for less civilized people. There were other popular conceptions. Many Americans before 1937 looked tolerantly upon the Chinese as a race of peaceable laundrymen and cooks.

The heroic resistance of the masses of the Chinese people against Japanese aggression did much to defeat the believers in Dr. Fu Manchu, and at the same time modified the prevailing idea that the Chinese are Confucian pacifists. There is possibly no foreign people concerning whom the average American is fundamentally more ignorant than he is about the Chinese, but he is nevertheless convinced that the Chinese are our friends, and are fundamentally all right.

We know little about the people of Japan, partly because the leaders of the Japanese people have apparently not wanted us to understand them. This means that we have had a series of impressions of the Japanese, all of them partly untrue. It is doubtful if we will form an accurate picture of these people for years to come.

Gilbert and Sullivan played an important part in the development of Anglo-Saxon misconceptions of the Japanese. *The Mikado* has done much not only to entertain its listeners but also to create a dangerously false impression of the little men of Titipu. It is notable that our ideas concerning Oriental peoples in general have been profoundly affected by motion pictures and popular books which have created a romantic fog through which the truth is often not to be discerned. The romantic ignorance of the American people regarding the Japanese and other Asiatics has been reinforced by a callow assumption of complete racial superiority.

It is well for us to remember that there was a time in the not distant past when Americans looked with benevolent friendliness on the Japanese, who were regarded as giant-killers during their war with Russia. There was a great deal of pro-Japanese feeling during that war, and among intellectuals of the period there was a profound interest in the Japanese people aroused and nourished by such writers as Lafcadio Hearn. The latter regarded the Japanese as the modern Greeks, and apparently was convinced that they embodied most of the more worth-while human virtues.

America's friendship with Japan rapidly deteriorated in proportion to Japan's rise as an international power. Part of the deterioration was our own fault, growing out of our arrogance and our unwillingness to deal with Japan on equal terms. In any event, the Japanese militarists have created concerning the Japanese people as a whole an indelible impression on the American mind. We look upon the Japanese as cruel, crafty, and utterly untrustworthy. It is hard for most Americans to conceive of any large number of decent people in Japan. It will be many years before the Japanese and American peoples will be able to deal with each other on an open and friendly basis.

# II

One of the most important bonds between Americans and Asiatics has been the Christian missionary movement. The motivation of this movement is the Biblical command, "Go ye into all the world and preach the gospel." The fundamental assumption of the missionaries is that they bear "good tidings and great joy" concerning the one true way to salvation.

There have been many kinds of missionaries. Some by their fanaticism have discredited the whole movement, others have been unofficial ambassadors and have done much to create international good will based on mutual understanding. Many missionaries have grown in wisdom through their contacts with ancient cultures, and have become zealous spokesmen in America for the people they were sent to convert to Christianity.

Missionaries have been for the average church-going American his only direct contact with remote alien peoples. The missionary movement has thus become a matter of considerable sociological significance, and must occupy a prominent place in this discussion.

American missionary activity has been constant in the Near East since 1820, when the ten-year-old American Board of Commissioners for Foreign Missions began operations in Turkey, Syria, and Palestine. Pliny Fisk was the pathfinder. He was followed in Syria during the middle of the nineteenth century by such men, well known in the America of their day, as Dr. Henry H. Jessup, Dr. Cornelius V. A. Van Dyck, translator of the Bible into Arabic, Simeon Calhoun, the "Saint of the Lebanon," and Daniel Bliss, who went out for the American Board in 1855 and ten years later founded the Syrian Protestant College (later the American University of Beirut) of which he became the first president. In Turkey at approximately the same period was the famous Cyrus Hamlin, who provided bread for the ill-fed British soldiers in the Crimean War, and later founded Robert College of Constantinople.

During the "Great Century" of religious development other denominations in addition to the Congregationalist, Presbyterian, and Dutch Reformed churches, which united in the American Board of Commissioners for Foreign Missions in 1826, promoted work in the area, though the three original churches continued to exercise the majority influence. When separate Presbyterian and Dutch Reformed mission boards were later established, the Near Eastern field was divided among them by agreement. The Congregationalist in Turkey, the Presbyterians in Syria and Persia, the Dutch Reformed in Mesopotamia (Iraq) and Arabia, the United Presbyterians in Egypt, and a legion of representatives of other missions in various parts of these countries have kept alive in America a vigorous concern with the spiritual affairs of the Near East. And since spiritual affairs are inseparable for practical purposes from physical and cultural affairs, there has been a constant stream of information flowing back from abroad to large areas of American Christendom.

The impetus of the missionary effort gave rise to the establishment of schools, primarily in order to overcome the widespread illiteracy of the Near Eastern countries at that period, and thus make possible the reading of the Bible and religious literature. The existing Arabic type was found to be inadequate for the printing requirements of the mission, so the missionaries designed a new font, which was cast in Leipzig, in 1849, under the direction of Rev. Eli Smith. This type style, which was used for printing Dr. Van Dyck's translation of the Bible, is still used throughout the Arabic-speaking countries and is still universally known as American Arabic.

Since there was in the early eighteen hundreds no satisfactory system of secondary education in operation in the Near East, it was a natural step for the missionaries to create high schools and then colleges in order to develop the capacities for leadership in local churches and in the governments of the countries themselves. Some of these colleges remained under the control of, or closely related to the mission boards, like Anatolia College, originally of Marsovan, Turkey, and now of Salonika, Greece, or the American University of Cairo, Egypt. But because the cost of higher education was greater than mission boards could usually afford to support, a number of these institutions were developed under separate leadership and came in time to obtain the financial backing of a large American clientele of their own.

The outstanding example of institutions of this latter type is the group of six great colleges which, for administrative efficiency, have been organized into the Near East College Association. The component institutions in the Association, with the dates of their establishment and latest enrollment figures, are as follows:

| Institution | Estab. | Enroll. |
|---|---|---|
| Robert College of Istanbul, Turkey | 1863 | 1100 |
| American University of Beirut, Lebanon | 1866 | |
| International College, (formerly of | | 2267 |
| Smyrna, Turkey, now of Beirut) | 1903 | |
| American College of Sofia, Bulgaria | 1860 | 480 |
| Woman's College of Istanbul, Turkey | 1890 | 470 |
| Athens College, Athens, Greece | 1925 | 450 |

All of these colleges are chartered in the United States and each has its own board of trustees. They all conform to the best American educational standards and their graduates have a recognized status in the field of American education. Robert College has a high ranking engineering school, to which the Turkish government now sends a number of selected students. The American University of Beirut has first-class schools of medicine, pharmacy, and nursing which have practically created those professions in the Near East.

It would be beyond the scope of this discussion to consider the service which these institutions have rendered to the Near East, but it is pertinent to look at what they have done for American-Near East relations. Quite aside from the fact that they and the other American philanthropic enterprises have built a firm foundation of friendship between the Near Eastern peoples and the United States, they are a living monument of American interest in the Near East. Combined, these six institutions alone represent an investment of some $21,000,000 in plant and endowment. On the faculty of the American University of Beirut alone have been graduates of nearly 120 American colleges and universities. Many of these former teachers have become experts on Near Eastern affairs, and most of them have been enthusiasts on the Near East, spreading the light of knowledge and interest among their associates at home. At the present time there are many former teachers of these colleges serving the Government at Washington in various capacities related to the Near East.

Within the past three years the Near East College Association has begun an effort to provide information on the Near East for people in America, regardless of whether or not they have actively supported the colleges in the past. The Near East Service, which was started by the Association in 1939, publishes a printed and illustrated *Quarterly;* a monthly *Bulletin* giving brief interpretations of recent Near Eastern events; and a series of "Special Articles," published by the Service when material is available, dealing in detail with some particular aspect of life or thought in the Near East. Typical of the last are the series of articles on Religious Sects of the Near East: Christian, Moslem, and sects neither Christian nor Moslem. All these publications are distributed to annual members of the Near East Service, the avowed purpose of which is "to interpret the Near East to the West."

Another organization which aroused a great interest in a considerable part of the Near East was the Near East Relief, set up in 1915 to help save the lives of and settle in new areas the refugee peoples uprooted as a result of the first World War. It has been called editorially "the greatest single charity in the history of the world." Concentrating originally on the Armenians driven from their homes in Turkey, the Near East Relief did noble service also with the Greeks transplanted from Turkey during the exchange of populations following the Smyrna fire in 1922. Nearly $116,000,000 was contributed by Americans to the Near East Relief, which blanketed the country with its urgent appeals. Probably more Americans learned of the Near East through this agency than had ever before known anything of it except that it was an area on the map.

Unfortunately, in its concentration on the refugee appeal, the Near East Relief painted a very black picture of Turkey and the Turks, conveying widely the erroneous impression that they are uniformly cruel, heartless, treacherous, and untrustworthy. It tended to confirm the stereotype described at the beginning of this chapter. The history of modern Turkey demonstrates the falsity of this view, and it is with considerable justification that the Turkish people resent it. Rightly or wrongly they hold the Near East Relief responsible, and they have opposed the operation in Turkey of the Near East Foundation, which continued some of the work of the Near East Relief when the latter was liquidated in 1930.

The Near East Foundation, through its social and agricultural development work in Bulgaria, Greece, and Syria, has likewise contributed largely to the knowledge which Americans have of the Near East. Operating with a less intensive program of publicity than its predecessor and on a less impressive scale, it nevertheless obtains and merits the regular support of a large number of contributors. Until the recent catastrophe in Greece, its activities had been devoted less to relief work than to a constructive program of social welfare in co-operation with the governments of the countries involved. In Syria, the Foundation and the American University of Beirut have joined forces in a village agricultural program of great interest and significance.

Americans have been particularly interested in medical work throughout the world, and support for this phase of fundamental human service has been generously given to the East, both Near and Far. Medical assistance has by no means been monopolized by the Rockefeller Foundation, though that has been perhaps the most generous single agency. All the mission boards have been interested in medical work, possibly on the principle that the medical missionary, to quote Dr. Paul W. Harrison of Oman, Arabia, "is simply an extra-legible version of the Christian." But in many cases the medical aspect of mission work has gained the financial help of laymen who might otherwise have lacked interest. It would be impossible to list all of the medical missions in the Near East, but they exist in such widely scattered places as Muscat, on the Persian Gulf coast of Arabia, Meshed and Tabriz in northern Iran, Tripoli and isolated Deit-es-zor in Syria, and in various towns of Turkey, Egypt, and the Sudan. All have their fascination, and all more than merit the support they have been given at home.

By no means all of the medical work in the Near East has been governed by mission boards. One may cite the American Women's Hospitals in Greece and the American Hospital of Istanbul, Turkey, now in a splendid new home, as institutions under separate, private control. The work of Dr. Lorrin Shepard of Istanbul is a romance in itself, and has received considerable publicity in the American press. The hospital of the American University of

Beirut has also done amazing things to alleviate suffering in Syria. These and many others are links in the chain of human sympathy which binds America to the Near East.

An entirely different field which has attracted American interest to the Near East is that of archaeology. Every American student who has been exposed to a course in ancient history is aware of the fact that much of our knowledge of ancient times has been dug from the ground or gleaned from a study of ruins and monuments which alone remained as evidence that a civilization had passed away. A large number of American colleges and museums have sent expeditions to the Near East, which, because it was the cradle of Western civilization, is particularly rich in historic remains.

Every educated American is familiar with the pyramids of Egypt, and has probably seen pictures of Egyptian temples and tombs. The discovery which probably aroused the greatest popular interest in Egyptian archaeology was that of the tomb of Tutankhamen, opened by Howard Carter and Lord Carnarvon in 1922. Although in actual historic significance this find was hardly of greater importance than thousands of others, it captured the American imagination. For a brief period it even had its reflection in the styles of women's clothes—an indubitable evidence of widespread interest.

Heinrich Schliemann's verification of Homer by his excavation of Troy is familiar to most Americans who know who Homer was. The writings of James Henry Breasted, familiar as texts to students of ancient history, were based upon excavations in Egypt and other parts of the Near East. Archaeological expeditions from the universities of Chicago, Pennsylvania, Harvard, and Princeton are now far from being novelties to the American people. Though the publication of their findings may not be widely read, they have disseminated generally a considerable knowledge of the Near East.

Outside the universities it may not be fully realized at first thought how much public concern there is with the ancient Near East. Yet nearly every important city in the country has a museum with at least some relics of the historic past, most of which exercise a sort of fascination on those who observe them—and they are many. Although archaeological societies as such may be

neither numerous nor large in membership, the subject of archaeology is by no means without great popular appeal. Through it
as a medium the American people have, directly or indirectly, acquired a considerable, if un-co-ordinated, knowledge of the Near
East. And in conjunction with other phases of classical scholarship it has received sufficient financial support to make possible
such projects as the restoration of the Parthenon, the sending of
numerous expeditions for further exploration, and the establishment, on the field, of schools for the training of archaeologists.
Among the last may be cited the American School of Classical
Studies in Athens and the American Schools of Oriental Research
in Jerusalem and Bagdad.

Since the first World War, American interest in the Arabs has
tended to fade with the increased attention which has been given
to the plans for a Jewish national home in Palestine. Zionism has
been very largely supported by the contributions of American
Jews and it has brought Palestine well to the forefront of American consciousness. It cannot be said that Americans generally
have much awareness of the many problems involved in the proposal for the establishment of a Jewish state, but they have certainly been made aware of the plan. The Zionist movement has
done much to link America to at least a small part of the Near
East with bonds of personal interest.

A movement like Zionism, which is so largely of a political nature, is likely to provoke opposition from the friends of those
who seem likely to suffer by it. In this case the opposition has
been partly, as might be expected, among Americans of Syrian
or Palestinian or Iraqi descent, who supported the now defunct
Arab National League, devoted to presenting the Arab side of the
question. Another organization, the recent development of which
has been blocked by the illness or involvement in military or government service of some of its more active members, is the American Friends of the Arabs. This is much less closely connected
with actual Arab politics than was the League, and for that
reason, as well as for the fact that enrolled in it are many Americans of prominence and influence, it may perhaps be more influential in the United States. Although it is handicapped by its
representation of a comparatively voiceless minority, the Ameri-

can Friends of the Arabs has brought to a considerable audience an interest in Near Eastern affairs.

There has been a certain vogue to organizations of "American Friends," but their activity has fluctuated with the prominence in world affairs of the countries to which they were devoted. For example, both the American Friends of Turkey and the American Friends of Greece were very active following the first World War, during the period of reconstruction whose miracles succeeded that conflict. After a season of quiescence, the American Friends of Greece has been recently revived and is devoting itself to securing aid and sympathy for the Greek people in the hour of their present agony. The American Friends of the Near East, another similar group, has been more constantly active because of its close association with the operations of the Near East Foundation.

Here, then, are some of the channels through which knowledge of the Near East has reached America. No mention has been made of American commercial interests, which are fairly extensive; nor of Arabian oil concessions to American companies, which are astonishing; nor even of the spiritual ties which link Christians, Jews, and Moslems to the cradle of world religions. All these deserve mention. But even including them it must be admitted that our knowledge of the Near East is more often than not scanty and partial. Yet it is encouraging to note an increasing interest among Americans in the wider horizons. Motion pictures and popular books which have created so many misimpressions, have also fostered a constructive interest, or at least a healthy curiosity, concerning alien peoples. Missionary and philanthropic work have contributed greatly to an intelligent mutual understanding between Americans and the diverse population of the Near East.

## III

The first contacts of the English-speaking peoples with India were purely predatory. It is shocking to the average reader of our generation to encounter men like Warren Hastings and his virile colleagues who conquered the Indian Empire for the Honorable East India Company in the seventeenth and eighteenth centuries. For many years the Company skimmed the cream of the wealth of India. Not only were there few attempts to help or understand the oppressed people of Southern Asia, who suddenly found themselves victims of aggression, but there was active hostility on the part of commercial and military interests towards any efforts to improve the conditions of Asiatics.

As the people of Europe became increasingly civilized, the British took over the conquests of the Honorable Company, and conditions began to change for the better at about the time of the American Revolution. These changes were in no small measure a result of the pressure brought to bear by church groups in England, who insisted on launching missionary enterprises, which, later reinforced by American missionary societies, have resulted in the enrolling of some 8,000,000 Hindus as Christians. Schools and colleges were established for the benefit of all social classes in India, and much of the progress that has been made by these people in the past 150 years may be traced to the influence of Christian enterprises.

American contacts with Indians have been strong in the missionary field. Some of the greatest figures in the Protestant church have devoted their lives to the betterment of the people of India, and have done much to create in America good will towards India. Such men as E. Stanley Jones, the Apostle of the Indian Road, and Sam Higginbottam, beloved agriculturist, have been unofficial two-way ambassadors between India and the American people, and their books have exerted considerable influence on public opinion in America. There is a strong reservoir of friendliness towards India in America, and in India towards America, which is a monument to the work of generations of missionaries.

Indian art and philosophy have also exerted strong influences in intellectual circles. The philosophy of non-violence, which is indigenous to India, has found an enthusiastic following among many Americans, and has had an important part in the growth of pacifism in America. There is a strong sentiment of respect in this country towards the intellectual accomplishments of the people of India. The manifestations of this respect range from the ridiculous to the sublime, from an American prize fighter practicing Yoga to improve his punch, through sundry Hollywood cults, theosophy, and offshoots of Buddhism, and culminate in a growing intelligence concerning India and its problems.

It is characteristic that many servants of imperialism have been conquered by the wealth of India's culture as evidenced by the following list of outstanding British societies devoted to bettering relations between India and the West:

British Indian Union, 43 Chalkhill Road, Wembley, Middlesex—for friendship and understanding between the two races.

Central Hindu Society of Great Britain, 43 Chalkhill Road, Wembley, Middlesex—for exposition of Hindu philosophy and for better mutual understanding.

Central Indian Colonial Association, 170 Adelaide Road, London, N.W.3—to further interests of Indians living in British Colonies.

East India Association, 3 Victoria Street, London, S.W.1—"to promote, by all legitimate means, the welfare of the inhabitants of India generally."

The Indian Society (Arts and Letters), 3 Victoria Street, London S.W.1—to promote the study of Indian art and literature.

Muslim Society in Great Britain, 18 Eccleston Square, London, S.W.1—to further interests of Islam and Islamic Institutions.

Royal Asiatic Society, 74 Grosvenor Street, London, W.1.

Royal Central Asian Society, 8 Clarges Street, London, W.1.

Royal Society of Arts (India and Burma Section), 18 John Adams Street, Adelphi, London W.C.2.

Society for the Study of Religions.

World Congress of Faiths, 2 Victoria Street, London, S.W.1.

School of Oriental and African Studies, Christ's College, Cambridge.

It is well for Americans, who sometimes are hypercritical about British influence in India, to remember that there is a strong pro-India sentiment in Britain, and that many Britishers have devoted their lives to helping the people of India.

Most of what has been said above concerning relations with India can be repeated for the East Indies. In recent years the Dutch government has dealt with the peoples under its control with friendly paternalism, and has frequently discouraged missionary enterprises; this has hampered the formation of strong links with the American people. It was difficult even for tourists to make the acquaintance of the Indies, because visas were frequently hard to obtain. The discovery of Bali precipitated a flood of round-the-world tourists, and created a smoke screen of romantic notions, as well as arousing a lot of healthy curiosity. Had American missionary enterprise been encouraged, knowledge of the Dutch East Indies might have matched that of other areas of Asia.

# IV

If the total result of the work of the various sociological and educational organizations interested in China and other Eastern countries has been to create a strong bond of understanding and friendship between the peoples of North America and the population of most of the Asiatic mainland, it may well be asked why tension has arisen with Japan. Our inter-cultural relations with the Japanese people have in some ways been better developed than has been the case with other northern Asiatic peoples. Furthermore, the material civilization of the Japanese has more nearly approached our own, and therefore it might have been supposed that it would be more natural for friendship to exist between the Japanese and the American peoples than between the Chinese and the Americans, with whom there were fewer material things in common.

Another question which might fairly be asked is whether the impressions that the American people have gained through the organizations herein discussed have been objective and fair. There are those who dislike the Chinese, and maintain that the organizations which have helped to create pro-Chinese feeling in the United States have done so at the cost of honesty.

It may be several years before it will be possible to make an objective study of our cultural relations with Japan. However, certain factors in Japanese-American relations stand out. There has been for years a rigid control in Japan of most of the activities of foreign agencies. Thus, the work of missionary and educational bodies in Japan has been much less free to develop without hindrance than has been the case, for example, in China. It has been said that whereas returned missionaries from China frequently spend their time propagandizing for the Chinese, returned missionaries from Japan often spend their time apologizing for the Japanese. This situation holds true for most objective observers, regardless of their affiliations.

Japanese propaganda in the United States has been largely of an official nature designed to make Americans see the Japanese people as the Japanese government wished them to be seen. Thus the Japan Society for years carried on a successful campaign for the propagation of Japan's cultural gospel. This campaign emphasized Japanese art, the tea ceremony, flower arrangements, Japanese gardens, and the other genuinely fine aspects of a highly complex society. This propaganda was an effective smoke screen which did much to obscure the dangerous elements of Japanese civilization. The essential lawlessness of the Samurai spirit was carefully hidden. The poverty of the masses in Japan, the organized prostitution of the Yoshiwara districts, the struggle for power between the various military cliques, the gradual elimination of all visible vestiges of liberalism, the flagrant violation of international obligations, all these things were carefully camouflaged. Every effort was made to direct our attention towards pleasanter matters.

The Japanese government circulated large quantities of exquisitely designed and printed booklets extolling the glories, beauties, and superiorities of Japan. Choosing at random, we note the following titles: *Tea Cult of Japan; What is Shinto?; Floral Art of Japan; Castles in Japan; Japanese Noh Plays; Japanese Food; Japanese Music; Kimono: Japanese Dress; Japanese Industrial Arts; History of Japan.* There were many others, all uniting to give a highly colored picture of a Never-Never Land.

The conducted tours of American educators, business men, and community leaders were another part of the same program. These good Americans paid very little and had a splendid holiday. Many of them were awarded free transportation in the laudable name of fostering mutual understanding. They saw only what they were supposed to see, and it was only the wiser ones who realized what was happening, who could penetrate the veneer and see the reality.

It appears in retrospect that in the years preceding Pearl Harbor, Japan carried on one of the most ambitious and intense programs of "cultural" propaganda in America ever attempted. As a result, a good deal of genuine knowledge of certain choice aspects of Japanese life was acquired by a substantial number of Americans. Of more immediate concern to the militarists who ruled Japan was the fact that many Americans were greatly befuddled. They could not believe much evil of Japan, and were unwilling that Washington should disturb our "historic friendship" in any way. This hampered military preparations by America and strengthened a state of mind which made it easy for Japan to trap us at Pearl Harbor.

The most sinister aspect of Japan's "cultural" program in America was her purchasing of the tongues and pens of several American writers and speakers. This problem as a whole cannot as yet be seen in proper perspective. Yet it is shocking to know that a leading American periodical with a long and honorable tradition could be bought and controlled by American citizens acting for Japan, and that a former member of the American Consular Service could be indicted as a Japanese agent.

It is too early to draw conclusions from Japanese-American cultural relations, yet we venture to suggest that cultural ties created and maintained by governments will almost inevitably be governed by ulterior motives. Genuine understanding is more likely to be a product of spontaneous and unhampered private contacts.

## V

Our friendship with China, and the more accurate of our ideas concerning the Chinese people, are based on our past contacts through Americans who have traveled or lived in China. These have included business men, casual travelers, members of the diplomatic, consular, and armed services, missionaries, scholars, and writers. Of them all, the missionaries have become the principal spokesmen for China, and have succeeded in passing on their conception of the Chinese to the American people. They constitute a tie which binds together in friendship the Chinese and American peoples.

The American missionary in China has generally enjoyed far better opportunities to understand the Chinese people than have his fellow Americans in other fields of endeavor, since he has been motivated mainly by a desire to serve the Chinese. This attitude has been, in the minds of the people, a marked contrast to that of the average foreigner in China. The business man, the diplomat, and the consul, have frequently been connected with imperialistic enterprises. The Chinese have therefore often trusted Christian missionaries, while looking upon other foreigners' agents generally with cold suspicion.

Missionaries have generally made it a point to master the Chinese language, and to become acquainted with native customs. While this has been done with an ulterior motive, in order to enable the missionary better to present his cause, it has usually resulted in geniune sympathy and understanding, and has made the missionary an earnest friend of the Chinese people. The thousands of American children of missionaries who have been born and reared in the heart of China, have been bilingual from the beginning, speaking Chinese and English with equal facility. On their return to the land of their fathers, most of them have become energetic propagandists for China.

There have been many Americans in business and official circles in China who also have become familiar with Chinese languages and customs. But what has been called the Shanghai Mind was long an unpleasant reality. This mentality was distinguished by varying degrees of contempt for everything Chinese. Too many Americans in China insulated themselves as far as possible against contacts with the Chinese. They had their clubs and their cliques, and proudly assumed the White Man's Burden of superiority.

Missionaries are, of course, not the only Americans who have befriended China. Many business men have been equally loyal, and sometimes more objective in their friendship. There are Americans who hold positions of great importance in our diplomatic services, and in the army and navy, who learned during their official residence in China not only to speak the language fluently, but to hold the people in great esteem.

Yet as a whole the missionaries have been the middlemen of friendship between China and America. They have created an enormous amount of good will for America in China; and in America, they have acted as impassioned partisans of China. They have exerted considerable influence not only on American public opinion through their churches, but also on the State Department. Whereas the American Missionary Movement started out exclusively to convert the heathen in China, it has become one of the most effective unofficial programs of inter-cultural education the world has known, and has laid the foundation not only for military collaboration between America and China, but for co-operation in creating a just, new order in Asia.

During the last seventy-five years the Protestants have far out-numbered Catholic missionaries in China, who had gained substantial numbers of converts in China as early as the fourteenth century. Furthermore, the Protestant enterprises have been dominated by Anglo-Saxons. Since 1900, Americans have outnumbered their British colleagues, and at times there have been as many as 5,000 Protestant American missionaries in China.

During the twentieth century American Catholics have gone to China in ever-increasing numbers. However, they are still relatively few compared to the Protestants, and they have in no way approached the latter as spokesmen in the Anglo-Saxon world for the Chinese people.

Compared to the Catholics, the Protestants have been late-comers. The result has been that of the approximately 4,000,000 Christians in China, at least three-fourths are Catholic. However, the Protestant influence in China is exceedingly strong, quite out of proportion to the membership of the various Protestant denominations. This is largely a result of the type of personnel sent to China by the Protestant churches. There has been a large percentage of university-trained men and women. To paraphrase Kenneth Latourette in his history of the Christian missionary movement, the flower of Protestantism has labored, and is still laboring, in China. These men and women have emphasized education and social service. They have concentrated on producing leaders, and have been successful in achieving a dominant position in many phases of the life of contemporary China.

Protestant missions were unknown in China until 1807. In that year Samuel Morrison arrived in Canton. He translated the Bible, wrote many pamphlets in Chinese, and endeavored to lay the foundation during his life for the study of Eastern languages in Britain. He did much to make possible the rapid expansion of Protestant missions in China during the latter half of the nineteenth century.

The contribution of the missionaries both to China and to their native lands may be best indicated by brief stories of individuals and their accomplishments. The first American missionary to China was Elijah C. Bridgeman. He went to China in 1830 as a guest of a New England merchant in Canton by the name of Olyphant, a gentleman who was so noted for his piety that his office was known to other foreign merchants as "Zion's Corner."

It is noteworthy that two years after Bridgeman's arrival he launched a magazine entitled the *Chinese Repository*, which was published in China from 1832 through 1851. In the words of its founder, this magazine was intended to spread among foreigners "information concerning laws, customs, history, literature, and current events in the Empire." Thus, the first American missionary to the Chinese people within two years of his arrival in China decided that one of his principal functions should be to combat ignorance and prejudice among his own people. The *Chinese Repository* is an invaluable mine of information, and is also a symbol of the accomplishments of the Protestant missionaries in educating the Anglo-Saxon world to understand and appreciate the Chinese.

In 1833, Bridgeman was joined by S. Wells Williams, a printer, who was sent to China by the American Board of Commissioners for Foreign Missions to develop a modern press which would spread the Christian gospel. Williams became one of the greatest foreign spokesmen for China. His books, *The Middle Kingdom* and the *History of China*, were for many years the best works of their type.

The American missionaries were not, however, the first to write in English on behalf of the Chinese. As early as 1818 an Anglo-Chinese College was established for the purpose of facilitating cultural interchange. This missionary institution was founded at Malacca, in the Indies, but was moved to Hongkong in 1843. It was originally intended that the College would enroll six European and six Chinese students, who would be trained to act as intermediaries between China and Europe. Those who lightly accuse the missionaries of intolerance would do well to investigate their purposes and accomplishments, even in the earliest days.

Among the thousands of Americans and British missionaries who have served China it is here possible to mention only a few.

James Legge, who arrived in the Far East in 1840, became one of the greatest sinologists, and was in his later years professor of Chinese at Oxford. Among his works are: *The Chinese Classics* (7 volumes); *The Religions of China; Confucianism;* and many others. Alexander Wylie, another Englishman, arrived in China in 1847, and contributed much to the interpretation of the Chinese people. Towards this end he learned French, Russian, German, Manchu, and Mongol, in addition to Chinese. He wrote voluminously on religion, literature, and science, and is credited with certain valuable translations.

An outstanding pioneer American was Justus Doolittle, who arrived in Foochow in 1857. In addition to being a successful missionary, he wrote a valuable book entitled *The Social Life of the Chinese,* which is still worthy of attention. An American Presbyterian, W. A. P. Martin, who arrived in China during 1850, wrote the popular *A Cycle of Cathay.* He was so loyal to the Chinese that the imperial government made him head of the first modern Chinese institution of higher learning, the T'ung Wen College in Peiping. The name of this college may be translated as mutual (or joint) culture (or learning), which indicates its purpose.

Many other missionaries made major contributions to the interpretation of the Chinese to Europe and America. E. T. Williams, an American from the Middle West, was a missionary who became an author, resigned from his mission to serve in the American diplomatic service, and eventually became the head of the Department of Oriental Languages and Literature at the University of California. Special mention should be given to Arthur Smith, who wrote several standard books on the Chinese, and exercised considerable influence on President Theodore Roosevelt, with the result that America returned the Boxer Indemnity to subsidize higher education for the young men of China. Dr. Smith was warmly seconded by Bishop James W. Bashford, author of *China, an Interpretation,* who was a missionary statesman of the first rank.

The use of the Boxer Indemnity to educate young Chinese was a master stroke in diplomacy, and did much to cement Sino-American friendship. Tsing-hua University still exists as a vindication of American policies in the Orient. The young Chinese who received their higher education through the Boxer Fund have done much to promote Sino-American friendship.

Missionaries have likewise made contributions of the greatest importance in the field of linguistics. A large number of Chinese language texts and dictionaries were prepared by missionaries, among whom were Baller, McIver, MacGillivray, Goodrich, Douglas, Chalmers, and Fenn.

Christian missions in China have long emphasized education and medicine in addition to evangelism. Hundreds of schools and hospitals were established in many parts of China. These institutions required for their operation a large number of specialists in medicine, in the sciences, and in other departments of learning. While they were contributing their services to the Chinese, many of them also learned from the Chinese, and made available to the European world the results of their investigations.

While most of the foreigners in China lived in the cities, a large proportion of the missionaries, including specialists, lived in remote sections, and traveled through almost every part of the country. The result was that they became the explorers and pioneers, and their reports formed the basis for much of our knowledge of China. Typical of this aspect of their interest in China is the West China Border Research Society, which was founded in Chengtu during the early years of this century with the purpose of exploring the Tibetan borderland, and making available to Europe and America information concerning one of the least known populated areas on earth. This organization consists primarily of members of the various missions operating along the Tibetan border. Such men as James Edgar have for many years been exploring the Tibetan mountains, and the reports which he and his associates have made constitute a large part of the existing information on this frontier region.

Among the first western scientists in China were missionaries and men of missionary background. For example, Harry R. Caldwell wrote *South China Birds,* a standard work, and also has contributed monographs in entomology and other fields of natural history. Claude Kellogg, of Fukien Christian University, and Burl Slocum, of the University of Nanking, among other missionaries, have contributed to our knowledge of Chinese entomology. Franklin D. Metcalf, who taught at Lingnan University, did distinguished work in botany. Dr. R. Gordon Agnew spent many summers in Eastern Tibet studying the relation between diet and the decay of teeth. The area he chose was ideal, because he found a great range in altitude and an equal variation in diets. His discoveries constitute a major contribution to the science of oral hygiene. The American parent who gives his child vitamins to control the development of his teeth owes a personal debt to Dr. Agnew.

One reason for the prominence which has been attained by the missionaries in the sciences in China is the development of Protestant Christian colleges and universities. Some of these institutions have been in existence for seventy-five years. They have brought to China hundreds of highly trained specialists who have done much not only to develop their fields in China, but to advance the cause of science in general. They play a major role in the intellectual life of modern China.

The following is a list of the Protestant Colleges in China:

| Institution | Estab. | Enrollment 1941-1942 | 1943-1944 |
|---|---|---|---|
| Fukien Christian University | 1915 | 403 | 463 |
| Ginling College | 1915 | 210 | 280 |
| Hangchow Christian College | 1897 | 919 | 228 |
| Hua Chung College | 1924 | 148 | 151 |
| Hwa Nan College | 1908 | 72 | 115 |
| Lingnan University | 1893 | 800 | 574 |
| Nanking, University of | 1888 | 793 | 1,099 |
| St. John's University | 1879 | 1,420 | 2,000 |
| Shanghai, University of | 1906 | 870 | 283 |
| Shantung Christian University | 1864 | 468 | 461 |
| Soochow University | 1900 | 1,318 | 320 |
| West China Union University | 1910 | 763 | 1,149 |
| Yenching University | 1870 | 1,156 | 380 |
| Totals | | 9,340 | 7,503 |

In the autumn of 1941 there were 115 institutions of higher learning of all types in China, as compared with 108 in 1937. The largest prewar enrollment was 41,922, as compared to more than 45,000 after four years of war, a figure that is reported to have reached 50,000 in the autumn of 1942. In 1937 the "American" colleges enrolled 15.3 per cent of all college students in China; this proportion had climbed to better than 20 per cent by the time Japan started the Pacific war.

The Christian Colleges have earned their present status in China by preserving sound intellectual standards, and by devoting their energies to serving the best interests of the Chinese people. There are approximately 11,000 living graduates of these colleges. An investigation of the latest Chinese *Who's Who* reveals that about one half of all the college graduates therein listed were graduated from the thirteen Christian Colleges. The Chungking Government contains a large percentage of these men and women. Since 1928 relations between the Government and the Christian Colleges have been increasingly cordial.

These colleges represent an investment in American funds of nearly $20,000,000. In the years 1943-44 they will receive for their support over $2,000,000 from the United States, in addition to substantial sums from British, Canadian, and Chinese sources. The Christian Colleges in China are a co-operative enterprise involving four nations, and have been one of the principal media for cultural interchange between China and the West. It is estimated that there are 800 men and women now living in the United States who at one time or another were connected with the colleges in China. These people as a group are highly educated and articulate. They have individually occupied many positions of prominence in the United States, and frequently have become unofficial envoys to America for China.

Most of the cultivation of popular interest in China by the missionaries has been indirect, but there has also been a vast amount of direct information disseminated through the churches. In order to maintain interest in the missions of China, the church boards have found it necessary to keep a large number of returned missionaries busy lecturing, and to distribute large amounts of literature. Examples of this publicity may be seen in the releases of the various mission boards, which range from reprints of personal letters received from missionaries to expensive brochures. The Associated Boards for Christian Colleges in China, which administers the endowments and obtains new funds for the work of the China Colleges, issues a quarterly bulletin with a circulation of more than thirty thousand, together with numerous book-lets descriptive of the Christian Colleges. The Board of the Methodist Church distributes as many as a million copies of a single item in its publicity program. Lastly, many missionaries have extensive personal mailing-lists. In one instance, 1,500 men and women regularly receive reports from their missionary in China. Thus the churches and the institutions they have sponsored have built in America a vast good will for China, and an active interest in her affairs.

Some of the missionary publicity has been of a high order. The Missionary Education Movement, an interdenominational organization, has presented a reasonably objective picture of life in foreign lands, and has done a great deal to educate the American people. Such recent pamphlets as *The Amazing Chinese*, by Willis Lamott (1940), and *China Rediscovers Her West*, a symposium (1940), have a genuine educational significance.

# VI

To examine any comprehensive list of books on the Orient is to be impressed by the number of people who have written of their adventures in strange lands, and have endeavored to interpret the peoples of these lands. It is difficult to assess these contributions to inter-cultural understanding. Much that has been written is deplorably bad, yet in these veins there is considerable gold. Such excellent books as those of Pearl Buck have assumed substantial sociological significance because of their great and deserved popularity. Doubtless thousands of Americans have discovered for themselves through reading *The Good Earth* that the Chinese are human beings. But space does not permit an evaluation of the influence of popular books. This survey must limit itself primarily to organizations and institutions of sociological importance.

The American Council of Learned Societies issued in 1942 a *Directory of Organizations in America Concerned with China*. The booklet lists some 105 organizations of various types. Many are primarily concerned with enterprises in China, but they also influence American opinion by their activities in this country. Other groups and institutions are frankly interested in interpreting China to America. The China organizations as a whole have exerted a major influence on public opinion in the United States.

It is interesting to note that 45 of the 105 organizations listed are definitely connected with Christian groups. In many other organizations there is a strong indirect church influence. This is natural because such a large proportion of American residents in China have been missionaries. The significant fact is that a large majority of the men and women, of all types and opinions, who return to the United States after sojourning in China become partisans for the Chinese people. Former residents of China tend to band themselves together to work for China. This loyalty of "Old China Hands" to China is a psychological phenomenon which not only is unique, but has become an important political and military factor.

It is also notable that important financial organizations have shown for many years an interest in the welfare of the Chinese nation. In this connection, the Rockefeller Foundation and its affiliates have done much for China. The great Peiping Union Medical College, one of the largest and most creative institutions of its type in existence, is a Rockefeller gift to the Chinese people. Since 1928 the China Medical Board, supported by Rockefeller endowments and grants, has been devoted to supporting the Medical College in Peiping.

The Rockefeller Foundation also is contributing directly to the support of other worthy enterprises in China. The Foundation has fostered the development of rural reconstruction, mass education, public health, scientific agriculture, and various branches of higher education. It also grants subsidies to a number of Chinese universities, and has played a major role in developing the science departments in several of the Christian Colleges in China.

The American Rockefeller Foundation has assisted several colleges and universities to develop Far Eastern studies. The Foundation has helped the American Council of Learned Societies to support seminars on Far Eastern studies, and has granted subsidies to the Institute of Pacific Relations. Space is lacking to list all the constructive benefactions of the Rockefeller Foundation in the field of Sino-American relations. Certainly it is one of the strongest ties binding together China and America, and its activities are also important in other Asiatic countries.

The estate of Charles M. Hall, who developed a successful process for the extraction of aluminum from its ores, has been another important factor in American relations with Asiatic countries. The estate invested a total of $13,963,688 in colleges and schools in Japan, China, India, the Near East, and the Balkans. The Harvard-Yenching Institute was endowed by the estate with $6,354,788. The Institute promotes Chinese cultural studies in China and the United States, and is affiliated with the following universities in China: Yenching, Fukien Christian, Nanking, Shantung Christian, Lingnan, and West China Union. The work of the Institute in America centers at Harvard, where it has created a magnificent library of Chinese and Japanese books. Instruction is provided on both undergraduate and graduate levels.

The American Oriental Society is another important bond between East and West. It was founded in China by American scholars in 1842. During the past century its scope and its membership both have grown. Now there are 843 members, devoted to "the cultivation of learning in Asiatic, African, and Polynesian languages and cultures and the publication of books and papers on these subjects." The light of this society was long obscured by the bushel of public indifference. The recent growing interest in Oriental languages and culture should make it possible for the society to fulfill the aims of its founders, who one hundred years ago expressed the hope that the American Oriental Society would serve as a bridge between the cultures of the East and the West.

The Institute of Pacific Relations is an international organization with national councils in Australia, China, Canada, Great Britain, the Netherlands, New Zealand, the Soviet Union, the United States, and the Philippines. The membership of the American Council is more than 1,200; headquarters are in New York. The activities of the IPR are manifold, including the promotion of meetings, the publication of pamphlets, periodicals, and books, the production of radio programs, and subsidies for research. The American Council has been increasingly active in the interpretation of the Orient to America.

The American Council of Learned Societies has done much to foster the development of sound scholarship in Oriental subjects.

This organization was founded in 1919 "to co-ordinate and advance humanistic sciences in America"; its membership consists of twenty-one learned societies. Through its Committee on Chinese Studies the Council has exerted a formative influence on sinology in America, and through other committees, on the development of Indic, Arabic, and other Oriental studies. The Council sponsors research projects, and has published a number of important works.

The average American is only indirectly influenced by the activities of learned societies. His principal contacts with China have been through church organizations, and through the activities of charitable enterprises. In the *Directory of Organizations in America Concerned with China* there are listed fourteen oganizations, such as United China Relief, interested in the relief of China's wartime needs, and many others, such as the Associated Boards for Christian Colleges in China, which participate in relief enterprises while carrying on their regular activities.

The East and West Association is a newcomer, founded as recently as 1942. Neither a relief organization nor scholarly in its approach, not committed to any faith or creed, and nonpolitical, it seeks an unsentimental approach to an understanding between peoples. Its methods are fluid, suited to the community in which it works, and therefore its avenues are many and varied. It presents series of lectures in cities, in co-operation with a committee representing the city's own educational, church, labor, minority, and other groups. It furnishes to colleges, men's and women's clubs, and other organizations authoritative speakers and entertainers, for the most part people from the countries of the Near, Middle, and Far East. It supplies to museums, schools, libraries, and other centers visual and auditory aids for teaching about other peoples. It works with groups of its own members in forming social and co-operative study groups so that people of varied backgrounds can meet and share their cultures on a basis of everyday living. The emphasis of the entire East and West program is on the human level; of coming to know people and their problems through their modern culture patterns as well as through their historical and political backgrounds.

China in modern times has been a land of calamities, and every great natural or man-made cataclysm has aroused a response in

America. Organizations have come and gone, and each has made its contribution both to the American and the Chinese people. In soliciting funds from the former for the latter, the giver has been educated to understand the needs of the receiver. The receiver, in turn, has been taught to regard America as a land of plenty and of good will, and to consider the Americans as friends. Some of the relief organizations, such as the American Association for China Famine and Flood Relief, have made important contributions to the education of America.

# VII

In conclusion, then, as historical facts clearly demonstrate, there is full reason for Americans to feel that they have definite connections, more firmly established than many are aware, with the Eastern world. There is full reason, nevertheless, for an effort to strengthen those bonds yet more. The East will inevitably play a role of increasing importance in the future affairs of the world. It is not too early for Westerners to comprehend its growing power, and it would be well for them to cultivate their knowledge of it from the Far, through the Middle, to the Near. Whether they meet head on in violent opposition, or peacefully as understanding friends, will depend, for our part, on how conscientiously we seek to know and appreciate, as individuals with qualities of culture and character to be respected, the inhabitants of these Asian lands. It is the part of wisdom for us to open up all possible channels for the interflow of mutual understanding, thus strengthening and increasing in number and effectiveness the many "ties that bind."

John Gould Fletcher

# THE ORIENT AND CONTEMPORY
# POETRY

## I

THE diffusion of literature, or—to describe the process
more accurately and closely—the way in which a literature has
been able to renew itself and to alter its direction by means of
contact with some form of literary expression practised in another part of the planet, is a fascinating subject. Those who are
unfamiliar with world literature are likely to suppose that the
masterpieces in this field are the product of great minds, who,
through their work, cover great areas of human experience,
guided by nothing better than their "inspiration." The more
eager and persistent student will, sooner or later, come to the
deeper problem of why certain literary forms came into being,
as well as the question of why certain languages guided them to
this achievement—and, allied to this, he will inevitably discover
that the attempt on the part of certain literary creators to trans-
pose a given form of literature from one language into another
has frequently been responsible for new literary awakenings in
lands remote from the birth of the original form.

It is with such a group of literary creators that this essay will
mainly deal; a group which originated in England, had its adherents in both England and America, and was known by the expressive name they gave themselves, as the Imagists. Professor
Glenn Hughes, in the only complete history written of this literary group (*Imagism and the Imagists*, Stanford University
Press, 1931) has stated, correctly, that the Imagist movement began with a meeting of a few people interested in the writing of

145

poetry, at a restaurant in London, in the early spring of 1909. Present at the first meeting were T. E. Hulme, F. S. Flint, Edward Storer, F. W. Tancred, Joseph Campbell, and Florence Farr —the last two being recent arrivals from Ireland. The group were highly dissatisfied with the way that poetry in English was being written, and were determined to do something to improve the general quality of contemporary poetry. Hulme, their unquestioned leader, was a man whose interests were equally philosophic and literary; he had done much independent study in both French and German philosophy and literature, and had undoubtedly read the French Symbolist poets, with their dislike of Victor Hugo's verbosity, to great advantage. Flint, who had carefully taught himself to read and write French, was his able second; he was much interested in the new French *vers-libre* forms.

Within a month of its formation, the group was joined by Ezra Pound, the first American present, who had just published his first book in London, under the title of *Personae*. As Flint and other chroniclers have accurately stated, up to that time Pound's poetry had been mainly influenced by the Provençal troubadours, by the early Italian poets of Dante's circle, by Rossetti and William Morris, Robert Browning and the early Yeats. With his restless desire, natural to an imaginative American expatriate, to conquer new poetic territory, and his flair for discovering new poetic talent, Pound felt at once at home with this group. His mind was intrigued with their 'doctrine of the image': a theory whereby the production of poetry was made dependent on the production of new and concrete images in words. Hulme, whose philosophic position in regard to the writing of poetry was already fully worked out, and who was prepared to insist upon such clarity of statement as made his pupils see "each word with an image sticking on to it, never as a flat word passed over the board as a counter" was prepared to demonstrate the 'doctrine of the image' by means of examples worked out on a blackboard. He was in full reaction against Victor Hugo, Swinburne, and the other romantic poets who were "always flying, flying over abysses, flying up into the eternal gases." He wanted poetry to return to the hard, the definite, the precise, the dry; he demanded a poetry that would present a continuous working up of pictorial analogies between the real world and the world of the imagination. Poetry to him was not inherent in any given metrical form, and for that reason he was disposed to favor the recent French experiments in *vers libres;* it was inherent in the power of metaphorical expression, which alone could create appropriate images; and for that reason, he favored the shorter poem over the long.

The group, as Flint later stated, "died a lingering death at the end of its second winter"; but before that event occurred, two important incidents in relation to it had happened. In the first place, the American poetess, Hilda Doolittle, whom Pound had known back in his early American days, and who was trying to restore to English poetry something of the metric freedom, as well as the poetic vividness, of early Greek lyric poetry, decided —following a brief visit by Pound himself back to America in the winter of 1909-10—to come over and settle in London. She then met the members of the group, and was acclaimed by them, as a perfect example of Imagism—although she made no attempt, as they did, to write on modern subjects. In the second place, the author of this essay, in the same spring of 1910, had himself met Hulme in an editor's office in London. Hulme had fished out of me that I was interested in the writing of poetry, and he promptly invited me to take part in the meetings and discussions of the group. My painful shyness—of which I was acutely conscious—as well as the effort I was then making on my own account, to write poetry according to models provided by the early French Symbolists, forbade my responding to Hulme's invitation. And so my efforts were to continue, single-handed, along somewhat parallel lines, until the day in late May of 1913, when—with my series of *Irradiations* worked out and complete—I was destined to meet Ezra Pound in Paris.

The reader may well ask, at this point, "Just what has all this to do with Oriental poetry and its influence upon contemporary English and American poetry?" The answer is, that it has a great deal, as anyone will see who reads further in this essay. None of these early theorists of the image had, one presumes, read much Oriental poetry, either in the original or in translation. Goethe's *West-Oestlicher Diwan*, as well as Edward Fitzgerald, and Wilfred Scawen Blunt's adaptation from the Arabic—which Pound admired—were no doubt, familiar territory; but the attempt made by James Elroy Flecker to follow Persian models, as well as the *Ghitanjali* poems of Tagore, which may themselves owe something to the Chinese, and which were enthusiastically hailed by Yeats in the early months of 1913, lay still in the future. On the other hand, we have Flint's word for it that the group was much attracted, from the first, by Japanese *tanka* and *hokku* forms (presumably someone among them had read Lafcadio Hearn or Basil Hall Chamberlain); and as Flint added, "we all wrote dozens of the latter, an amusement." The obvious conclusion is, that something in the conciseness of Japanese poetry, as well as its pictorial quality, early attracted the Imagist group.

We who are aware of the immense cultural debt long since owed by Japanese literature and art to the Chinese, are also aware of how little effect these Japanese forms—which have acted on Japanese poetry as a deterrent rather than as a factor favoring full development—can have had upon developing the Imagist group in the direction of a better understanding of Oriental poetry. They might as well have tried to write poems modeled upon the Persian *ghazel*—as the Georgian poet James Elroy Flecker, actually did a little later—as to have confined their attention solely to the *tanka* and the *hokku*, except for amusement, as Flint says. Whether they were aware or not that a great body of poetry existed in the Chinese language that was very highly Imagistic in its essential qualities, I do not know; but the fact remains that Flint, in his own early account of the genesis of Imagism, makes no reference to Chinese poetry, which would encourage a negative conclusion. However, I myself, though not then a member of the group, was becoming increasingly aware of the importance of Chinese poetry; I make no apology, therefore, for interposing at this point a purely personal narrative.

Sometime about the year 1910, I first became aware of the fact that the Chinese people had known a great literary flowering, and had enjoyed great writers of their own. I do not know how this intimation was first brought to me; I know only that I had been familiar with some of the great products of Chinese pictorial and sculptural art since the days when I, as an undergraduate at Harvard, had first walked into the Oriental Wing of the Boston Museum of Fine Arts, and had looked at the treasures magnificently displayed there. It was during the same early period of my studentship at Harvard (1902-1907) that I avidly read through the writings of Lafcadio Hearn; first as a translator of certain French authors—Gautier and Flaubert—whom I had come to admire, and secondly, as an interpreter of Japan. I did not realize at that time that Hearn, great prose writer as he was, was quite unaware, from the outset, of the immense spiritual and cultural debt which Japan had owed to China; and since he was handicapped, as a man, by the myopia which enabled him to see only the objects nearest at hand, he had necessarily refined upon and exaggerated the contributions that the older culture of Japan (already passing away while he wrote about it) had to make to mankind. What he said concerning a people whose lives were regulated by Spartan self-discipline, but who had continued to make an art out of the minute and the subtle, excited me by contrast with the raucous, bustling America I knew, but it actually influenced me very little at the time. After all, as an eager young student, I wanted a culture which was somewhat broader, which responded more completely to the flowing and diverse interests which underlay mankind.

This broadly human element I finally discovered in the Chinese; but I did not become acquainted with them as a people with a literature of their own, till around 1910, when I had already settled in London. Just what book first introduced me to them, I do not know; but I suspect it was Herbert A. Giles' *A History of Chinese Literature*, published in 1901—a book which I still possess and still find worth reading. This led me to Giles' predecessor, James Legge, and to Confucius; but Legge's more than Scotch matter-of-factness, as well as his utter inability to appreciate any poetical qualities in the Chinese written character, repelled me. I received, at the same time, far more enlightenment from the pages of Judith Gautier's *Le Livre de Jade*, first published in 1867, and revised early in the twentieth century. This I found totally delightful; though Chinese scholars have told me it is quite inexact. Cramner-Byngs' *A Lute of Jade*, published in 1909, and consisting largely of rather romantically colored adaptations of Giles and some French or Latin translators, also charmed me when it first appeared; but with the real pioneer effort in French, the Marquis d'Hervey-Saint-Denys' *Poesies de l'Epoque des Thang*, a magnificent piece of scholarship published in 1862, I was quite unfamiliar at the time, and did not see a copy in fact until shown one by Ezra Pound, about a year after I came to know him, early in the spring of 1914.

It is difficult for me to say just how deeply I was affected by the first Chinese poems I thus read in European translation; I am sure however, that although they gave only hints of the great riches of Chinese literature, they acted on me as a revelation. In common with all the advanced poetry writers of that period, I was in full revolt from the Victorians, with the sole possible exception of Browning; it seemed to me that all the English poets, from Shelley and Wordsworth onward, had tried too hard to make poetry teach something, preach something, bear the abstract connotation of a general moral lesson—when the real business of poetry was to state, and state concretely, just what had moved the poet, and to leave the reader to draw his own conclusions. True, the Pre-Raphaelites of the seventies, eighties and nineties had tried to get away from too much Victorian moralizing, but only William Morris, to whom poetry meant the return to heroic mythology, had made much out of Pre-Raphaelitism; and Morris had the advantage of long familiarity with old folk beliefs behind him. The attempt that the Georgians were then making, in the England where I lived, to revive the pure nature-lyricism of the early Romantics by reliance chiefly on Blake, rather than on Keats, Shelley, and Wordsworth, seemed to me rather artificial and forced; I recall that it was obvious to me that few of the Georgians knew anything concerning French poetry, just then concluding some fifty years of extraordinary development under the Symbolists; and so they seemed merely sentimental and naïve, where the French poets were mature, passionate, and subtle. W. H. Davies' poems were to me minor efforts in a falsely pastoral convention; James Stephens was Irish, a rougher and more erratic kind of Yeats; the early Masefield of the *Everlasting Mercy* seemed merely a cheap flash in the pan; W. W. Gibson was frankly dull; Brooke was clever, but just another precocious playboy; James Elroy Flecker charming, but rather too consciously exotic, in the manner of Leconte de Lisle and his favorite Parnassians. The only Georgian that seemed to me to matter was Ralph Hodgson, of all the Georgians the least fecund in output, but the richest in intensity and charm. All of them would, I felt, be better poets had they ever read this poem turned into my own English from Judith Gautier's French version:—

"One day, through the foliage and the perfume of the flowering trees, the wind carried to me the sound of a distant flute.

"I cut then a branch from a willow-tree, and fashioned of it a flute, and responded with a song.

"Since then, at night, when all are sleeping, the birds have heard a conversation conducted in their own language."

This, with its hint that it is only through art that man can aspire to rival nature, seemed to me to contain a lesson that the Georgians would do well to learn. Also there was this, written by the same poet, Li-Po, and found by me later on in Hervey-Saint-Denys' translation:—

Close to the city, enveloped in waves of yellow dust, the crows assemble to pass the night.
They fly cawing, above the trees; they perch on the branches; the males call after their mates.
The wife of the soldier, seated at her task, is weaving figured silk;
The crying of the crows comes to her, through the lattices purpled by the last rays of sun.
She stops her shuttle. She thinks with discouragement on him she awaits here for long;
She goes silently to her solitary cot, and her tears fall like summer rain.

Both of these poems—and many more like them—seemed to me to point out the Chinese poets had used their imaginations to identify themselves with the objects they wrote about. That Li-Po had probably never actually cut for himself a flute, and held conversation with the birds in their own language; that at best he had only pictured the wife of a Chinese soldier in a city besieged by Tartar cavalry, was of minor importance. He had done what Wordsworth had failed to do: "to choose situations and incidents from common life, and to relate or describe them throughout, in a selection of language really used by men; and at the same time, throw over them a certain coloring of the imagination, whereby ordinary things should be presented to the mind in an unusual way; and further, and above all, to make these incidents and situations interesting by tracing in them, truly though not ostentatiously, the primary laws of our nature."

It was to this conclusion that I had been driven by my own investigations into such Chinese poets as I could find available in either English or French translation, shortly after completing the series of my *Irradiations* at the close of June in 1913. As I have said publicly in another place than this essay, the *Irradiations* themselves owed a great deal to French Symbolist poetry, notably to Verhaeren, Francis Jammes, and to a forgotten book—*Les Fêtes quotidiennes* by Guy Charles Cros. These poets had taught me that the commonplace incidents of our lives—the vision of a child asleep in a baby-carriage, the aspect of great carts piled high with pots of flowers rumbling off by night to a city market—were as valuable subjects for poetry as Tennyson's "Locksley Hall" or Hugo's interminable efforts to match the godlike sublimity of history. Small wonder, therefore, that when Ezra Pound told me, sometime in the winter of 1913-1914, that he had fallen heir to the notes left behind by the late Ernest Fenollosa, who had died in September, 1908, and that these notes contained the translations of several quite excellent and important Chinese poems, I was invincibly curious. And sometime during that winter—after I had already finished my own *Sand and Spray; a Sea-Symphony*, the first of a series constructed according to a pattern which was, strictly speaking, my own—Ezra Pound showed me some of these translations, now grouped together in his work under the title of *Cathay*.

To say that I realized that these poems, so far as I was concerned, represented to me an enormous revolution in English poetic technique, would be an understatement. I had already, during the late summer of 1912, made some attempts at something similar, both as regards subject matter and technique. Let me quote two of these, both taken from my *Visions of the Evening*, published in the spring of 1913:

We will sleep in the high-pillared pavilions of late summer
    nights,
Watching the mists take vague and altering reflections
From the crimson lanterns, the towering tripods of flame
Set all around the hall, overflowing with golden lights.

We will slumber or we will drink, while the crimson-robed,
    dark-eyed dance girls
Weave a few wayward paces 'mid the cups and flowers on the
    floor. . . .
Let us sleep in the high-pillared pavilions of late summer nights,
Watching the moon's blue breath on the mirror of the pond.

There were some other lines to this as first written, lines voic-
ing a somewhat Omar-Khayyamish mood in philosophy, but not
germane to the chief substance of the poem, which aimed to present the image of a night spent camping in the American woods,
in an unfamiliar way. The other poem is even more explicit in
its direction:—

The lanterns dangle at the ends of long wires, the breeze bobs
    them to and fro.
My soul is in love with that lazy lantern dance.
Oh how the autumn gusts through the dark gardens
Rattle them together, rending their crimson sides!

This, recalling a far-off garden party I had witnessed as an
extremely young man in Arkansas, was actually entitled in my
book, "From the Chinese." In reality, its substance was no more
taken from any particular Chinese poem than was the substance
of certain other experiments in the same book, labeled "From the
Japanese," actually taken from that language. I knew nothing of
either. What had happened was that I had somehow, as a poet,
guessed at the way the Orientals had constructed their poems.
The parallelism of construction, casting back and forth from the
observer to thing observed, is surely manifest: and the self-same
quality is omnipresent in Ezra Pound's *Cathay*.

Unlike Pound, these experiments had been made without the
benefit of reference to Ernest Fenollosa's literal translations. I
had, though, read carefully through his *Epochs of Chinese and
Japanese Art*, but without any explicit reference to my own
poetry. The general construction of the metric cadence in these
examples is, at least, remarkably similar to the *Cathay* poems. And
the point about the *Cathay* translations is this: that every succeeding Chinese translator, beginning with Arthur Waley, whose
first book appeared in 1918, has, with very few exceptions, es-

sentially followed the metric scheme set up by Pound. This form —ignoring the "rhymes" and the "tones" of the Chinese originals— directly follows the Chinese construction of the phrase and is therefore the most nearly correct vehicle for translating Chinese poetry we have.

It was only after I had read the *Cathay* translations—taken as Pound said, "from the notes of the late Ernest Fenollosa, and the decipherings of the Professors Mori and Ariga"—that I threw overboard my own scruples, which had forbidden me up to then to take part in the Imagist movement, and proclaimed myself truly an Imagist. The Chinese influence and example seemed to me to fortify the whole case for Imagism, which in H.D.'s early poetry, as in that of Aldington, had depended too closely and exclusively on Greek or Latin models. Greek art had already offended me with its academic naturalism; the work of the early Chinese artists, whether in painting or in sculpture, seemed to me very much superior; could not something of the same sort be said also against Greek poetry? Flint's position, as a modern experimentalist taking off from the achievements of the French Symbolists, was far more sympathetic. Indeed, there was at least one poem by Flint that seemed to me rather Chinese, in its implications:—

> On black, bare trees a stale cream moon
>     hangs dead, and sours the unborn buds.
> Two gaunt old hacks, knees bent, heads low,
>     tug, tired and spent, an old horse tram.
> Damp smoke, rank mist fill the dark square;
>     and round the bend six bullocks come.
> A hobbling, dust-grimed drover guides
>     their clattering feet to death and shame.[1]

It was, then, thanks to the Chinese influence altogether that I myself became an Imagist, with all that the term implied. And when Miss Amy Lowell, in April, 1915, published the successor to Pound's *Des Imagistes* Anthology (which had appeared in the spring of 1914) under the title of *Some Imagist Poets*, I was proud and happy to take my place in its pages; for it seemed to me that my own combination of French Symbolism and of Chinese image-making had made of me as much an Imagist, as the influence of Greek poetry had made H.D., or the influence of Latin poetry plus Flint, had made Aldington.

## II

It is now clear that the Imagist group, as such, did not derive its impetus primarily from Chinese sources. The initial push to the movement had been given by T. E. Hulme, a speculative philosopher and a critic rather than a poet; he had been ably abetted in his initial purpose of getting rid of the vague rhetoric of Hugo and Swinburne by F. S. Flint, who—like Hulme himself—had dipped deeply into French Symbolism. Ezra Pound, who was trying, even then, to alter the rich but rather over-mythological early style of Yeats into something more vivid and direct, had come and listened, and become convinced by Hulme's demonstrations; H.D., who had, with the help of many early Greek lyrists, written herself back into a world which stood out in complete contrast to the world of twentieth-century London, had attended some of the meetings, and her earliest poems—duly printed in *Poetry* of Chicago in January, 1913, and labelled "Verses, Translations and Reflections from 'The Anthology,'" meaning of course, the Greek Anthology—had been agreed upon by all as perfect examples of Imagism. Richard Aldington, as a self-confident young man then just emerging on the career of writer, had entered the group, to be strongly influenced by both H.D. and Flint; I, too, had entered, rather belatedly, in the early months of 1914, only after the first Imagist anthology had been published. Miss Lowell had come to London in the summer of 1913, having—like most of us—previously read much French Symbolist poetry; she had threatened to take charge of the movement from the start; but had gone back to Boston, and was not expected to appear in London again till the summer of 1914. The main sources of Imagist Poetry were still to be found in Greek, Latin, French, and in Pound's Provençal; the Chinese influence, if it existed, was only a vague something in the background; and I cannot myself recall discussing Chinese poetry with any members of the group except Pound and, somewhat later, Amy Lowell.

But if French Symbolism be taken for the father of Imagism,

Chinese poetry was its foster-father. I have already pointed out that, in my own case, it was Chinese poetry alone—in such translations as I could then find—that finally convinced me of the validity of the new school. And Pound, by obtaining from Mary Fenollosa her husband's papers, sometime in 1913, had inevitably taken the same direction. He now had in his possession, besides the *Cathay* material, a long and extraordinary essay "The Chinese Written Character as a Medium for Poetry"—an essay which he jealously guarded as a most precious possession and allowed no one to see for a long time, before giving it out to the public.

Fenollosa's contention in that essay was that the Chinese language was the most perfect poetic instrument to be found in the world, because of its ideogrammatic constituents. It perfectly combined the element of pictorialization and of temporal continuity. Fenollosa agreed that the primary act in the creation of poetry was the forging of metaphor—Hulme had spoken of the "continuous working up of analogies," meaning precisely the same thing. To a reader of Fenollosa's essay, it almost seems that, at times, the author of this remarkable document was ready to argue that the Chinese characters are in themselves metaphors: "Poetic thought works by suggestion, crowding maximum meaning into the single phrase, pregnant, charged, and luminous from within. In Chinese character each word accumulated this sort of energy in itself."

This recalls somewhat the theory set out by Richard Wilhelm, the great German sinologist, in whose work Doctor Carl Jung, the Swiss psychologist, has become so interested: that the continuity of Chinese culture (despite all disasters) has been due to the fact that the Chinese possessed an unbroken record of ideographic language. But it is easy to see in what direction Fenollosa went much further; and how many pitfalls there were in his doctrine, when pushed to extremes by such an extremist as Ezra Pound. For Pound, as the jealous guardian of Fenollosa's legacy, immediately leaped to the conclusion that the thing to do was to reduce Imagism to further intensity, and to pack into every word of his resultant poems all the pictorial overtones which Fenollosa had previously found in Chinese characters.

Whether this new direction on his part was responsible for the coolness that now sprang up between him and T. E. Hulme, I cannot say; but in the spring of 1914, I was destined to hear a great deal, through Pound, of a new art-movement he was starting, to be called Vorticism. The new group consisted of Wyndham Lewis, who was writer as well as artist; Edward Wadsworth, a painter; Jacob Epstein, the well-known sculptor; Henri Gaudier-Brzeska, the young Franco-Polish sculptor whom Pound had recently met and befriended; and Pound himself, along with one or two others. Pound worked hard on me to get me to take an interest in the movement, and even offered me a chance to lecture to the public on my own theories of poetry. I had, however, other concerns for the moment, and in July of that year, at the same time that the new group got under way with their famous little magazine *Blast,* which soon after vanished—thanks to the more reverberant blast of the First World War—Miss Lowell did return to London, prepared to push the Imagists further along by bringing out, at her own expense, a series of annual anthologies. She and Pound immediately quarreled over the editorship; with the result that when the first of this series of anthologies came out in the spring of 1915, it had no editor at all, and was deprived of the services of Ezra Pound.

In saying this much, I am, however, already getting in advance of my main story; which is, as far as I am able, to trace the impact of Chinese poetry upon the consciousness of some modern Western poets; which impact, I believe, took place at first exclusively through the group known as the Imagists. My secondary purpose is to trace the same impact through my own work. I had already, at the close of January, 1914, written my "Blue Symphony," which was at first intended as an exercise in the pictorial manner of such Chinese poets as had already come my way; and then—as I have already narrated in my *Autobiography* —had, during the course of writing this poem, suddenly run across, by accident, some of Hans Bethge's German translations of old Chinese poems, serving as a choral background to Gustav Mahler's orchestral symphony, *Das Lied Von der Erde,* then being given its first public performance in London. As I have elsewhere stated, the effect of the discovery of these translations was electric. "As I listened to them [the Bethge translations] it seemed to me that the poem I was now writing was the same poem that many of these old Chinese poets had already written.

My modern loneliness, exile, despair, fled across centuries of time and thousands of miles of space and was joined to theirs." This rediscovery of the Chinese made me feel that my chief business was to see to it that the direction taken in my "Blue Symphony" was fully followed up; and accordingly, the whole series of my "Symphonies" was then and there begun. To continue with them was now my chief concern.

Pound, however, was certainly off on another tack. In the spring of 1913, he had been strongly and emotionally moved by the beauty of many faces seen in a city crowd as he descended from his train at a station of the Paris Metro. He wrote a thirty-line poem, according to his own account, about this; six months later, he shortened it, adjudging it work of 'second intensity'; a year later, he made the following *hokku*-like sentence:—

> The apparition of these faces in the crowd;
> Petals on a wet, black bough.

Flint was also doing much the same thing when he reduced an earlier and much longer poem that had appeared in his first book, into the sixteen-line lyric of his *Cadences,* well known under the title of "The Swan." I was doing something of the same thing when I was condensing my personal emotions as detailed in the "Blue Symphony" into what could be pictorially and vividly stated in a whole series of Symphonies. But the effect of Pound's 'one image poem,' as he called it, was, as it was more intense, more potent. It really compared favorably with such a well-known Japanese *hokku* as the following:—

> Fallen flower returning to the branch;
> Behold! It is a butterfly.

The question of the relation of the Japanese *tanka* and *hokku* poems to the Imagist movement, or to the older Chinese poems, is a difficult question; and since I write, not as a professional sinologue, but as a poet who happens to have derived much from reading translations of both Chinese and Japanese poetry, it is one that cannot be fully resolved here. My feeling at the time was that the direction taken by this poem—which was put forth by Pound himself as a pure example of what he meant by Vorticism, was largely wrong. Pound has said, in relation to it: "the image is not an idea. It is a radiant node or cluster; it is what I can, and must perforce call, a vortex; from which and through which and into which ideas are constantly rushing. It is as true for the painting and the sculpture as it is for the poetry." In other words what was produced here was as close an approximation to an ideographic poem as the English language could bear. Pound had not read Fenollosa's essay for nothing.

Nevertheless, the English language, for all that, remains non-ideographic; and the relation of certain beautiful faces seen in a Paris Metro station to petals on a wet tree branch is not absolutely clear. Morever, the relation of the Chinese classical poets to the Japanese *tanka* and *hokku* poets is, psychologically speaking, like the relation of full-grown and mature human figures to a group of rather small and temporarily attractive children. The *tanka* or the *hokku* poem is nothing more than a sketch; the Chinese poem presents a full picture. Though many attempts have been made to justify the limitations of Japanese poetry—the best being in my opinion, the book on *The Spirit of Japanese Poetry* by Yone Noguchi, whose poetry also had had, since 1912, some effect on my own—yet the fact remains, that the more Japanese poetry one reads the more one realizes that every Japanese poet is forced, by the exigencies of the form, to resemble every other Japanese poet. It is exactly as if every major English poet had been compelled to write nothing but sonnets—or rather, it is even worse. The Chinese poets, by contrast, are richly endowed; they have in their possession a medium in which all their important experiences can be fully displayed.

While I was writing the series of "Symphonies," during 1914 and early 1915, I was content to abide by the Chinese influences that had been absorbed in the translations I had found accessible; and was prepared to resist Pound's Vorticism, which seemed to me to point in the direction of Japanese *tanka* and *hokku* poetry, rather than towards the fullness of experience which I had already found in Li-Po, Wang-Wei, Tu Fu, and Po Ch'u-I. Chinese poetry was used by me as a crystallizing influence, an achievement accomplished along parallel lines to modern Imagism, which achievement helped to show Imagism the paths it could follow. It was also so used by Miss Amy Lowell, who—after my return to American in the last months of 1914—became my chief literary mentor, and my closest friend. There are many of the shorter poems in her *Sword Blades and Poppy Seed*, published in October, 1914, which betray that preoccupation with the concrete occasion which is common to both Chinese poetry and to Imagism. There are even vividly pictorial sonnets here, like "The Temple," and "A Tulip Garden," which could not have been what they were without some reference to Chinese models in their author's mind.

It occurs to me, at this stage to point out that such has always been the way of poets. They obtain much from poetry written in other languages, somewhat in the way that a hungry man is prepared to taste an unfamiliar dish rather than go without food. The same process goes on also in art and in music. Painters learn from other painters, and musicians from other musicians. But in the case of poetry, when certain technical devices native to one language flow over into another one, all that can be transmitted in the long run is, not a direct imitation, but a unifying spirit. All the sinological expertness in the world could not have directed the Imagists more clearly to the thing to be found at the core of old Chinese poetry: the attitude of man to nature, which was not that of the romantics, nor of the contemporary Georgians, nor—as it proved—that of the more recent intellectualist poets, but was Chinese, and I might even add, Taoistic.

It was only when the "Symphonies" were finished, during the first three months of 1915, that I turned back along the lines already marked out by Pound's Vorticism, and became again attracted to the possibilities of Japanese, rather than Chinese poetry. The poems then written under what might be called the *tanka* influence, are the ones assembled under the general title "The Ghosts of an Old House," in my *Goblins and Pagodas*, published in 1916, and those brought together in my *Japanese Prints* published two years later. The specific occasion that prompted me to pursue this path was the memorial exhibition of the Clarence Buckingham Collection of Japanese Prints, at the Art Institute of Chicago, in January and February of 1915. As examples of an art of the people, rather than an art produced for feudal and aristocratic consumption, these *ukiyo-e* masterpieces especially appealed to me, an American. In repeated visits to the Art Institute exhibit, I strove to give to many of them their poetic equivalents.

Let me examine one of these equivalents, based on a print showing a *daimyo* attempting to embrace a lady, who is resisting his ardor:—

> Force and yielding meet together;
> An attack is half-repulsed.
> Shafts of broken sunlight dissolving
> Convolutions of turbid cloud.

The reader will immediately note that no attempt is made to follow the Japanese *tanka* or *hokku* pattern of syllables. All I was interested in was all that Pound had been interested in, in his Metro poem: to produce an objective equivalent in words, to the object I saw. With the attempt, made at much the same time by Adelaide Crapsey, to produce a metrical equivalent of the *tanka* form in the so-called "Cinquain," I was then unfamiliar. My poem attempted to state the precise effect of the *ukiyo-e* artists' vision, in abbreviated form.

The difficulty with a poetry such as this is that it confines its creator to the fragmentary impression. The links between impression and impression, as well as the power to contrast one impression with another, are lost. What Fenollosa—mistakenly, as I feel—girds against in his essay under the name of the 'copula-sensation,' is lost. This applies particularly to my "Ghosts of an Old House" poems. Fragments of what should have been a linked-together experience are arbitrarily juxtaposed. The best of the older Chinese poets have not shared this fault. One feels in them a continuous power to move from experience to experience: they do not adopt what Amy Lowell, reading these Japanese-inspired experiments of mine, called "the unrelated method."

The Japanese manner, or as much of it as I could temporarily employ, soon lost interest for me, in favor of a more complex attempt to relate my own capacities as a poet to my American background; though Miss Lowell herself later produced a brilliant specimen of its use in continuous development in her "Twenty Four Hokku on a Modern Theme." There are probably also other examples of Japanese adaptation to be found in the poetry of Wallace Stevens—who has as well studied Chinese

161

models. I do not feel today that it has much value, except as an exercise. Though poetry should be, as the Imagists said, primarily objective, the subjective element is a fairly continuous undercurrent, and cannot be banished without undergoing the peril of making the poetic process frivolous in itself.

# III

The effect of Imagism was not what the Imagists intended; instead of drawing attention to the value of much vivid, direct, objective, and clear poetry in early Greek, early Chinese, or latter-day French periods, the result of the Imagist anthologies published through Miss Lowell from 1915 to 1917 was to promote what may be called the free-verse controversy—which sooner or later degenerated into the succeeding prose-poetry controversy.

A file of clippings now in my possession reveals the fact that the academic critics were chiefly irritated by the novelty of the Imagist form. The Imagists had also, in addition to practicing new forms, forsworn the vague cosmic and optimistically prophetic subjectivism that was so rampant in the works of Tennyson, Meredith, Swinburne, and Whitman. So those critics who did not attack the Imagists on the grounds of lacking form, melody, rhythm, took as their ground of attack the Imagists' preoccupation with objects immediately to hand, which they qualified as myopic; while the Imagists' preoccupation with their own personal experiences was a clear mark of their egoism. Whether these critics were named William Ellery Leonard, O. W. Firkins, or Padraic Colum, such was their burden of complaint. Colum even went to the lengths of saying that many of the poems included in Miss Lowell's first anthology were far more egoistic in tone than those of Byron.

Other critics, such as John Livingston Lowes or Conrad Aiken (both of whom later repented) pointed out that the range of experience native to Imagist poetry was at best fragmentary, their lines prosaically insipid, and that models of the same kind of poetry could often be found in many prose works, especially novels, where they were embedded in the narrative. This led directly to the prose-poetry controversy.

The writer of this essay once took part in a discussion of just what was meant by the term *vers libre*, which the Imagists continually employed; though this term was in many cases abandoned in favor of a better term: poems in unrhymed cadence. The discussion occurred in the columns of an English weekly journal in March of 1917, and T. S. Eliot was this writer's opponent on that occasion. Eliot argued that there was a distinction to be made between prose and verse, and that "the ghost of some simple meter should lurk behind the arras in even the 'freest' verse, to advance menacingly as we doze, and withdraw as we drowse. Freedom is only truly freedom when it appears against the background of an artificial limitation."

To this the writer reluctantly agreed, though he denied that there was any fixed and abiding dividing line to be made between prose and poetry. The controversy, however, then went on into the question whether such a thing as the prose poem could, or should, exist. All this is given here as a sample of the reaction provoked by the Imagists in critical circles.

Eliot, however, has repeatedly shown—whatever his critical theories may be—that, as regards rhythm, he stands firmly with the free-verse promoters: while the degree to which he is indebted to Imagist practice may be illustrated by some lines which I now extract from the opening of his *Journey of the Magi:*

> 'A cold coming we had of it,
> Just the worst time of the year
> For a journey, and such a long journey.
> The ways deep and the weather sharp,
> The very dead of winter.'
> And the camels galled, sore-footed, refractory,
> Lying down in the melting snow.
> There were times we regretted
> The summer palaces on slopes, the terraces,
> And the silken girls bringing sherbet.
> Then the camel men cursing and grumbling,
> And wanting their liquor and women.[2]

Surely the thought here is divided into just such parallel phrases as one finds in most Chinese poems—with the leading constituents of the whole picture pointed up by alliteration, especially in the first lines, according to the Anglo-Saxon practice.

Nor can Eliot's poetry, or even this specimen of it, escape the charge leveled at the Imagists, of being too exclusively personal to its creator. There is far more of Eliot's individual and exclusively personal experience embodied in every line he has written, than his critics have yet suspected.

One may say here also that if the Imagists were personal to the point of cultivating their egos exclusively, so too were some of the very best Chinese poets. A great many Chinese poets were, in fact, disappointed office-seekers or fallen favorites of some Emperor's court or the other; retiring into the wilds, they took up the careful cultivation of their egos in the face of nature, as a compensation for their failure in a more sophisticated sphere. The Imagists, similarly, were in many cases seeking some individual way out of the mechanistic barbarism of our times, by writing about nothing but what had directly moved them personally.

Moreover, to confute the pedants and the pedagogues, there is abundant evidence to show that Chinese poetry was not always the matter of "flat" and "deflected" tones, of limited rhyme-schemes, and of overworked classical allusions that it became about the time of the Sung dynasty. Arthur Waley—who once freely acknowledged to me the metrical debt his fine Chinese translations have owed to Pound's *Cathay*—has, in one of his volumes, pointed out the existence of long descriptive pieces, irregular in form, and called *"fu"* by the Chinese; these are in fact, prose-poems, though the prose types employed resemble more closely Amy Lowell's once notorious "polyphonic prose," than straightforward stuff. In short, the Chinese poets only became pedantic in the employment of rules to govern their prosody, as their own impulse towards poetry decayed.

For the rest, Imagism did not set itself the task of transmitting directly the *substance* of classical Chinese poetry. Every generation of poets, Eastern or Western, is faced with the same conclusion, of coming to terms in some way with the times in which they happen to be born. That they not infrequently find themselves at odds with their times is a visible fact, to be deduced not only from Western, but also from much Chinese poetry. My contention throughout this essay is that the Imagists, being dependent on such hints as they could find in accessible translations, constructed a poetry rather more akin to the Chinese *spirit* than the critics have hitherto suspected. Chinese poetry became for them a crystallizing influence, rather than a model to be slavishly imitated.

Moreover, in the case of a language basically so different in its construction from English as classical Chinese, it is easy to see that any translation must, of necessity, be inexact as regards its ability to transmit all the shades and overtones of original meaning. I. A. Richards has, indeed, made this fact the basis of one of his volumes, in which the impossibility of translating Mencius into reasonable English is graphically displayed. The Chinese ideogram, as Fenollosa points out, presumably derives from primitive picture writing: though the question of why certain radicals have been combined to form given words, is still quite obscure in fact. Any attempt to give the complete 'feel' of the ideograms in English, is sure to lead to much over-elaboration; which was just what misled Amy Lowell, when with Florence Ayscough's assistance, she produced the translations embodied in her book known as *Fir-Flower Tablets*. The concision of the ancient Chinese is lost, under a spate of English phrases.

No translator, therefore, can render classical Chinese exactly; to do so would require the construction of another language upon the same basis. About all that can be given is an approximation, a hint that, after all, despite all the barriers of language, the Chinese spirit may have its counterparts in the West; and that 'all men are brothers,' whatever their language, learned at the knees of their parents. Let me therefore conclude this section of my essay by quoting a short piece of old Chinese poetry, by Liu Ch'e, Sixth Emperor of the Han dynasty. Here is how it appears, in the versions of three different translators:

> The sound of rustling silk is stilled,
> With dust the marble courtyard filled;
> No footfalls echo on the floor,
> Fallen leaves, in heaps, block up the door:
> For she my pride, my lovely one is lost;
> And I am left, in hopeless anguish tossed.[3]
> —*Herbert Giles.*

> The rustling of silk is discontinued,
> Dust drifts over the courtyard.

There is no sound of footfall and the leaves
Scurry into heaps and lie still.
And she, the rejoicer of the heart, is beneath
  them;
A wet leaf that clings to the threshold.[4]
                         —*Ezra Pound*.

The sound of her silk skirt has stopped.
On the marble pavement dust grows.
Her empty rooms are cold and still,
Fallen leaves are piled against the doors.
            Longing for that lovely lady,
How can I bring my aching heart to rest?[5]
                         —*Arthur Waley*.

Each of these poems might be taken by the judicious reader as
an acknowledgment of the debt we all owe to Chinese literature,
and as a partial promise to repay.


# IV

Poetry is an act of communication. What is communicated in
poetry is not the emotion of the poet, but the objective equivalent of that emotion stated in words (just as what is communicated in painting is not what the painter sees, but the objective
equivalent of his vision stated in colors and in forms; and what
is communicated in sculpture is the objective equivalent of the
sculptor's vision stated in the formal planes of wood, bronze, or
stone). All art is primarily making; and beauty is "that which
seen pleases"; a definition on which both East and West can
agree. Poetry is therefore an aesthetic object made up out of
words, with the purpose in view of communicating something.

Therefore, the good student of poetry must be one exception-
ally sensitive to words, both from the point of view of their
external musical qualities as sound, and from the point of view
of the way they affect one another in the construction of the
phrase or the sentence. Poetry might also be termed the highest
possible articulation of human speech; that is to say, it is human
speech heightened by the sense of rhythm that we naturally derive from the muscular activity of our own bodies, and guided

by the creative imagination. As to what the imagination is, and how it works, I must refer the reader to Coleridge, and to that famous passage in Chapter Fourteen of *Biographia Literaria* for the only satisfactory definition. Whatever its imaginative constituents may be, a good poem is so bound up in the language in which it is written, that translations of poetry from one language to another are notoriously difficult, unless the translator happens also to be a poet.

Poetry, through its words, aims at producing in the reader something of the same state of mind the poet recalled when he set down the words which form the external content of the poem. These words usually combine objective observation and subjective feeling in a novel and unusual way. The most accepted method, for poets of the West at least, to combine these mental constituents is by means of metaphor, as Fenollosa long ago pointed out. A metaphor is an image, that is to say it is an analogy drawn between something in external nature and the feeling that arises within the observer. Therefore Shakespeare was producing a perfect short Imagist poem when he wrote, in *Hamlet:*

> But see, the morn in russet mantle clad,
> Walks o'er the dew of yon high eastern hill.

There is, however, one important qualification to be made. Inasmuch as we may suppose the reader of poetry to be a person possessing a wide range and diversity of interests in life, there is no reason why a poet—however Imagistic his intention—should not use his material with the purpose of being philosophic, didactic, satiric, sentimental, or merely vivid. Imagism, in its manifestoes, simply said "Be as concrete as possible"; not "Do not teach anything." However, it is possible to construct poems consisting solely of a single natural observation without commentary of any sort. This is precisely what was done in Japan, first by the composers of *tanka* and later by the *hokku* poets.

With the limitations of the Japanese method I have already dealt; therefore I shall not attempt here any recapitulation. The same limitation does not apply to the great Chinese classical poets. Indeed, theirs is probably the greatest body of poetry arising from natural and familiar fact that we have in the world. However, the Chinese poetry still possesses certain marked limitations in subject matter from our Western point of view, which may have been the reason why so many Western poets have recently been turning away from it, since the days of the Imagist reform. With these limitations I must now deal.

As Arthur Waley in his *A Hundred and Seventy Chinese Poems* pointed out, the love of a man for a woman is not a theme often touched upon by Chinese poets, after the period of the Han dynasty. To the Oriental, sexual relationships were supposed to have nothing to do with either companionship or sympathy; these feelings the classical Chinese poet reserved entirely for his friends; with the result (according to Waley) that fully one-half the poetry in the Chinese language deals with the theme of parting with one's friends. Another large number of Chinese poems deals with the theme, common enough in a country where sexual relationships were entered into purely for biological reasons, of the deserted wife or concubine; such poems, as Waley has stated, were written indifferently by poets of either sex, and were thought of as being vaguely allegorical, as recalling the thwarting of public ambitions on the part of their authors, who belonged to the official mandarin class. Moreover, an enormous majority of early Chinese poems are infused with feelings more closely akin to the Taoist or the Chinese Buddhist conceptions of the interrelations of man and nature, than to the severely social and ethical conceptions of the official Confucianism. Finally, as the older Chinese literature grew, a process took place within it that is closely paralleled by Chinese art; the copying and imitation of older models became universal, leading to the mannered artificiality of almost all Chinese poetry produced later than the twelfth century.

Even more serious than all this, from the Western point of view, is the fact that Chinese poetry deals very infrequently with the supernatural. Such a poem as Po Ch'u-I's "Everlasting Wrong" does indeed stand in "garish isolation," not only to the main body of that poet's work, but to the general tendency of Chinese poetry. Except for Ch'u Yuan's famous "Li Sao," with its marvelous description of "the genius that roams the mountains, clad in wisteria and girdled in ivy," and its supernatural machinery, I can scarcely recall another Chinese poem that takes the supernatural very seriously. The Chinese Taoist, or the Chinese Buddhist, in distinction alike to the primitive Buddhist or to the Christian ascetic, kept his eyes fixed upon nature, in order to discover the secret workings of her laws. A Chinese Dante would be impossible; such speculations as to the spirit-life of the dead would have been thought of as being both impious and dangerous. Human life, in all its variety and continuity, not the otherworld, was important to the Sons of Han. Indeed, it is precisely the otherwordly side of Christianity—that blend of Greek mystical speculation and of Hebraic moral precept—that has, for good or ill, set its mark on all Western poetry, and made of it something so much more complex in its mingled intellectual and emotional striving than anything present in the classical Chinese poets, that the Chinese seem naïve by comparison.

For example: the Chinese poet might refer to a seascape as being blue or gray, calm or stormy, but never "terror-stricken." Such metaphorical adjectives are as good as unknown. Also the long, farfetched simile is quite unknown in Chinese poetry. The reason is that the simile was almost undoubtedly developed among European poets in order to heighten the spiritual impression to be made by their work. By referring some material fact to some other fact more extraordinary (and the more farfetched the comparison, the better according to most "moderns"), the poet proved that he was one visited by the Muses, or under the direct inspiration of a God. It is curious to note that no Chinese poet ever laid direct claim to such divine inspiration (except possibly Li-Po, who claimed to find it in drunkenness); that that there is a connection between this fact and the absence of long similes in Chinese poetry, is, to my mind, not to be doubted.

The Chinese poet, then, was one readily content with his human limitations: he was not one who 'neglected to consider the ultimate fate of the body,' to quote a phrase from a quite celebrated Chinese poem.

The Western European poets were not so easily satisfied: they were driven alike by their background of mystical and otherworldly Christianity, as well as by their own ingrown nationalism —even more rampant after 1918 than before—and by the monstrous pride of Western secular science (always promising a new world to be set at man's disposal, and always devising some new brand of sheer hell) into a renewed affirmation of the supernatural element in poetry. They escaped, after 1918, from 'Weltschmerz' of a new kind of disordered romanticism, explored only by the Expressionists in Germany and the surrealists of France, by proclaiming for themselves, "a new order." A more introspective and more complex kind of metaphysical poetry, derivable from Rilke, or from Donne, or from Paul Valéry, full of the most farfetched metaphors and similes possible, became fashionable in Western literary circles. This poetry, more and more common since T. S. Eliot turned aside from his earlier Imagism to explore his own "waste land," has already shown itself to be strong in dogmatic assertion, but weak in powers of communication. And so Imagism, as a opening path that had, from 1910-12 onward, led largely in the direction taken previously by many great Chinese poets, became a neglected path—at worst a passing phase, at best an experiment that might expect to receive a few passing pats from those professors who at least realized that it led to a reconsideration of poetic form.

In the highest poetry of the West that we have—the poetry of the Greek tragedians, of Dante in Italy, of Shakespeare and his contemporaries in England, of Goethe and some of his contemporaries and immediate followers in Germany—the linguistic expressions used by the poet always appear to be fused directly with the thought: the style becomes the man. This is not true of many of the most recent and "advanced" modern poets now writing in English. In their eagerness to get away from anything that smacks of sentimental romanticism, they have attempted to recreate the style of Donne, and to apply it to the material of the present day; forgetting that an intellectually adopted manner, without corresponding emotional stress, makes only for pedantry, not poetry; and that Donne himself most frequently justified his style when his feelings were most completely engaged. In these ultramodern poets—I might cite Mr. W. H. Auden, as a good example—thought has so far outrun verbal expression, that the authors concerned seem to be seeking for means of expressing some range of thought that is altogether so peculiar to themselves as to be inexpressible in any definite terms that we know. Poetry, to them, has become a means of communicating, to an increasingly dwindling audience, ranges of experience so far removed from the normal that only the practical and patient reader can make anything out of them. These poets have therefore been forced to defend themselves continually against the charge of obscurity.

A prolonged and a careful study of the Chinese poets, who have always so gracefully and completely succeeded in stating their thought, would do much towards clarifying the muddled intentions of the modern poet. It might even succeed in bringing poetry back into popular favor, as the most natural and complete way we human beings have of defining our attitudes to existence.

However, it is quite useless to deny that there are whole ranges of human experience familiar enough to us, which were seemingly quite foreign to the best Chinese poets of the Han, 'Tang, and Sung dynasties. These poets were, one and all, trained as civil servants under the old Imperial system, on which the stability as well as the continuity of the Chinese people rested. A great number of them, owing to dynastic intrigues or for some other reason, failed of political advancement and took up poetry as a means of consoling themselves. We in the West would find it somewhat comic if poetry were to be practiced widely by disappointed politicians (I am far from saying that our kind of politicians would not be benefited if they only knew a little more about poetry). Our conception of the poet is that of a man who necessarily stands completely aloof from local politics, with his mind fixed on values greater than the temporal. We have even become suspicious of poets who write as events move them, who are moved primarily by external occasions to compose their poetry; forgetting that one of the greatest, Goethe, in his conversations with Eckermann, qualified his own poetry as being entirely "occasioned."

The character of the classical Chinese poet, as a member of the official mandarin class, limited him to themes familiar to this class. The poets of the West, drawn from every class in the community, have long since claimed all human experience as their province. It is useless, therefore, to attempt to create an influx of influence from the Chinese poets upon the West, by means of any strict line-by-line analysis and comparison of specific Chinese poems with specific Western ones. What we have to achieve is a transmission, not of detail, but of general method: and this transmission, I feel, took place not only in such Imagist poets as freely acknowledged their debt, such as Amy Lowell, Ezra Pound, and myself, but also in others who have similarly displayed an objective approach akin to the Chinese. For instance, I might refer the reader to poems by William Carlos Williams, Marianne Moore, and Wallace Stevens. The thing that all these poets have in common with the Chinese, is neither a precise similarity in subject matter, nor a direct imitation of form; it is rather a spirit of intense observation, of patient surrender to truth, of complete identification with the object. Such poems as, for example, William Carlos Williams' "The Red Lily," or Marianne Moore's "The Monkeys," or Wallace Stevens' "The Bird with the Coppery, Keen Claws" could not have been the same poems as they are, if the older Chinese poets had never existed; which is far from saying that any of them bear any external resemblance to any particular Chinese poem.

Since the affinity that may exist between the Chinese poets of the past and the Western poets of the present day is altogether a matter of approach, rather than of detail—and since the Imagist poets largely discussed in this essay were those who felt this affinity most keenly over a wide range of subject matter—it surely follows that for most of us, unfamiliar as we are with Chinese ideograms, the best way that we can assimilate the Chinese influence is through the study of translations, and by comparison of these with the work of the Imagists, as well as with the work of those Western poets—three of whom I have already mentioned—who have felt the Imagist influence most keenly. Such a study, I am assured, would result in giving to the Imagist poets a position far higher than they now have in most academic circles. It may be true, as has frequently been stated, that none of the Imagists were great poets. (No one seems to know just what a great poet is, until a long time after the person most concerned is safely dead; and at least one poet who has recently been proclaimed as great, W. B. Yeats, was undoubtedly influenced in the development of his final manner by Imagism, though to this was added a habit of mind more Celtic than English.) But the Imagists, at least, opened up a pathway between East and West that seems to me, at least, one better worth pursuing than the "intellectualist" direction taken by the most recently discussed group of English poets. That is their historical importance in literary history.

In Chinese thought, from antiquity down to the present day, there has been no separation made between human nature and external nature; and it is for this reason that the Chinese poets have so easily been able to shift their attention from one to the other. The same unity between what is without and what is within has controlled all traditional Chinese philosophy. Confucius and Lao-tzü did not really differ as regards the object to be sought for by wisdom, but only as to the means to be employed to attain it.

We in the West today stand at the end of a long watershed of human history. Since the days of Descartes and of Newton, that is to say for the last three centuries of Occidental development, science—whether pure or applied—has ruled over the Western mind. Western science has been governed by the assumption that all the phenomena of matter, of organic life and growth, of the development of personality, of instinct and of reason, have been controlled by causes external to us; that any gaps in our knowledge concerning these causes can only be remedied by the acquisition of more scientific knowledge; that it is only through such knowledge, not through an instinctive faith or an imaginative vision, that man can become in any way master of his own destiny. Nevertheless, no amount of science can tell us why, in the present conflict, we Americans should take our stand upon the basis of those human rights that are affirmed in the Constitution of the United States. That we should affirm the four freedoms of man in the teeth of Axis opposition, throughout the world, is not a scientific, but an ethical fact; and science is, ethically speaking, neutral. Our ethical direction towards democracy is not given us by scientific knowledge but by instinctive faith and imaginative vision; and this is also true of the direction that has now been taken by the Chinese people.

The Chinese people have been forced, by the external circumstances of the last half-century at least, to take up one Western innovation after another; and they were well in process of making a successful readjustment to the ideals of our Western democratic ways of life when—thanks to Japanese aggression—they were forced to the defense of their soil and their final right to govern themselves; a defense which surely, when the history of this war is written, will outrank any other in the field. With the downfall of the older Imperial system, much of the traditional knowledge and the culture of the Chinese people has inevitably disappeared; so much has already lost its contact with the Chinese earth, like the Chinese objects now scattered and reassembled in our Western art museums, that one often wonders how much can be transmitted to the future, even by the Chinese themselves, concerning one of the greatest and longest lasting civilizations which this planet has ever known. But the Chinese people have, since 1937, shown so strong a principle of instinctive solidarity within themselves, as well as such a stubborn and persistent determination to remain masters of their own destiny, and to endure everything rather than to fall under the control of a military clique directed from Japan, that we now have good cause to hope, not only that full Chinese independence may be restored, but that the older Chinese culture, philosophy, fine art, and craftsmanship may also be revived and revitalized, in forms more appropriate to the needs of today.

We of the Occident can best help the Chinese to this consummation by studying for ourselves and understanding more completely the great fundamental landmarks of Chinese culture, in architecture, sculpture, painting, literature, and philosophy. "Who helps another, helps himself" applies here, no less than in the political and economic sphere, where China's continuance as an active combatant on the side of the Western democracies becomes every day a matter of more critical importance. Thus, in the return for the great cultural wealth that the Chinese have already given to us, we of the West can see to it that this culture is not only preserved but restored to its proper functions and proportions. Such, rather than the restoration of bygone European culture, now—so far as Europe itself is concerned, utterly destroyed and made waste, thanks to the Nazi conceptions of race and nationalism—should be our American destiny, for the next thousand years. "When both our central being and outward harmony are carried to the point of full perfection, heaven and earth are in a state of tranquillity, and all things will be nourished and flourish."

*William York Tindall*

# TRANSCENDENTALISM IN CONTEMPORARY LITERATURE

FOR a good many years writers of England and America, troubled by the civilization around them, have turned to the East. To some it has meant mystery, color, and freedom from habit; but to more it has promised a spiritual enlargement which the West appears to have denied. Contrary to the general opinion, the temper of much of the best contemporary literature is religious, and, not infrequently, religious means Oriental. Three important writers of the present century will illustrate the point: William Butler Yeats, the greatest modern poet; D. H. Lawrence, one of the most celebrated novelists; and Aldous Huxley.

In order to understand their histories and their work it is necessary, however painful this may be, briefly to consider the state of their world. It is a place where machines have suddenly multiplied the population and elevated a class without what Mr. Eliot likes to call sensibility. The popular education decreed by this class has at once spread knowledge and spread it thin. The sudden concentration of people in cities has killed the local roots which nourish sentiments. And what seems worse, science and materialism have destroyed for many writers the religious traditions upon which their feelings once centered and their art.

Isolated from an audience by these changes and denied public expression, many writers write for themselves alone or for a few friends. Henry James, for example, and James Joyce, slamming the doors of ivory towers, pursued in privacy an elaborate, great art which increased the confusion out of doors. But other artists of equal stature have remained outdoors to seek their own and the world's cure. Deprived of their fathers' belief but feeling its need and believing belief as necessary for their art as it was for Dante's, they have turned not to private literature but to private or all but private religion according to their capacity. The invention or discovery of some substitute for the religion they had lost or, to put it in more general terms, the search for spiritual satisfaction in times apparently hostile to it constitutes what is known as the romantic movement. Sometimes the substitute for religion is another religion, sometimes a devotion to objects which are not normally adored, such as animals, flowers, or music. Adolf Hitler, discussing Wagner, is reported to have said: "His music is my religion. I go to his concerts as others go to church." To the religious impulse persisting out of church or in the absence of suitable objects T. E. Hulme gave the name of "spilt religion." This definition of romanticism would be more pleasing if it did not define so well a state that persists.

Although a few gifted, emotional men like Gerard Manley Hopkins, G. K. Chesterton, and T. S. Eliot rediscovered Christianity, many more have adopted extraordinary religions which, since the West seems at fault, have commonly assumed an Eastern character. For the literary man, wandering in Mr. Eliot's waste land or between Arnold's two worlds, theosophy has been a favorite resort, but sometimes his choice has fallen upon an Oriental or pseudo-Oriental system which, if more respectable, is equally synthetic. The somewhat more respectable synthesis is Huxley's choice, while theosophy contented Yeats and Lawrence.

At the risk of boring the theosophist with what he is almost sure to know, I should like to review the essentials of his belief. In 1875 Mme. H. P. Blavatsky, the founder of the Theosophical Society, arrived in New York from Tibet where certain adepts, she announced, had filled her with philosophy. Her Tibetan masters, if any, appear to have been liberal Buddhists and Hindus, united no doubt by a spirit of compromise. Although theosophy contains Western ingredients such as anthropology and all sorts of Orphic, Kabalistical, Hermetic, and Pythagorean matters, the essence of Mme. Blavatsky's system is a mixture of Buddhism and Hinduism, including reincarnation, karma, and nirvana. Like yoga, which it loosely embraces, theosophy is a method of introducing the particular soul to what Mme. Blavatsky called Anima

Mundi. This is accomplished not by meditation and discipline but, tempered perhaps to the convenience of Westerners, by ceremonial magic, symbolism, and good intentions. Such practices and such beliefs, she said, were once maintained in Atlantis and, after its submersion, obscurely survived in the doctrines of Egyptians, Aztecs, Rosicrucians, alchemists, and most of all, Far Easterners of all varieties. Her aim was less to spread Oriental religion than, through Oriental religion, to recover Atlantis. But in the absence of Atlantis theosophy remains substantially Oriental.

Like Henry More, Emerson, and Irving Babbitt in their times, Mme. Blavatsky and her disciples in theirs were discontented with a civilization alien to the spirit. To destroy rationalism they sought the irrational and the profound; to remedy the familiar they sought the exotic and the remote; to cure Western materialism they sought its opposite. In place, for example, of Darwin's notions about the rectilinear descent of beasts, which they considered bestial, they proposed the circular ascent of spirits. Their immodest proposal takes its place in the romantic tradition with Emerson's Oversoul, Walpole's gothic castles, Bergson's metaphysics, the music of Wagner, and the *Herrenvolk* and other noble savages of countless inventors. That Mme. Blavatsky's conceits have also failed to cure what may be incurable cannot be held against them. It is unfortunate, however, for the mutual understanding of East and West, but, considering the character of romanticism, not unnatural that so many writers of our time saw the light of Asia through the imperfect eyes of Mme. Blavatsky.

# I

In her capacity of middleman between East and West, this extraordinary woman enlightened Yeats, who was ready to receive what she had to offer. For some years he had held the biologists and physicists responsible for the materialism of the West and for the spiritual limitation that accompanied it. Darwin, Huxley, and Tyndall, he complained in the early 1880's, had robbed him of the religion of his youth and had given him nothing with which to replace it. Forced by his intellect and their teachings to accept materialism, he was miserable under it and he longed for something to satisfy the persistent, irrational yearnings of his soul. The Church of Ireland would no longer do. The new materialism disagreed with his sentiments. In this quandary he discovered theosophy, which was not only as hostile to Darwin as he was but offered his soul, without apparent offense to his intellect, the expansion it desired.

Yeats first encountered this romantic mixture of the irrational, the exotic, and the occult in the works of A. P. Sinnett, the London representative of Mme. Blavatsky. In 1885 Yeats read Sinnett's *Esoteric Buddhism* (1883), which tells of cyclical reincarnation in a manner calculated to inflame the weary Darwinist. Thus inspired, Yeats, together with A. E., Charles Johnston, and John Eglinton, founded in Dublin a Hermetic society. The members, instructed by a Brahmin philosopher from London and by an Orientalist of Trinity College, read papers to one another. After this preparation they were chartered in 1886 by Sinnett as the Dublin Lodge of the Theosophical Society. At the Monday meetings of the "household," as it was known, they discussed Blavatsky's *Secret Doctrine* and the yoga aphorisms of Patanjali, or they watched A.E. and Yeats experimenting with ceremonial magic on the floor, or they listened to Annie Besant, Mohini Chatterjee, and other visiting adepts. The members of this seminar never quite recovered from it. Charles Johnston spent his life translating yoga aphorisms, the *Bhagavadgita*, and fragments of the *Upanishads*. A.E., whose devotion to Mme. Blavatsky knew no limits, not only based upon her teachings the mystical practices which he recorded in verse and prose, but seems even to have based his economic theories on *The Secret Doctrine*. When he was not rereading Blavatsky, he was reading the *Upanishads* to which she and Emerson had led him. Unlike A.E., Yeats never achieved mysticism, for which he wanted the temper; but moved by a more restless curiosity, he emerged from the Dublin Lodge, which contented A.E., and visited Mme. Blavatsky, now in London, to add personality to doctrine.

Curiosity and further need next impelled Yeats to add the Kabala to his Oriental library. In 1887 he joined the Order of the Golden Dawn, a London society of alchemists, Rosicrucians, and Kabalists under the leadership of Liddle MacGregor Mathers, author of *The Kabala Unveiled* (1887). George Moore was right to suspect the extent of Yeats' knowledge of the *Zohar;* for although Yeats displays some acquaintance with the ten *Sephiroth,* the Kabala defies the casual understanding. Such knowledge as he possessed was found in the introduction to Mathers' book, which had been inspired by French commentaries. Ignorance, however, did not keep Yeats from copying out in Hebrew characters the *Shem Hamphorash* (YHWH or Jahveh) with its seventy-two possible variations, a favorite Kabalistical exercise.

This recreation, however, proved meager when compared with what awaited Yeats when he visited Paris during the 1890's. At this time Paris was the center of occult studies. Surrounded with alembic and gallipot and under the frightful auspices of the Sabbatic Goat, alchemists hunted the formula for Hermetic gold; in crypt and sewer or worse, Satanists celebrated the black mass; while in back parlors disciples of Eliphas Lévi ceaselessly interpreted the Kabala. The principal cult of many was *L'Ordre Kabbalistique de la Rose-Croix,* over which presided Stanislas de Guaita, disciple of Lévi, magus, alchemist, Rosicrucian, and Christian Kabalist. Yeats read Lévi, took part in Kabalistical orgies with his followers and with those of Saint-Martin, an eighteenth-century mystic; and on one occasion at least he paid the great de Guaita a visit. To the pleasure of being a poet, Yeats observed, was added that of being an adept. Darwin, Huxley, Tyndall, and the British middle classes were temporarily forgotten. And on the poet's return to London memory made the quotidian more tolerable. It is plain that these visits to Paris took the place for Yeats of going to church on Sunday. His essays of later years contain fond accounts of his sabbatical excursions, and the short stories about Michael Robartes which he wrote while memory was fresh, "Rosa Alchemica," "The Tables of the Law," and "The Adoration of the Magi" (de Guaita was a magus), preserve the occult atmosphere of Paris no less faithfully than Huysmans' *Là-Bas.*

These stories were not the only works Yeats wrote under the spell of theosophy and the Kabala. His impressive edition of the prophetic books of William Blake, in whom he recognized a fellow adept, is also colored and shaped by Blavatsky and Mathers. For much of the esoteric matter of *The Shadowy Waters, The Unicorn from the Stars, The Hour Glass,* and other plays Yeats consulted his Parisian memories. In *The Countess Cathleen* rioting students of the National University detected an odor of "Buddhism," and their diagnosis, if not their conduct, was correct. Yeats' essay entitled "Magic" (1901) describes his Hermetic interests and reveals the theory of poetic symbolism for which he was indebted more to Mme. Blavatsky than to Verlaine or Mallarmé. It was her idea in *Isis Unveiled* that objects, myths, and events of this world are linked by magical correspondence with Anima Mundi or the memory of nature, and, as Yeats puts it, "this great mind and great memory can be evoked by symbols." Yeats' aim in poetry was less to find a verbal formula for a state of mind in the manner of the French Symbolists than by using Irish symbols as a magus would to call down upon himself and his readers the influence of the Spirit. The poet became enchanter, his poetry incantation and a kind of devotion. Few of Yeats' poems in *The Wind Among the Reeds* (1899), except for those on elemental spirits, appear to owe their matter to Blavatsky, but most of them were written according to her prescription.

The Irish middle classes, refusing to be enchanted, preferred their own form of devotion. While Yeats fought for ten years a hopeless fight with the "mob" and whetted his style upon it he had little time for the occult. From 1901 to 1917 when his marriage to an occultist inspired him again, his chief connections with the East, except for an occasional reference in a play, were his introductions to *Gitanjali*, translations from the Bengali by Rabindranath Tagore (1912), and to his friend Ezra Pound's edition of Ernest Fenollosa's *Certain Noble Plays of Japan* (1916). These Noh-plays shaped all of Yeats' subsequent plays for maskers and dancers and provided an "aristocratic" refuge from journalists and the mob; for his Japanese imitations were to be performed in the privacy of a drawing-room for fit audience though few. Pound lent this Eastern ivory tower to a Westerner defeated by the West, but Pound's interest in the *hokku* and in Confucius, who, despite one's natural impression, was known to the West before Pound recommended him, seems to have left Yeats unmoved.

In 1917 Yeats published a long essay, *Per Amica Silentia Lunae*, only the second part of which, entitled "Anima Mundi," need detain us. In order to free his mind still further from the world of matter, says Yeats, he had frequented mediums, despite de Guaita's warning against them; he had delighted in images which evoked transcendental sensations; and he had even brooded over abstract technical words which time has turned to poetry. This is a cloudy way of saying that in addition to the ivory tower of aristocracy Yeats needed Anima Mundi once more; for nothing is less like the Irish middle classes than Anima Mundi. As he pursued meditation to the point of trance, deliberately provoking visions from the great memory where all things are stored, his guide for the moment was Henry More's *Immortality of the Soul,* a work proving the existence of daemons and other spirits and richly informative about their deportment after the death of the body. But "Anima Mundi" is Blavatsky's word for what More, who was familiar with Latin, was content to call the Soul of the World. Yeats was improving More by Blavatsky and making Blavatsky and de Guaita respectable by Cambridge Platonism. Under this decent disguise they presided over these fancies. In this sense *Per Amica Silentia Lunae* is remotely Oriental in origin and also in the sense that Henry More's congenial wisdom was founded largely upon Plotinus, Hermes, and Pythagoras, who are as close to the East as Mme. Blavatsky. If to the impatient Orientalist Yeats' Orientalism seems secondhand, it is only because it was secondhand—or third.

Mediums to Yeats, as witches to More, proved the existence of Spirit; but mediums were even more helpful. One of them, Yeats' wife in fact, received and dictated his next important essay on the Spirit, leaving for Yeats little of the author's chore apart from syntax. This product of supernatural collaboration is called *A Vision* (1925). After some attempt to mystify by attributing its inspiration to the *Speculum Angelorum et Hominorum* (the Latin, I am afraid, is Yeats' own) by Giraldus and to an obscure Arabian tradition, Yeats admitted that while he and his wife were near Los Angeles shortly after their marriage certain daemons, accosting Mrs. Yeats in her bed, had started communicating. On subsequent nights these daemons, who seem to have been preoccupied with pneumatology, psychology, and history, told Mrs. Yeats, while her husband took notes to her dictation, that the progress of the soul may be represented by the twenty-eight phases of the moon, arranged around a gyre or wheel. Each phase, except the full moon and the dark, which are spiritual holidays, is the incarnation of a psychological type according to the proportions of light and dark in that phase. The bright or antithetical fortnight includes the better sort of men, the artists and heroes; the dark or primary phases embody objective men. Each soul makes the circuit of reincarnation several times before its release from time and destiny into the thirteenth cone; and between incarnations the soul follows a prescribed course of memory, purgation, dream, and sleep. During the dictation of this scheme frustrating, earth-bound spirits jumbled the daemonic messages by a sort of occult static; and good or bad smells told Yeats of the absence or presence of these wicked shades that he might be on his guard and take or refuse to take notes as the case might be. After several years in which the family could have enjoyed little repose, the talkative spirits finished their mission, Mrs. Yeats shut her mouth, and Yeats his notebook. If this elaborate system was dictated by daemons there is nothing more to say except perhaps for a word of astonishment or awe. But it is possible that Yeats was deceiving or deceived and that the work is his own synthesis of more or less Asiatic wisdom.

Multiplied by four, his system resembles the spiral chain of reincarnation around seven planets as taught by Sinnett in *Esoteric Buddhism* and by Blavatsky in *The Secret Doctrine*. Their authority seems to have been the Buddhist wheel of destiny around which spirits move until they escape from time into nirvana. But the Buddhist wheel does not involve the moon, which Yeats could have found in the bright and dark fortnights of the *Upanishads*. Yeats frequently cites these Hindu fortnights as parallels lending authority to his own; but what he cited as parallel may be source. It would not be difficult to impose Hindu moon upon Buddhist wheel. For the states of soul between incarnations Yeats could have found what he wanted in the *Upanishads* or in treatises on yoga. But the conflict of opposites and the alternating cycles of history which also turn upon Yeats' wheel seem to owe less to Asia. They come perhaps from Plato, Empedocles, Hegel, Vico, and Spengler, with all of whom Yeats was on familiar terms.

Though Occidental in origin, Yeats' philosophy of history has an Oriental bearing. In his system two opposite civilizations, the antithetical and the primary or the spiritual and the secular, alternate every two thousand years. At present Europe is nearing the end of a primary period, beginning with Christ, and characterized by materialism, democracy, and heterogeneity. Asia, on the other hand, and by Asia here he meant the Near East, is aristocratic and spiritual. Yeats looked hopefully toward the begetting by Asia on Europe of a new spiritual era in Europe to begin about the year 2000. By his wheel of history Yeats explained to himself, since few readers now dared to invade his privacy, his dissatisfaction with the modern Europe which had imposed privacy and occultism upon him. And by his wheel Yeats explained his love for an Asia which seemed to represent his dreams of aristocracy and religion or Europe's opposite. The synthesis of West and East in Yeats' system, with its emphasis upon the East, epitomizes the destined union of those conflicting opposites.

Meanwhile questions occur to the Western mind. One may ask how a poet could produce a system so formidable and abstract as this. But Yeats had a gift for abstractions, which he detested; and he admits that he wrote *A Vision* to purge his mind of abstractions, leaving it free to create poems. If one asks how seriously Yeats, a man of high intelligence, took his synthetic doctrine and what purpose it served, one may recall his own answer to these questions. He says somewhere that although his critical mind mocked, he was delighted. He felt that a poet needs a philosophy, a religion, or a myth in order to excite his passions, and, failing to discover a suitable myth in modern Europe, he turned inventor. His system was to him what theology was to Dante, opium to Coleridge, or alcohol to Poe. Poe may have been a drunkard because he liked to drink but Yeats was an occultist for the sake of art. The dictating daemon who said, "We have come to give you metaphors for your poetry," knew what he was talking about. Many of Yeats' best poems, the best poems of our time, were inspired by his system; and whatever has that effect, though it may pass our understanding, compels, if not adherence, our most genial applause.

That memorable poem "Sailing to Byzantium" was so inspired. Byzantium, situated between East and West, is Yeats' image for the aristocratic and spiritual place of his desires. The lords and ladies to whom he will sing bear little resemblance to the English or Irish audience. His song of "what is past or passing or to come" cannot but suggest a phrase in Yeats' own translation of the *Mandookya Upanishad:* "Past, present, future—everything is Om." The sages who "perne in a gyre" are Asiatic masters, spiritual advisers to Yeats and his aristocrats. The nature from which Yeats will be free is not only his senility but Europe and the cycle of time and destiny. Byzantium is a poetic equivalent of nirvana, shaped to the needs of a modern European. "Two Songs from a Play," an equally distinguished poem, is based upon the wheel of history as suggested by Plato's "Timaeus," Vergil's Messianic eclogue, and Shelley's chorus from *Hellas.* The poem tells of the transition from the Asiatic, antithetical period, symbolized by "Babylonian starlight," Plato, and "Doric discipline," to the new order of Europe, symbolized by Christ. Pythagoras, who appears in several of the later poems, symbolizes the Orphic sage, half Asiatic and half Greek. If romanticism is the pursuit of a spiritual ideal in unpropitious times, these poems are romantic in theme. But in manner they are what we have come to associate with the classics. The language, unlike Wordsworth's, is general. The order of words is natural. The manner is as grand as Gibbon's. Nothing of our time approaches more closely the feeling of Ben Jonson and Racine. It is both pleasing and odd that the Oriental and the occult, which have served romantics so faithfully, should have inspired these classical poems.

Some of Yeats' early romantic poems, such as "Anashuya and Vijaya" and "The Indian upon God," written during the 1880's, deal with Brahma and Hindu worship. In some of his poems of the 1930's, such as "Meru," in *The King of the Great Clock Tower*, Yeats returned to these Far Eastern themes. This return was due to his friendship with a learned yogi named Shri Purohit Swami, whom Yeats met in 1931. Through conversation with this initiate Yeats was enabled at last to bid Blavatsky farewell and to see his Hindus plain. As a sign of his sainthood the Swami had received during his initiation as his own stigmatum the bump on Buddha's brow. Deeply moved, Yeats saw in this mark and in the asceticism and courtesy of its owner an intimation of Asia at its best "and where it is most different from Europe." In his enthusiasm Yeats went so far as to compare the

Swami with the theologians of Byzantium. This spiritual man had been sent by his master, a man sublimer than he, to act as apostle to the West. Although provided with a letter from the founder of the *Bharat-Dharma Mahamandel*, the Swami was unable to secure an audience with the Pope. Failing to win this eminent convert, he had to rest content with Yeats, who in 1932 wrote an introduction to *An Indian Monk* by the Swami. All his life, said Yeats, he had borrowed from the East, selecting for admiration everything that was least European, "as though groping backward towards our common mother." Here at last in this book of ancient Hindu discipline he had found a philosophy which satisfied his intellect and imposed unity upon the occult experiences he had enjoyed throughout his life. In 1934 Yeats wrote an introduction to the Swami's *Holy Mountain*, an account of his master's initiation on Mount Meru. After noting some further corroborations of his great wheel in the *Upanishads*, Yeats devotes his essay to a technical account of yoga, posture, meditation, and ultimate union with the Self, for which he was indebted to the Swami's translation of the *Yoga-Sutras* or aphorisms of Patanjali, upon which Yeats had cut his teeth in Dublin, and for which, when the translation was printed in 1938, he provided another introduction. Meanwhile in T. S. Eliot's *Criterion* (July, 1935) Yeats published an essay on the *"Mandookya Upanishad"* in which he analyzed Om or Aum and discussed Tantric yoga or sex as a way to God. It was not for nothing that Yeats called himself in one of his last poems a "wild old wicked man."

The climax of Yeats' Oriental career was marked by his collaboration with the Swami in a translation of *The Ten Principal Upanishads* (1937). Dissatisfied with the "muddy English" of previous translations, Yeats gladly lent himself, during a holiday in Majorca, to this task. The Swami, knowing Sanskrit and English, put the *Upanishads* into English which Yeats put into English. In the introduction to this work, Yeats tells of A.E.'s interest in the *Upanishads* and says of his friend something which has a wider application: "He expressed in his ceaseless vague preoccupation with the East a need and curiosity of our time."

Though old and ill, Yeats undertook these labors not only to satisfy his own curiosity and need but to assist young poets, who, like Dante, needed their myth. Yeats' dream of a school of Irish poets finding their excitement in the *Upanishads* instead of in the politics that Yeats deplored was not realized in his lifetime nor may it be in ours. Of the generation after Yeats, James Joyce, who once attended A.E.'s conventicle, made fun of Yeats' theosophy in *Ulysses*, though yielding to none in his admiration of the poet; and Sean O'Faolain, a younger man, regards Yeats as a lost leader. Ignorant of theosophy, young English poets like George Barker and Dylan Thomas prefer another kind of madness. Yeats himself, untrue to his ideals, devoted most of his last poems to Irish politics and love.

## II

Love suggests D. H. Lawrence, who, no less impatient with Europe, faced Eastward in his turn. His original Methodism impaired by Darwin and Huxley, but his aspiration unconfined, Lawrence also devised a private religion. Because the West seemed materialistic, rational, and, in a word, Western, Lawrence made a cult of the primitive, the irrational, and the Eastern. To him the East meant the primitive and the unintellectual, but, since the East meant theosophy to him, his interpretation is not surprising.

Between 1912 and 1915 Lawrence read *Isis Unveiled* and *The Secret Doctrine* by Mme. Blavatsky, together with several works by Annie Besant and by Rudolph Steiner, the German theosophist. For a time he subscribed to *The Occult Review*. This literature, plus a little anthropology, formed the substance of the religion which, preached in essay and novel, was intended to explain himself to himself and to save the world. Traces of theosophy appear in "The Crown," an apocalyptic essay Lawrence wrote in 1915, but the ideas about the conflict of opposites in the same essay came from those semi-Oriental early Greek philosophers who also fascinated Yeats. The essays of Lawrence's later years, filled with casual references to Om, the Third Eye, the ankh, the serpent with his tail in his mouth, and the "Sanskrit joys of Purusha, Pradhana, Kala," show the extent of his theosophical learning. From theosophy, distorted by anthropology, Lawrence gained his understanding of the Egyptians, Hindus, and Etruscans who are rarely absent from the thoughts of his fictional characters. As a theosophist, however, Lawrence was even more eclectic than Yeats, being more of a Dissenter perhaps. Rejecting reincarnation and Anima Mundi as too abstract, Lawrence took from Mme. Blavatsky what he found congenial. In this, of course, he is not unlike other theosophists.

Lawrence adored Atlantis, which although located underneath a Western sea, has become, through the endeavors of Mme. Blavatsky, an Eastern Utopia. What we consider Oriental today or, indeed, what we consider Mexican, is but the corrupt tradition of Atlantis to which one must return for the real thing. In this return Lawrence followed his leader, as the preface to his *Fantasia of the Unconscious* ingenuously shows. Lawrence's most theosophical and also his best novel, *The Plumed Serpent* (1926), deals with the quest for Atlantis through its Mexican vestiges. Working through Aztec symbols, especially Quetzalcoatl, the cult of Don Ramon in this novel attempts to revive the West. Lawrence had not forgotten *The Secret Doctrine*, nor was he indifferent to Blavatsky's disciples. Among the anthropologists whom he consulted for this novel was Lewis Spence, authority on Atlantis and Rosicrucian of Los Angeles.

In his later years, pursuing a more authentic East, Lawrence read several of the Vedas, of which he liked the *Rigveda* best for its air of primitive animism. His devotion to *Siva* may have been increased by Coomaraswamy's *Dance of Siva*, which he read and liked. Lawrence also found an affinity in the *Upanishads*. One who is more familiar with Lawrence than with the East will be struck on looking into the *Upanishads* by their resemblance in doctrine, rhetoric, and atmosphere to Lawrence's essays and novels. But, to put the horse before the cart (or *proteron hysteron*), the *Upanishads* resemble Lawrence because he resembled the *Upanishads*.

As might be expected, he loved yoga, to which, in the preface to *Fantasia*, he admits a debt. He could have learned something of yoga from his friend Earl Brewster, who, although a Buddhist, was not unfamiliar with Hinduism. Lawrence could also have learned something of this discipline from the *Upanishads*, but true to his spirit, he preferred a less reputable source. This was *The Apocalypse Unsealed* (1910) by James M. Pryse, who had been one of Mme. Blavatsky's twelve resident disciples. For a time Pryse was a member of the Dublin Lodge along with Yeats and A.E., but, responsive to the Westward course of empire and of spirit, he soon departed for Los Angeles, where he is still inactive. Pryse's book is a theosophical application of yoga to the Apocalypse of St. John, a perpetual favorite of the apocalyptic mind. The account of the *chakras* in Lawrence's *Psychoanalysis and the Unconscious* is as near to Pryse as Pryse is to yoga. The initiation of Don Cipriano and the spiritual exercises of Don Ramon in *The Plumed Serpent* are based upon the initiation described by Pryse. And Quetzalcoatl, the feathered snake, is not only Mme. Blavatsky's serpent with tail in mouth but Pryse's Kundalini, the serpent coiled at the base of every yogi's spine. Like certain yogis, Lawrence was also able in this novel by putting sex to a transcendental use to make it suitable for Puritans. *Apocalypse*, Lawrence's last effort to improve the West, is modeled closely upon *The Apocalypse Unsealed*.

Lawrence's popularity attests his appeal. As he found an affinity in the East, our age, seeking the transcendental and the deep, has found an affinity in Lawrence. But unaware that much of Lawrence is theosophical yoga or Blavatsky fictionized, his readers can hardly be expected to proceed through Lawrence to the East or, using the word in the sense of near-beer, even to the near-East. Some of his literary disciples, however, have penetrated his meaning. Henry Miller, for example, the American novelist who is even more romantic than his master, is a devoted reader of Mme. Blavatsky.

Although they were inspired by much the same sort of thing and for similar reasons, Yeats and Lawrence differ in all other respects. Yeats was an artist first, an occultist second and for the sake of art. Lawrence was an occultist first, an artist, if at all, for the sake of doctrine. Lacking Yeats' critical detachment and his craft, Lawrence allowed what he knew of the East to increase his romantic impatience with limits, including form. The effect of the East, as of everything else, depends upon the hands into which it falls. If they are shaping hands, the effect is art; if not, not.

# III

Aldous Huxley, another of Lawrence's disciples, came to the Orient without benefit of Blavatsky. Science and the war had prepared the world for his disgust, emptying it of meaning and value. Huxley expressed his disgust in desperate, frivolous novels, in which Yeats, reading them years later, found what he called an almost Buddhistic hatred of the world. This hatred and a suppressed yearning are, as we have seen, the customary preparation for a spiritual career. The religious and moral temper which Huxley had concealed beneath his cynicism came to the surface in *Those Barren Leaves* (1925), a novel in which a leading character, repenting his fashionable desperation, climbs a mountain, discovers his soul, and communes with the universe. This tentative, fictive flight prepared Huxley for actual flight in Lawrence's company. Upon their first meeting in 1915, though attracted by Lawrence's profundity, Huxley had been enabled by youth and intelligence to resist conversion. But he succumbed to Lawrence upon their second encounter in 1926. Ignorance of theosophy and Lawrence's silence about his sources permitted Huxley to remain unaware of the Oriental character of Lawrence's thought. As the portrait of Lawrence in *Point Counter Point* shows, his appeal was personal. Though never quite happy about Lawrence's obscurantism, for Huxley is a learned man, he was pleased with the emotional relief which Lawrence offered to the worldly and the wise. Then Lawrence died, taking his personality with him; and the disciple cooled. But he remained a seeker. Prepared by Lawrence for spiritual expansion, but too nice to yield to Blavatsky, Huxley found what he wanted at last in Gerald Heard, her modern equivalent. Heard's omniscience won Huxley, who could never resist omniscience; and Heard had profundity too. In 1935 master and disciple were active in Canon Dick Sheppard's Peace Pledge Union, which promoted a scheme of non-violence like that of Gandhi and from equally Indian premises.

The philosophy which Heard offered to Huxley's desire, a synthesis of Buddhism and Hinduism, is expounded in *The Third Morality* (1937) and *Pain, Sex and Time* (1939). In these tracts Heard says that scientific materialism not only ignores the spirit but promotes fear, greed, and violence, the sins of the Western world. The only hope of salvation lies in Eastern transcendentalism, adapted to the West from the theory and practice of the Vedantists and the Buddhists. The individual, and through him society, can be saved by a diet of vegetables, by posture and exercises for the spine, by deep breathing, and by systematic meditation after the manner of the yogis, until, transcended, the self unites with God. Tantric yoga shows how the energies of sex may be used to enlarge the consciousness. The eightfold path of Buddha and "concentration between the eyebrows" free the spirit from the body and from time. The Sankara philosophy is of help in a way that escapes me. By these means, under the direction of a "Neo-Brahmin," small monastic groups of the devout will transcend their personalities and the world. Omniscience opened many books to Heard, but one of his principal debts is to Irving Babbitt's *Dhammapada*, which contains an excellent account of Buddhistic meditation, its practice and effect, together with a defense of Buddha against the skeptics of the West, who, after reading Babbitt's earlier books, might be inclined to dismiss Babbitt and Buddha as romantics. Babbitt's essay on Buddha differs from the essays of Heard in sounding reasonable.

In his capacity of disciple Huxley repeated the ideas of Heard. *Ends and Means* (1937) is Heard's *Third Morality* under a different title, in order to confuse the public, perhaps. The novels Huxley has written since his conversion are also propaganda for Heard's Oriental synthesis. *Eyeless in Gaza* (1936) is the story of Huxley's conversion. Desperate, materialistic Anthony Beavis (Huxley) meets Mr. Miller (Heard) who prescribes diet, exercises for the spine, and meditation. Greatly improved, Beavis joins a pacifist organization led by Miller and preaches non-violence to the materialists of London. Between sermons he meditates in his closet, exclaiming "Peace, peace, peace," as if he were commencing a *Upanishad*. In *After Many a Summer Dies the Swan* (1939) against a background of skeptics and materialists Huxley projects the figure of Mr. Propter (or Gerald Heard), who conducts in California a little Oriental cult of vegetarians and meditators living in separation from the world. In his garden this Neo-Brahmin passes his time transcending personality ʌnd time when he is not preaching Gerald Heard to the unbeliever.

In 1937 Huxley accompanied Heard to America. After investigating telepathy in Carolina and Quakerism in Pennsylvania, in search of corroboration, they retired to the neighborhood of Los Angeles. There Huxley meditates and writes for the cinema. There Heard meditates and writes detective stories under another name in order to earn a living, for, despite his endeavors, he is not yet independent of his body.

I owe my information about Huxley's most recent state to Mr. Thomas E. Barensfeld of the University of California in Los Angeles. For the past year or two Huxley has been associated with the Vedanta Society, which maintains in Hollywood a chapel resembling, in its degree, the Taj Mahal. Here, to Aldous Huxley and Miss Marion Davies, a fellow communicant, Swami Prabhavananda of the Ramakrishna Mission expounds the *Bhagavadgita* on Tuesdays, and on Thursdays the yoga aphorisms of Patanjali. Thus instructed, Huxley wrote an enthusiastic Foreword to Swami Nikhilananda's *Gospel of Sri Ramakrishna* (1942), an introduction to a system which, according to the prospectus, has also pleased Bergson, Gandhi, and Irwin Edman. To Professor Edman, for example, Ramakrishna seems "the real thing in metaphysical mysticism." The November-December, 1942, issue of Swami Prabhavananda's *Vedanta and the West*, a periodical devoted to Ramakrishna, contains an excerpt from the *Bhagavadgita*, meditations by two local Swamis, and a meditation entitled "The Magical and the Spiritual" by Aldous Huxley. By mortification of the intellect Huxley rises once more in this meditation to Reality, from which he excludes as dangerous such psychic phenomena as elementals, pixies, and table-rappings. In this way he detaches himself not only from limits but also from the neighboring Rosicrucians and theosophists, with whom the Vedantists, though much less *infra dig*, might be confounded.

The influence of Huxley and Heard may be detected, perhaps, in the recent conversion of Christopher Isherwood, author of two novels and collaborator in poetic plays with W. H. Auden. Soon after his arrival in Los Angeles, Isherwood fell under the power of Heard's Swami, renounced literature, the movies, and the world, and proceeded to meditate in the convenient desert whence he emerges occasionally to assist the Swami in public devotions. It is said in the magazine *Horizon* for January, 1944 that Isherwood is now little better than a hermit. The influence of Heard and Huxley may also lie behind Somerset Maugham's recent preoccupation with yoga and the Hindu scriptures. In *The Razor's Edge*, 1944 (a title taken from the Upanishads) Maugham's American hero is converted to Hinduism, gives up his inherited capital, and returns from India to New York, where, driving a taxi for his bread, he enlightens his fares. It would be improper to conclude that Maugham shares these unearthly sentiments; for he refers to himself in this novel as "earthy" and he lives, after all, in New York and the Carolinas and not in Hollywood.

# IV

The histories of Yeats, Lawrence, and Huxley illustrate a tendency in our day not unlike the Transcendentalism of an earlier day in New England. But these three men are only a small part of the new transcendentalism, and the Oriental is only one of its many aspects. Surrealism, which reveals its nature by its name, is a more secular example of the same tendency. And the introspective novel has produced the equivalent of religious meditation. *The Waves* by Virginia Woolf, for example, ends with the extinction of personal identity and a union with all things which differs only in namelessness from that of the Buddhists and yogis. All over America and England literary men have come to resemble James Joyce's Mr. Bloom who, at one point in *Ulysses*, ascended rapidly from Dublin "to the glory of the brightness at an angle of forty-five degrees . . . like a shot off a shovel." These transcendentalists are not a group united by locality or friendship like their predecessors in New England, but they have been forced into a pattern by the times and by their romantic aspiration. The reader will have noticed recurrent patterns in these three exemplary histories, the pattern, for instance, of materialism attended with detestation and yearning and followed by theosophy or Hinduism. And the reader may also have noticed the strange recurrence of Los Angeles. To that city Heard, Huxley, and James M. Pryse, contriving to go East and West at once, retired to meditate, and it was there that Mrs. Yeats received the daemons. The attraction of this place for spiritual men and even for spirits is plain. But I am not sure that I know what it means.

*William Ernest Hocking*

# LIVING RELIGIONS
# AND A WORLD FAITH

IF ONE were still able to travel by train from the New Harbor of Dubrovnik to Serajevo, climbing noisily (and smokily) up the mountain slopes bordering the fine estuary of the Ombla, he would be aware of a swift change of cultural as well as of physical climate. The Dalmatian coast bears everywhere the Roman and Venetian mark in architecture and religion; there are a few Greek Orthodox Churches and numerous Jewish synagogues. But as one reaches Mostar he sees minarets as well as steeples and domes. And at Serajevo it is evident that the religion of Mohammed is a lively factor in the community. Christianity, Judaism, Islam—three religions of Asiatic origin, dominate the Balkan peninsula. At Spalato, Mestrovic's gigantic statue of Bishop Gregory set up in the ruins of the palace of Diocletian symbolizes the almost complete submersion of the religious influence of classical antiquity, both Roman and Greek, under these faiths from the East.

Except in point of proportion the story of the Balkans is repeated everywhere in Europe and America: whatever forms of religion are alive among us we owe to Asia. We are less conscious of the presence of Islam than of Judaism and Christianity, hardly at all aware of Hinduism. Many do not realize that there are (or were) active Moslem missions in England (as at Woking in Surrey), Germany, and France; and that besides the monumental mosque in Paris built to signalize the fact that France was a great Moslem power, there are active mosques in Brooklyn and Chicago; nor that Bahai is an offshoot of Islam, as the Vedanta movement with a dozen American centers is an offshoot of Hinduism.

There are no religions indigenous to Europe and America which compare with these religions from Asia either in their present vitality or in their influence on our civilization. This fact has sometimes been taken as a reproach against the religious originality of the Western world. Sometimes it has been taken as an argument that religion itself is a peculiar Oriental export, not really suited to our mentality, which we should do well to lay aside quietly, with all due gratitude for its historic services.

To comment on the latter point first, it is not at all certain that these historic services have been finished. What they amount to, in sum, is supplying the fecundity and the backbone for all that we call "Western civilization." This has been chiefly the work of Christianity. The Christian version of Roman-Stoic law, eked out by canon law, and administered by officers of the church, tided Europe over its darker hours of disorder, and laid the foundation for all civil law in Europe. The common law of England and America is an offspring of Anglo-Saxon conscience under the guidance of the church. The whole conception of the rights of man is directly traceable to Christian conceptions of human nature, and with that, all we call individualism, liberalism, democracy in the modern sense. The art of Europe, including architecture, music, painting, sculpture, was shaped by the medieval church; likewise its literature and philosophy. And as for its science, which we are inclined to think of as the result of a revolt against religious authority, and especially as one point which sets us off from everything Oriental—the whole development of scientific method in the seventeenth century, with its spirit of revolt—not against religion nor Christianity but against the authority of Aristotle and the Bible in matters of logic and science, is demonstrably an application of Christian ethics to the study of Nature, and was carried on by men who regarded themselves as more religious than those who criticized them. No historian can explain why and how what we call the modern era arose in Europe and America and nowhere else, who does not recognize the religion of Europe and America as one of the parents of that era.

And though we owe so much to Christianity, it is not at all

clear that we yet know what it means. It still seems strange to us
—otherworldly, remote, extravagant, impractical—in short 'Oriental.' Probably the Orient does in fact understand it better than
we do. This means that we claim too much when we say we have
taken our religion from the East: it has not yet been completely
taken. We still have to learn religion from Asia, both in terms of
the living religions which are there, and in terms of Asiatic versions of Christianity. Certainly, the learning business has to go
in both directions; but our own culture will lack catholicity,
poise, and security until we know what we have to do with religion in an age which is rightly committed to the humanistic
spirit and the technology which is the gift of science.

As to the other matter—that we ought to be ashamed to take
our religion from Asia—there are two things to be said. First, that
religion is always original or nothing: nobody can use the religion of anybody else but himself. Whatever he accepts by way
of suggestion or teaching from outside has to become his own
conviction before it can do him any good. And as he appropri-
ates it, he remolds it and produces his own version, even when
he accepts it most humbly as the authoritative word of God.
Second, the Western world is not behind in religious fecundity.
Every ethnic region of Europe has produced its religious forms,
still discernible in the undercurrents of folklore. There have
been magnificent pantheons among them, from the urbane Olym-
pians of Greece to the stormy Aesir, denizens of Asgard (from
two of whom, Odin and Thor, we derive the words Wednes-
day and Thursday—our weekday names remaining obstinately
pagan). And with these there have come splendid poetic literatures, mythologies, theologies, and parable-wisdoms. There have
not been lacking efforts to resuscitate some of these buried cities
of the spirit or to recover for use some of their ideas. Lutoslawski,[1] for example, labored over the doctrine of transmigration as
found in the Polish epics in order to show that it was an improvement on either the Hindu doctrine, associated with Karma, or
Plato's picture of rebirth. But these European religions remain
local reminiscences, held in the subconscious mold of peasant
usages or absorbed into the framework of the dominant faith.
Why, then, have the great Asiatic religions taken their place?
The fact, I believe, is neither accidental nor humiliating: it is an

inevitable consequence of the nature of religion and its history. I shall try to make this evident.

# I

Religion is man's practical dealing with the enduring auspices of his destiny, his communion with what is eternal and total in his world, conceived as a source of direction to right living. By definition, religion reached toward what is universally true, that which concerns all men alike, no matter of what place, color, sex, race, or nation. Its nature is, therefore, to unite men in the consciousness of a common lot and obligation. Wherever it arises, and however it expresses itself, its whole meaning is to find that one reality and that one law which are valid for all mankind. At the same time, every religion, having its local origins, dealing with the less tangible sides of the world, having to use symbols, metaphors, and appeals rather than market-literalities, is steeped in localism. Belonging as it does to the working balance of a culture, it grows with the given culture, and the early religions naturally observe the limits drawn by language and political control. It is this paradoxical union of the local and the universal by which we have to understand the strange facts of religious history and dominance.

The strain between the local and the universal is relieved by the fact that the worshiper is usually unaware of the local quality of his religion. The Arab does not think of his religion as Arabian: it is his way of dealing with Allah, who, in his view, is the God of all men: so far from being felt as local, it is his way of escaping from localism. But he has something specific to do about his faith; he must make his prayers, and in doing so, orient his prayer-rug toward Mecca. He may well be wholly unconscious that in tethering his religion to a particular point in space, he has thereby separated himself from—let us say, a Japanese for whom a certain brass plate in a temple near Nara marks the spot where Amaterasu Omikami began the creation of the world. It is not the Arab but the outsider who finds that this Arab's religion has an "Oriental" flavor, or if he the outsider is a connoisseur, an Arab flavor, racy with the grandeur and masculinity of the imagination of the great peninsula.

And let us notice, too, that whatever the strain may be between the local and the universal, it does not amount to a contradiction. No religion is more local than Hinduism: it is steeped in the atmosphere of the land whose name it insists on keeping: it is a vast tree with a thousand branches and a thousand roots, almost oppressive to the European-American taste by the exuberance of its imagery and the fruitiness of its sense of life. Yet it is just Hinduism which distills itself into the most ethereal of all essences: its Brahman, the absolute being, is devoid of all describable attributes, has no temples, is not worshiped, stands one might say for a sort of dark North Pole in the night sky of the mind. It is as if Hinduism, as it strove to give an exact account of its faith, derived from its soil enough energy to reject every trace of the soil, every trace of the earth itself and of human life, everything that could serve as an identifying mark, and in the guise of Vedanta spread everywhere like a religious ether, pervasive and nonresistant.

This case of Hinduism suggests what happens to a religion as it becomes thoughtful. It becomes aware that its *truth* has no national boundaries, and on that ground, it begins to travel.

It is likely to be handicapped in this undertaking by the fact that a religion does not consist of truth alone; if it did, the problem of a world faith might be much easier. A religion is always a truth (embodied in a creed), a ritual, and a code. The moral code is likely, in early stages, to embody much of the common law of the community and therefore to be so characteristic as not to be applicable to other groups: the Hindu sacred law (*The Book of Manu*) could not be practiced in China. And as for the ritual, these symbolic observances belong so much to the special histories and feelings of the groups in which they arise that they are with difficulty so much as understood by others. Primitive peoples hide their rituals, not because they are ashamed of them, but because they do not wish to expose what is so closely bound up with their own feelings to an unsympathetic eye: early ritual is inherently private to its group—which is one reason of course for the exceptional curiosity it awakens in anthropologists and others. It is for this reason that a great Hindu like Gandhi, whose creed is in many respects coincident with Christianity, has no inclination to identify himself with Christianity. When he says that God has set his lot in India and that he must remain Hindu, he means not that his beliefs are different but that his religion is inseparable from the code, the ritual, and the sacred literature of his people (including their development and reform), and cannot lightly migrate with the universal scope of their thought. The name Rama is to him the most friendly and homely name of God.

Now Gandhi is certainly right about the localism of the whole concrete working of a religion: it has to have roots in the place it lives in. But if this were the last word, we Americans neither ought to be nor could be using Asiatic religions. God knows what religion we would have—possibly Druidism, if we have a Celtic rill in our veins! For a migratory people, localism presents difficulties, and certainly cannot be the determining factor. But there is a state at which *religion itself becomes migratory;* and this stage was reached in India itself. For Buddhism is an Indian product, and Buddhism is inherently a traveling religion. By its own view of its teaching it was incapable of staying at home; and its wandering saved its life, for after a time it died out in India, and lived only in its newer homes—Burma, Ceylon, Siam, Afghanistan, Tibet, China, Japan. Christianity likewise almost abandoned Palestine, spreading to the north and west. Islam, the third among the great traveling religions, has still its central hearth in Arabia and Palestine, but its great mass of adherents lie across southern Asia and northern Africa. What is the peculiar point of view of the traveling religions?

In my judgment it is a matter of religious maturity. It is a phase which was bound to come with full religious self-consciousness, favored by a long history of civilization. (We may leave Islam aside for the moment, since Mohammed was largely influenced by Judaism and Christianity as he met them in Arabia, the other "religions of the Book" as he called them.) The simple reason why we are all using Asiatic religions is that Asia, having a longer consecutive religious history, and producing the men of genius who were able to read the meaning of this history, reached this stage first. What they did was so well conceived that there is no more reason for rejecting it—in the interest of a specious originality—than there would be for rejecting the alphabet or the multiplication table as "Oriental" because these too were first elaborated in Asia. Every part of the world has its indigenous religion; but only in Asia did the local cult have time to come to full flower and send its seeds, detached from the mother plant, to the four winds.

The local religions of Europe have not traveled, because they were not ready to travel when the era of traveling was on. The Germanic and Scandinavian cults had not been ripened by that wide political experience which plays its part in tempering and saddening the human spirit. Not only were they unchastened and unremorseful with respect to their own inherent powers of right living, they had not encountered that experience of political disillusionment which could make a mental distinction between 'the world' and 'the spirit,' or between 'the realm of appearance' and 'the realm of true being.' In brief, the problem of evil, as an accompaniment of high political civilization, could not so much as be formulated by these European cults: they were exuberant, thoughtless, and aggressive; like the Wends of whom Carlyle wrote, their peoples had to be "damped down into Christianity." And if something was extinguished in them—as no doubt it was—they endured the chastening because there was opened to them, at the same moment, a whole new dimension of moral experience which they were able to recognize—not as Asiatic—but as their own. The West-bound religion of Asia engulfed them only because it showed them their own destiny in the concrete. Those who wish to decry Christianity in Europe call it an 'Oriental religion.' Those in Asia who wish to decry the Christianity which Europe and America have at times tried to bring back to it have sometimes called it a 'Western religion.' Very likely it is both, in various details; since a much-traveled religion, like a much-traveled man, will bear traces of all the regions in which he has been at home. But in its original out-push it was neither; it intended to be simply "the way" for men everywhere; its founder never heard the word "Christian"; he considered himself a Jew, calling for a reform or a reconception of the Jewish faith such as would shake off its local restrictions. Five hundred years earlier a young Indian, Siddhartha, whom we now call "The Buddha" or "The Enlightened One," had undertaken a similar liberation of the local religion of his people. He offered his "way" (under the name of the Noble or Aryan

Eightfold-Path) not to Indians but to mankind. He never heard the word Buddhism. These religions traveled because they had to: having reached self-consciousness about what a religion has •to do, a local boundary became a self-contradiction.

They did not as a rule spread automatically, as science has done, throughout human history, but by propaganda. Of each it is said that the founder "sent forth" disciples to preach the message—a new function in the life of religion. The words attributed to Buddha are these:

> "Go, ye Bhikkus, for the weal of many, for the enlightenment of gods and of men; go not two together; let your abode be the shade of trees, your food what is given you . . ."

Whether words like these were actually uttered is less important than the fact that they expressed what the original groups of believers thought of their duties and acted on. These religions had reached the traveling-point, as water reaches the boiling-point. I suggest that we now test this theory by examining some of the significant circumstances attending the origins of the great traveling faiths.

## II

First note the circumstances that these religions (again excepting Islam) arose within a limited period of world history—let us say between the eighth century B.C. and our era. The eighth century we may take as the period of the great Hebrew prophets who, considering Jehovah as god of the whole earth, laid the foundations for present-day Judaism. About this time, India's forests were yielding an esoteric wisdom, Aranyakas and Upanishads, drawing from the robust polytheism of the Vedas a strict and abstract monism, the basis of the Vedanta. Here, in the sixth and fifth centuries B.C. Buddha appeared (562-482 perhaps). And almost precisely contemporary with him, Confucius in China (550-478); while Lao Tze, founder of Taoism, whose date is uncertain, may have been an older contemporary of both.. About the same time, various so-called mystery religions in the Near East and in Greece, symptomatic of the religious unrest of the era, developed traveling propensities. Socrates and Plato (fourth and third centuries B.C.) were not unrelated to the religious concerns of the time. In Palestine, the hill country of Judaea and Galilee offered retreats for reflective spirits, aside from the main travel routes yet not far from them; its rabbis were called philosophers by the Greeks. Alexander paid it little heed, though his teacher, Aristotle, was said to have conversed with one of these wise men from the hills. But when Rome absorbed the small land the stage was set whereby a local disturbance, started by a dreamer from Galilee, could become a world movement.

The greater traveling religions are all products of religious revolt or reform; all of them shake off as unessential some of the local characters of the traditional religion of their several regions; all of them emphasize the universal aspect of religion. All of them make religion an individual matter, and an inward matter, more concerned with motives than with visible conduct. As revolts, they had to be the work of outstanding personalities. And partly on this account they have all come to be identified by the names or titles of their founders; they are "founded" religions, in contrast to the great local background of religious tradition whose authorship (generally speaking) is as little known as the authorship of the several languages. To identify a religion as "the religion of the Buddha" or "the religion of the Christ" or "the religion of the Prophet" does indeed introduce a new localism, a note of partisanship which promises much future trouble in the way of the world faith; but it does, at least, set the religion in question free from the older localism of habitat or race or people.

Was this striking set of similarities among the traveling religions a coincidence, or was there something like a world situation to which these several movements were responses? One suspects that the latter is the case, because no matter how great the genius of a prophet, he can start no historic movement unless the minds of men are asking the questions to which he offers the answers.

Perhaps the world situation was this—that men began to be aware that there *is* a 'world.' It was a period in which contact, commerce, and conquest within the area of Asia, Egypt, and Greece were destroying cultural isolation without destroying cultures. The 'world' began to be thought of as a cultural pluralism, in which it was no longer possible for each one, having grown strong in solitude, to think of itself as the hearth of mankind, the rest being in peripheral twilight as 'barbarian' or 'gentile.' What was taking place was the Copernican revolution of the cultural universe; the center could no longer be securely located at home! When Rome came, it merely finished what had been going on: to all but Rome itself, the political disasters implied by the Roman conquests toppled the easy mental supremacies of all local deities. Local religion had begun to be under suspicion.

More than this: individual men were forced to realize that they could not find complete human satisfaction any longer in their careers as citizens of their own communities. Standing, in the social world, was full of accident and injustice; the problem of happiness or of 'salvation' could not be solved within the human social or political order. Religion, which had hitherto gone along with group life, inspiring its codes and sanctioning its loyalties, begins to pull apart from politics and address itself to the individual soul. The other world becomes important, and immortality a desired prospect, if there is any way to secure it. The career of the soul becomes the dominant theme of the religious 'way.'

This disaffection from the actual world and its natural ambitions does not need to go to the extent of despair, or what Gilbert Murray calls "loss of nerve," in order to present religion with its primary problem, that of the meaning of life. The distinction between the present world and another world is itself a source of profound unhappiness. How can a man wean away his desires and interests from the world in which he must act? He does not do so unless he is compelled to, not merely by circumstances, but by his thinking which convinces him that the separation *has to be made*, alike whether he is personally fortunate or unfortunate: the world if human experience is simply not capable of satisfying the demands of the human soul. Things at their best are finite and man is infinite; this is the root of the 'problem of evil' which religion now faces in its full scope.

The great traveling religions are, accordingly, religions of 'salvation.' Each gives its own analysis of the human dilemma; each offers its own recipe for cure; each gives its teaching as to what men ought to hope for, here and hereafter. These answers are diverse, and this constitutes a part of the problem of the world faith of the future. We shall speak of these differences. For the moment we have been concerned simply to see why religion, arriving at a certain maturity in Asia, naturally came to Europe and America from that source.

At the same time, we can understand why certain other religious movements of the same period did not have the same tendency to universal spread. The Confucian world view had its religious elements; but Confucius was a reformer in this field only in the sense that, leaning against the superstition of his time, he selected and simplified its working elements, and confronted the rest with a prudent pragmatism. For him the working element of religion was a belief in Heaven (Tien) as an appointer of human destiny; everyman had his task, and was bound to qualify himself to fulfil it. For the ordinary conduct of life, Confucius' genius was that of clarifying usage, with great loyalty to tradition, and much sensitiveness of conscience. He has given us one of the great religious sayings of all time: "He who offends the gods has no one to whom he can pray"—the self-created moral solitude of the man who holds himself able to defy duty. There was sufficient universality in the Confucian outlook to permit its spread to Korea and Japan; but China was, in the period we have described, still somewhat apart from the main current of Asiatic thought. Confucius reminds us in many mays of Socrates, in his concern for definitions of ethical ideas, and his indisposition to speculate. But through Socrates and Plato, the career of Greek religious thought took a directly opposite turn, emptying itself almost wholly into philosophy. Now philosophy, like mathematics, is universal by its nature, and neither requires nor can use the methods of preaching and propaganda. Socrates remained the inspiration of various schools of classical thought, especially of the Stoics; but he founded no community, and his thought entered namelessly into the body of Platonism, and thus of Western theology.

Judaism toward the beginning of our era was led into the way of spreading by propaganda. Its own dispersed situation, partly compelled and partly chosen, favored this type of activity. But the impulse subsided in favor of another method of advance. The true religion must indeed become the religion of all men; but this may occur either by transmission or by a gathering in. For Judaism the sense of the community on a family pattern was so strong as to decide the issue for the second type. Judaism was not to be given broadcast to the world, but the world was to be absorbed, so far as it could become worthy, within the Jewish community. The appropriate ceremony of acceptance, involving circumcision, resembled a ceremony of adoption. Judaism may thus be included among the traveling religions; but its mode of travel being corporate, its spread is at present limited to the multiplication of the community under its Law.[2]

# III

I said that the answers given by the great religions to the problem of man's suffering and moral misery in the best of civilizations were diverse. It will be sufficient to illustrate this point if we contrast the answers given by Buddhism and Christianity.

To Buddha, the outstanding defect of human life is suffering, to Christ it is moral aimlessness. Buddhism accordingly undertakes to save men from suffering; Christianity to save them from "lostness." Buddha finds the escape from suffering in cutting the root of desire. His "Noble Fourfold Truth" runs in substance as follows:

Life in all its aspects is suffering;

The cause of suffering is the root of all desire, which is the craving for individual existence and that separateness from others implied by individual life;

The cure of suffering must therefore be the extirpation of that root, the overcoming of the craving to be, as a separate entity.

The way to achieve this cure (the Noble Eightfold Path) is neither asceticism nor indulgence, but a middle path, in which a union of activity with periods of meditation works steadily to the disenchantment which is Enlightenment and Nirvana—eternal peace, a goal which may be attained while one yet lives.

Christ finds the cure for moral lostness in nothing short of a rebirth, in which the straggling affections of secular human nature are unified in a dominant affection, a love of God and neighbor which brings desire and ambition to heel without killing them off. For both Christ and Buddha, the important thing about any human being is not what he does but what he cares about; both have long anticipated the psychiatry of today by showing that 'integration' or peace can only come about by a rulership of natural desire under a single principle which puts first things first. But Buddha could not say "Seek ye first the Kingdom of God and his righteousness," for to Buddha there was no God in the usual sense—there was only the inexorable law of Karma (which carried over an uncured desire into another spell of existence and hence of more suffering) and the equally infallible law, his own discovery, of the escape from Karma, and therefore from further 'existence.' By the terms of his problem, the hope held out to men might indeed be called an eternal life, but not an eternal 'existence,' rather an eternity of unseparateness, the overcoming of individuality, Nirvana, the end of striving. For Christ the hope held out to men was also eternal life, but in a positive sense of personal continuance and effect; it took the vague form of an invitation to membership in a "Kingdom of God," an inner cure of the affections and an outer cure of human history, a long work like the slow leavening of an inert lump—at any rate, something to do.

It is easy to draw up handsome oppositions between these two teachings, and say that Buddha's goal is negative, Christ's is positive; Buddha's attitude toward life is pessimistic, Christ's optimistic; Buddha solaces the bewildered individual by getting him to resign all individual claim on life-satisfaction, Christ by making him individually precious in the sight of God, and a co-operator in a divine work. But these differences do not stand in stark contrast as the two systems are more fully understood; since the life of Buddha and his disciples, like that of Jesus, was one of active endeavor for the good of men. And the later history of Buddhism qualified many of the tenets of the early preaching. It is to be noticed, further, that Buddha and Christ were not asking precisely the same question, and hence their answers cannot be directly compared. Christ was not concerned for the cure of suffering; he tried to get men to face the certainty of 'tribulation' with joy. Buddha was not concerned with the category of sin; he was rather a psychologist who inquired how man might train himself out of his earth-bound impulsiveness through a sort of sublimation. Hence many of the observations of each might be accepted by the other, within their diverse frame. The valid comparison of Buddhism and Christianity, though there have been many attempts, has yet to be worked out. Especially must it be remembered that Buddhism, in the forms it assumed in China and Japan, taught that every man participates in the "Buddha nature," and that his chief task is to realize that devotion to his kind, that superiority to selfishness, that power which comes from inner control, which were characteristic of the great sage. In this respect, Buddhism has dignified the conception of the human individual for Asia, as Christianity has done in the West.

But when all is said, the world views are surely not identical. The one is personal, the other impersonal; the one lives in a universe whose reality is moral will, the other in a universe whose reality is moral law; the one is aggressive, the other pacific—except, we must add, in Japan, where Buddhism long ago, in two of its sects, acquired a militant flavor. The ultimate world faith, therefore, will have to be one in which these differences must be resolved.

We have, then, a group of religions each of which accepts the responsibility of spreading its way of life to all men. Arising in widely separated centers and moving in different directions, they have in some measure divided the world among themselves, no one of them being effectively universal. The problem of a world faith will raise the practical question of the relations of these religions to one another, and to the local religions which they meet in the course of their expansion.

Nowhere is there a religious vacuum into which the migrant can move. Buddhism encounters Confucianism and Taoism in China, Confucianism and Shinto in Japan. But it came rather as a supplement than as a contestant. Confucianism had no dogmas regarding the other world and the career of the soul after death which it cared to oppose to the new doctrine, rich with metaphysical analysis and imaginative tapestry, supported by vast tomes of esoteric wisdom, and bringing to the human scene a new sense of divine compassion and of moral appeal to the Buddha nature in each one. Buddhism in China released a great wealth of artistic genius, giving it new themes in architecture, painting, sculpture. But chiefly it dignified human life by making it, in its inner struggle with suffering and desire, the central theme of the meaning of the cosmic process. A Chinese could thus be a good Confucianist and a good Buddhist at the same time. There was of course a silent competition on the plane of subsistence; for an organization must have an economic basis: what is given to Taoist priests cannot be given to Buddhist monks. But on the religious plane, there was room for all.

Christianity has been as a rule more belligerent toward the local religions. Professing to supply all the religious needs of mankind, it has called for singleness of allegiance. Buddhism in China presented the paradox of a religion with no God and at the same time with many divine figures, Buddhas, Bodhisattvas, and saints. A multiform system can flexibly add to its number or find cross-identities, whereas a monotheism such as Christianity or Islam must set itself against the whole apparatus of polytheistic worship, especially the images of the gods. The march of Christianity has therefore been a demand for Either-Or decisions; the temples and idols of the "heathen" have had to fall. But here also the conflict has not extended to the ground-level of the local structure. The tenacity of folk-custom and festival has led to many local amalgamations, and the sagacity especially of the Catholic missionaries has seen possibilities of conserving rather than destroying many a local observance within the body of the new faith. Hence the Christianities of the German forests, the Druid countries, the Mexican mountains, the old Spanish Southwest are markedly different in temper: they are variations on a common theme.

In principle, since religion must be both local and universal, there should always be the possibility of uniting the mature, self-conscious superstructure of the traveling religion with elements of code and rite which belong to local feeling and history. But the problem is in each case a special one, since codes and rites are not separable from creeds; and the union, whatever it may be, must be natural and coherent, not an eclectic patchwork.

But the major problem of world faith arises when the great traveling religions encounter one another.

It belongs to the accidents of history that Buddhism and Christianity are themselves the result of a slow selection among various movements of similar nature—Buddhism and Jainism rising together in India; Christianity, Orphism, Mithraism, and other cults finding themselves together in the Empire. But these survivors, spreading in opposite directions, did not encounter one another, so far as we know, for several centuries; and then understood so little of one another that a romanticized Buddha, under the name of Josaphat, an Indian prince who in the tale was converted by the monk Barlaam, was innocently canonized by the Christian Church, both Byzantine and Roman (though later dropped by the Roman church)! In point of fact, their teachings are very unlike, and Buddha (who died about 480 B.C.) had he met the monk Barlaam, would have been from the monk's point of view sadly in need of conversion, and vice versa.

It belongs also to the accidents of history that Buddhism in its eastward progress encountered no other traveling faith. Its extension was pacific. Pandit Das Gupta's statement, at the opening of the new Buddhist temple at Sarnath, to the effect that Buddhism had never used force, nor inspired the use of force in its behalf, is well justified. He drew a damaging contrast between this history and that of Christianity. The early expansion of Islam brought it into Christian territory, in the Near East—Damascus, Jerusalem, Constantinople, the Balkans, Egypt, North Africa, Spain. Islam had its own methods of tolerating the presence of Christians in its precincts, as witness the division of the great church of Saint John at Damascus into two parts, the Christians using one half, while the other was used as a mosque! But the issue of ownership of the "sphere of influence" between these two religions was determined by the sword; and the political element in the establishment of Christianity in Europe and the Near East is one of the least creditable chapters of religious history. It has to be remembered, however, that from the fourth century onward Christianity had become identified with the maintenance of public law in Europe, tiding over a period in which secular authority was in confusion, and that it had created a "Christian" Europe largely through its power over the sources of legislation and teaching. Likewise for Islam, though to an even higher degree, the religion was at the same time a code of law and a government. For neither religion, during the centuries of Islamic growth, was it possible to separate church and state. With this consolidation of authority, a given territory had to be either Moslem or Christian; and the matter could not be settled by either prayer or philosophy.

We have now reached a point in the evolution of both politics and religion at which a degree of mutual independence is seen to be necessary to the health of both. Religion must influence law, if it is of any value at all. And government must have its religious presuppositions. But when they are united as organizations, religion is corrupted by patronage, the "extension of the faith" becomes an undercover pretext for the extension of empire, politics loses the correction of an independent moral judgment, and the relations between nations lose the tempering influence of a religion which is beyond every state, because it is effectively universal. We have not yet realized this ideal of mutuality and detachment between church and state; but we are sufficiently advanced toward it, so that the relations between the great faiths will henceforth be determined more by persuasion, on the ground of intrinsic merit, than by the political complexion of the world—assuming that the world of tomorrow will allow the free intercourse of faiths, and the free play of thought in regard to them.

Meanwhile, we have three or four promising aspirants for the position of world religion. It is hardly correct to call them competitors, for the impulse to spread is not a matter either of self-interest or of pride—though these motives creep into every man-staffed large-scale enterprise—but of duty in the meeting of human need. And since it is the consumer and not the promoter who, in the end, determines whether the need is met, whatever rivalry there is should be of the most frank and generous character, like the rivalry of physicians in the cure of disease. The presence of these many aspirants is itself an anomaly; if the plurality were acquiesced in, that would be equivalent to saying that there is no world religion at all, and is to be none such, but only a group of differing faiths having no way to settle their differences, since each appeals not to reason nor to experience but to the undebatable and uncompromisable finalities of revelation.

On the other hand, the magnitude of the field of dominance of each of the great religions is so great that we must accord to each of them a large measure of success in satisfying the religious craving of men; no other factor could have maintained them over so long a period. We cannot, then, be dealing with three falsehoods and one verity—one revealed and necessary way, and three works of the devil—with the fateful problem in hand of recognizing the true light; what we have is a variety of versions of truth, struggling through media of human expression, vagary, conceit, superstition—with the problem in hand of recognizing and releasing the essence of the matter, and with the large probability that each of the group will have its own unique contribution to that essence.

# IV

There are now two questions before us. What are the elements of agreement among these several aspirants? What are the outstanding differences, and what processes are at work to resolve them?

A certain amount of agreement seems implied in the common circumstances of origin of the traveling faiths. All religion accepts the reality of an invisible order of being which in some way both commands and satisfies the root-awareness of life. It implies belief in the extra-natural, which usually takes shape as a belief in divine personal beings. All the mature religions recognize in the human individual a 'soul,' that is to say, a phase of the self deeper than the current phase of conversation and the day's work, reflecting on and guiding the current excursions in view of the total picture of destiny: the soul is the self in its dealings with the whole, and therefore with the extra-natural world as well as the natural. All the traveling religions see and teach that the soul is in peril, life being an opportunity which may be missed. They teach that the obvious world attracts and blinds the vision so that spiritual things become obscure, and life runs to frustration. They all offer cure, and guidance to what we may call the cosmic success. All of them propose a code of life, which is in part a condition of the cure; and all of them, whatever their other precepts, include in the code a requirement of good will toward the fellow man, and a degree of detachment from the pressures of physical desire and greed and social ambition.

To the extent of this agreement, we may say that a world faith already exists. This does not imply that all the world assents to the items in which all the religions agree. The advance of science and of positivistic logic has carried with it a wide swath of negation of the first assertion of all religion, the invisible order as a moral order. To this wholly secular and this-worldly temper, all religion is 'Oriental' in the sense that it assigns reality to something not 'verifiable' by physical observation. This secularism now pervades the Orient, and in order to burn off that religious excess we call superstition proposes to burn off religion itself; it aims to reclaim for pressing mundane business the energy drafted off into the fruitless catalepsies of the mystic. If there is soundness in religion it will accept the ordeal, learn its lessons, and hold to what it perceives, seeing that science itself is an extra-natural structure of the soul, responding partially to a demand of the cosmos for truth. The truth about tangible things is not itself a tangible thing; nor is the truth about perishable things itself perishable. To Gandhi, Truth and God are interchangeable terms, and the scientist has but to become more fully self-conscious to see that he also is a worshiper. We need not therefore make secularism an exception to our statement that a world faith already exists.

All the great religions further agree that the soul has a career not limited to the physical life of man; they have their pictures of continuance or of supplementation. The notion of immortality, once vivid and near, burns dim today; but the concern it stands for, as a part of the problem of the meaning of life, is even more insistent as our noble social orders reveal their insecurity.

They agree also on another matter, and one which becomes the kernel of disagreement: all give a unique religious position to their founders. The names of Buddha, Jesus Christ, Mohammed, become the party-signs of religious cleavage, and present the most refractory obstacles to mutual understanding. They incorporate in themselves the contemporary problem of world faith in its sharpest form. To many minds, this represents the crowning perversity of the ecclesiastical nostrumizing of religion, and provokes a disposition to reach a common faith, as Professor Dewey does, by discarding once for all the entire specialized apparatus of the religious organizations. My belief is, however, that there is a reason for the apparent perversity, and that we shall move ahead toward religious understanding far faster if we inquire why it is that the great faiths all take this turn.

We may profitably remember that there have been repeated attempts in history to bring men together on the basis of what they already agree upon, discarding their points of difference, as though differences were less important than agreements, only to discover once more that likenesses are abstractions, and are never enough by themselves to constitute a living organism. Why, then, do the traveling religions give a special divine status to their founders?

# V

We may approach the answer to our question by asking another. Why do men make holidays of the anniversaries of the advent of an idea? If an idea is true and valuable, it has no mark of time and place about it: it belongs by its nature to all minds who can apprehend it. The announcers of important ideas may not wish to be remembered in connection with the ideas—and most of them have not been—yet science itself strangely rebels against the impersonality of its product, attaches Napier's name to a set of logarithms, Newton's to certain laws of motion, and a motley array of personal roots to the names of various species of plants and animals. This impulse signalizes the fact that however timeless an idea may be, it is only 'realized' when it is born in a time-occupied mind. And in proportion to the scope of the idea will men make holidays of such dates of birth. The "Noble Fourfold Truth" would on this score always be Buddha's doctrine. The "Ideas" of Plato have ceased to be merely platonic beings, since they are forever Platonic. Time makes a time-festival of its capture of the eternal. That is the beginning.

Buddh Gaya, the reputed scene of Buddha's Enlightenment, has long been a holy place for Buddhist visitors. As late as 1931 a temple was opened at Sarnath, near Benares, at the site of the ancient Deer Park where the story places the scene of Buddha's

First Sermon. Buddha himself taught the doctrine of non-permanence, non-God-substance, non-soul-substance, and the timeless peace of Nirvana as his own portion; contrary to the spirit of his own thought, he has become an object of personal devotion, in the course of the time-changes which his doctrine has suffered. The Buddha-principle is hardly separable from the Buddha-image. The Buddhist initiate professes, "I take refuge in the Buddha." In much the same way, with careful avoidance of any deification of Mohammed, Islam makes its confession of faith: "There is no God but Allah, and Mohammed is his Prophet." This is not intended to be mere grateful reminiscence; it could not on that ground alone enter into the creed.

We come nearer to the secret when we recall that the founders were not merely seers and thinkers but teachers, planting their ideas in living minds as the best way, perhaps the only way, of securing their continuance. They were concerned to make their ideas forces in history, and to this end their concern was "Have they understood? Will they transmit?" Intentionally or not, they begot communities, bound together by the destiny of the faith in a world of opposition. It was not irrelevant that the founders, as reformers—and in the religious sphere which is the most bitterly conservative of all spheres because the landmarks are so few—had to be fighters as well as dreamers. Such communities, which as Royce has well said, will be communities of memory and of hope, have also to be communities of struggle, burdened with the trust of the teaching: the nerving memory of the original founder-fighter was needed as the living spirit of the effort. He would be thought of as present with them; the career of his idea in history would be the continuance of his cosmic career. The full profession of the Buddhist monk is, "I take refuge in the Buddha; I take refuge in the Dharma (the Law); I take refuge in the Samgha (the brotherhood)." By a similar process to that by which corporations in modern law become legal persons, these communities took on quasi-personal life, promoted by but also promoting the lives of their members. In them, something of the divine nature of truth had not alone entered time, but had taken on an historic career. It belonged to the nature of the divine to act in this way in history; and this nature is identical in quality with the nature of the founder, freed by death from bodily limitations. To take refuge in him is equivalent to taking refuge in God-in-history. We now see why the founder's name, with various shadings of the superhuman attribute, enters into the creedal statements of the several faiths. It is because, consciously or not, they all agree on a farther point, that God must have a human and temporal aspect, and that the human scene is ennobled by his working presence there.

Neither Buddha nor Mohammed would have accepted the phrase I used above, "God in history." Not Buddha, for to him there was no Brahman, but only the divine law, saving men from suffering and the misery of endless rebirth. Not Mohammed, for to him the divine majesty is unreachable, ungraspable, unembodied in any finite form: Allah rules all things, inscrutably, but he "neither begets nor is begotten," and with that denial Islam feels a permanent gulf set between itself and the Christian doctrine of the Son of God. But the chief agency in working toward a world faith is to see beyond language to meanings, by the aid of a sympathetic interpretation, aided by psychology. In the sense I have mentioned, it is the idea of incarnation which has given each of the founders his salient place in the creed. It is this idea which Tagore's "Religion of Man" is calling for and which many a movement which regards itself as atheistic is unknowingly using.

As these implicit meanings become slowly emergent into the general consciousness of men, the abstract world faith already present becomes by so much more concrete, and the obstacles of creedal difference melt away, because the truth namelessly persuades. But it is important that differences should be worked through, not abandoned; for men must differ according to their insights in order that their union when it comes may hold *all* their truth.

*Ananda K. Coomaraswamy*

# UNDERSTANDING AND REUNION: AN ORIENTAL PERSPECTIVE

ANY discussion of a possible or actual influence of X on Y takes for granted their difference; and if we are to discuss the results of such an influence we must have some clear idea of the characteristics of X, the influence to be traced, and Y, the subject presumed to have been influenced. I have been asked to discuss the problem generally, but with special reference to the art of the theater and its significance.

It is obvious that understanding is prerequisite to reunion. Were it not for difference, "understanding" would be needless; were it not for likeness, "reunion" impossible. In what respects do the cultures of the East and of America differ, and by what kinships are they linked behind the scenes? One initial point must be emphasized, that the difference is only quite accidentally geographical. No problem would exist if we had American Indians only in mind, nor would any serious problem have existed if the ends of the earth had been brought together not now but in the twelfth century. The predicament is one of period and Zeitgeist. It is much as if one should ask: What, if anything, can Platonism and Christianity still contribute to the welfare of the modern world?

The Oriental culture and way of life are traditional, the modern anti-traditional; the one values stability, the other change or "progress"; one demands from art an adequate expression of truth, the other self-expression; for the one, art is a necessity without which nothing can be well or truly made or adapted to good use; while for the other art is a luxury to be enjoyed apart from activity and without bearing on conduct. The Oriental

215

dance, for example, is an intellectual discipline and always responsible to traditional themes; ours a gymnastic exercise and physical display or, like other modern arts, the self-expression of the artist's private emotional storms. The Oriental artist, even at a court, is really maintained by the collective patronage of a unanimous society; the modern artist depends on the precarious support of a clique that is only a tiny fraction of the whole community. As art dealt with themes which are and have been familiar to everyone, literate or illiterate, and whether rich or poor, for millennia, there had been no necessity to include in cultural curricula courses on "the appreciation of art." When every professional had his disciples or apprentices, there was little need for "schools of art" in our sense, but only for masters and pupils. In the East, the necessity for museums was not felt until the traditional arts had been almost destroyed by the contagion of modern civilization; just as when folksongs could be heard everywhere, no one "collected" them.

In saying this, I have not in mind the current conception of "fine art" but the more vital and universal view in which all the arts, whether of painting, music, weaving or agriculture, are simply the means by which the needs of man's body and soul are simultaneously provided for. In this sense all the arts of a people are, not a byproduct of their culture, but that culture itself, composite of the forms of their way of life, and the visible evidence of their character. Works of art are the "ornaments" of life only in that original sense in which one says that the mind is adorned by learning, rivers by water, or an altar by its furniture.[1] It is with the ways of life that are expressed in art, and the possible influence of one upon another, that we are concerned. The whole East has believed, with Plato, that such as is our music, such will be the nature of our political institutions, that "life is a complex phenomenon in which all the apparently autonomous aspects, social, political, economic, moral, and aesthetic, are interlaced and interwined together in such a manner that action in one aspect will have momentous incidence in all the others." [2]

For example, in Tibet, "Metaphysics, ritual, law, government, art, even dress and the conventions of politeness, fit together like a jig-saw." [3] As this quotation implies, correctly, such a harmony within a given culture is only possible upon the basis of the primacy of metaphysics. But the "first philosophy" is one and the same for all cultures, regardless of the dialect in which the common language of the spirit is spoken; and an agreement and reunion of these cultures, in which allowance can also be made for adaptation to all local conditions, can have no other solid foundation. The same will apply to the "reunion" of the churches (in a much broader than the customary sense of the word "church"); for whatever necessary differences distinguish these allegiances from one another, all are based upon a common wisdom "that was never made, but is now what it has ever been, and shall be for ever," [4] and to which, by the same token, no one people can lay claim otherwise than by right of common inheritance. I have used the word "reunion" advisedly, to imply that the present disunion of the cultures is a temporary, and strictly speaking accidental, predicament: "Where God is our teacher, all come to think alike." [5]

As the late Dr. Heinrich Zimmer remarked in his admirable introduction to La Meri's *The Gesture Language of the Hindu Dance*, "the Indian dance reflects the dance of the universe, whose transient gestures we all of us are. . . . Its function is to be an encyclopedic initiation into the manifold mystery of life." The history of Indian dancing can be traced through three millennia, and that of treatises on the subject through two. In the oldest books we find a God (Indra) described as "dancing his heroic deeds" and as "performing a metrical composition," and that it is a dance of the Gods that sets in motion the cosmic process. We find also that the ritual of the sacrifice, which is an "imitation" of what was done by the Gods in the beginning, includes the dance in various forms; and that there are many gestures which are common to the iconography of the deities, the performance of rites, and the expressive dance. These gestures are related to those that are familiar in everyday life. It is, indeed, impossible to detach a traditional art from its environment, and to consider it simply as an art form. Art is a part of life, and life itself an art.

Indian dancing and music have never been "emancipated" from their religious associations; even today their ensemble is performed in temples before the image of the deity which receives all the services due to a king. Even in what we should call secular contexts, the dancer begins with prayer, and the fundamental theme

217

is that of the inner life. Thus in the words of the *Upanishad*, we can say that "Those who sing here are singing of Him." The erotic themes of the Vaishnava songs and dances are not an imitation of human behaviorism but of the archetypal loves of Eros and Psyche, the *Liebesgeschichte Himmels*. Under these conditions there are no bawdy songs; the same are sung and in the same way understood by the religious and the prostitute. Like Dante and Milton, the Oriental author is not working primarily for aesthetic ends—*Non facit ars cantorem, sed documentum*—but employs his art, however artfully, to attract an other-minded audience to the essential theme of Liberation. Rhetoric is not an art of pleasing, but that of the effective communication of truth. The myths that are displayed by word and gesture are not abstracted from historical events, but true forever. If ever the West should be profoundly moved by Eastern art, it can be only to return to herself, temporarily forgotten.

One of the most familiar forms of Indian art in our museums is that of Śiva as Naṭarāja, Lord of the Dance, whose creative and destructive, fettering and liberating operation is conceived in terms of the theses and antitheses of a dance, of which the incessance is the manifestation of his sustaining power. From this cosmic dance all other activities, operations, and dances are, so to speak, excerpts; to the extent of its perfection, every performance "participates" in the divine operation; the principles of dancing are not of human invention, but revealed, and have been transmitted from generation to generation in pupillary succession. The standard of excellence is not one of the pleasure that may be felt by a given audience, but one of correctness; just as for Plato, the irregularity of human motions is to be corrected by an assimilation to cosmic rhythms. An educated audience is presupposed, one that will be pleased by whatever is correct in the performance, and displeased conversely. It is in the same way that the mathematician judges of the beauty of an equation.

The Oriental dance is a language. Its motions, or gestures, compose an organized vocabulary of constant meanings; that is to say, a given position of the hand has a basic significance, like that of a verbal root, but takes on innumerable shades of meaning according to the way in which the hand is moved and the whole context in which the gesture is made. In this way the dance becomes a vehicle for the expression of all kinds of meanings, from the simplest to the most abstractly metaphysical. We must not, however, conceive of the gestures as isolated from one another; they are strung together in rhythmic sequences, one melting into the next, as words are strung together to make a poem— "surpassing all one can imagine of smooth, unending motion." In other words, to dance and to enact are one and the same thing, and it would be tautological to speak of a "nautch dance," the word "nautch" itself deriving from a root that implies at the same time a mimetic gesticulation and the "registration" of the hero's or heroine's (not the dancer's) states of mind. Hence, in discussing the influence of the Oriental dance, we are really discussing that of the theater.

What do we mean by an "influence" in such a case? In Asia, India has played the part of Greece in Europe, and we know to what extent we are still here indebted to Greece, however unconsciously. The influence of the Indian technique can be traced throughout Asia, and far down into the South Seas. At the same time each of the other great cultures of Asia preserves its own independence and unmistakably local color. This unquestionable case of "influence" is therefore worth considering. The Indian influence on the drama of Eastern Asia cannot be isolated from that of Indian culture as a whole: the fact that these other cultures were based on essentially similar principles made the assimilation of new formulae possible and easy; there was nothing exotic in the Indian point of view; it could be assimilated without disagreeing with their own and without a merely manneristic imitation. One may say, perhaps, that an influence is liable to have been the more profound the less obviously it can be recognized in outward forms, which may represent nothing but a passing fashion, comparable to those of our own past periods of Chinoiserie and Japonisme; and also, that those who are already rich, can best afford to lend or borrow.

One cannot but feel, accordingly, to quote the French Orientalist Jean Buhot, that "No study of Oriental art will, I think, be very profitable to the West until some attempt has been made to imitate also the mental attitude of the East." [6] This mental attitude is incompatible on the one hand with that of our "scientific humanists," and on the other with that of our "aestheticians." It is putting the cart before the horse to suppose that such a gulf can be bridged by any borrowing of Oriental idioms, however they may please our eye or ear or otherwise intrigue us.

The same writer similarly doubts whether Eastern music "will ever find in the West the congenial, tranquil atmosphere which is essential to its enjoyment." Neither the dance nor music is presented in the East in great buildings with complicated machinery or for a particular class of "playgoers" or musical "fans." There are folk singers and court musicians, and performances in the open air and in temples and palaces, at weddings and other special occasions. Under some conditions, up to the present day in Java, for example, more than a year's work and immense sums of money may be expended by a prince on the preparation of a dramatic performance. But this does not mean that the people's money is spent only for his private enjoyment; on the contrary, the performance is open to the public, with only what might be called reserved seats for the patrons. It often happens, too, that members of the royal family are themselves expert members of the cast. Peasant and aristocrat share the same fundamental interests and understand the same arts.

Nowhere in the world is the dance more specialized than in Bali, yet

> The dancer in Bali is simply another of those anonymous artisans who are continually renewing its cultural life . . . The elegance of the *Redjang* dancers in their long black skirts, and the subdued brillance of their corsage and train, their delicate fluttering fans and lovely coiffure of flowers, covering the front of the head and outlining the great coil of hair that frames the head on one side, as one still sees in certain old stone figures of noble ladies, goddess or princess, could scarcely be surpassed. But it is not so much the dress which lends distinction to the wearers as they who wear marvelously the dress. They may have tucked up their skirts knee high to wade the stream which divides the village from the temple, they may have waited in the mud and rain, but they never look anything but supremely elegant. To picture them among ourselves we should have to imagine for them an ideally refined and

beautiful setting; but they are in perfect harmony here with the mud floor of the palm-thatched ground outside the temple, lit by flickering oil flames and surrounded by their equals, the whole population of a Balinese village, swarms of naked children, boys and girls with old *kains* about their legs, women in towel turbans with naked breasts, young men and old squatting on the ground with the perfect grace they so mysteriously possess.[7]

"Before the decadent period . . . (the Burmese) stage was an open space in the center of the orchestra, around which the audience sat . . . The stage scenery consisted only of a tree branch to represent a forest, and a property box to represent the throne";[8] just as in the Elizabethan drama which, "being without scenery and elaborate stage apparatus, made its appeal to the mind rather than to the eye."[9] Such pictures as this must be considered when we ask ourselves in what way Oriental dancing can affect us, whose notions of art and culture are bound up with exhibitions in museums and concerts in Symphony Halls on the one hand, or on the other with the notion of a communal singing and dancing in which everyone takes part and none is a trained expert. What, in fact, we cannot learn from the American Indians, we cannot any more easily learn from the East. To make a real use of all these things, our whole way of living would have to be transformed.

To give any impression of Oriental music as a whole would be very difficult, if only because of its great variety, necessarily implied by its application to all the varied occasions of life. An Oriental can readily understand and be moved by a Gaelic folksong or by the Gregorian chant, while hardly anything later than Bach will seem to him to be musical at all. His conception of music is in the first place linear and at the same time modal; almost everyone can recognize and discriminate between the rather large number of modes in general use. Just because there has been no development of vertical harmonization, a far more extended and varied development of melodic forms than can be imagined by our concert-goers has been possible.

Real Oriental music and dancing have rarely been seen or heard in America; but the rare and outstanding opportunities that have presented themselves have been deeply appreciated. These have been provided by Uday Shankar, Mei Lan Fan, and the Siamese royal dancers who performed at the Keith Memorial Theatre in Boston and in New York; none of those who saw these performances can ever have forgotten them. One or two Europeans who have studied Oriental music in the East have given recitals that have been deeply appreciated in rather limited circles. On the other hand, few Americans have been even aware of the rather humble but strictly traditional theaters that have been supported by the Chinese communities of Boston, New York, and San Francisco.

Oriental influence has certainly played a part in the current interest in masks and in the type of mask that has been made; and has, perhaps, something to do with the revival of marionettes. No large-scale production of shadow plays has been attempted, except in the sense that a movie is a kind of shadow play; the possibilities here are unlimited, especially for themes in which miraculous or supernatural effects are required. Among the earliest attempts to represent the Orient on the stage were those of Ruth St. Denis; the approach was romantic and far from scholarly, but imaginative and sincere, and at least at first a really Oriental atmosphere was created. Some composers, notably Ehrlich, have made extensive use of Oriental themes. Madame La Meri, author of the book referred to below, has presented Oriental dance sequences as nearly true to Indian feeling as would seem to be possible for a foreigner. Only a very limited amount of good Oriental music is available on records, and still less of Oriental dancing on accessible films. There are practically no records available of poetic recitative. We have not yet asked for these things from the East; to *ask* for them would be the "right demand that evokes the right response."

What may be, in the last analysis, a more far-reaching, although less tangible, influence of Oriental dancing and music has been exerted through a number of books, in which not only the technique and effects of these arts, but also their underlying philosophy, have been treated with sympathy and understanding. One of these was my own *Mirror of Gesture* (2nd edition, with Bibliography, New York, 1927), another the recently published and more fully illustrated book by Madame La Meri, *The Gesture*

222

*Language of the Hindu Dance* (New York, 1942). Beryl de Zoete and Walter Spies, enlarging on a theme already well treated by Miguel Covarrubias, in his *Island of Bali*, have produced a work of real genius in their *Dance and Drama in Bali* (New York, 1939); I do not know how anyone can have read such a book as this, or even looked at its marvelous illustrations, without being deeply stirred and impressed by the picture of what the arts can mean in a community whose erotic, social, religious, artistic, and economic activities are so inextricably interwoven as to make it impossible, even in a book, to break up the unity of their culture into isolated categories of experience.

In speaking of books we must not ignore many others that have been published here and/or in Europe and are available to American readers. For example, M. H. Aung, *Burmese Drama*, Oxford, 1937; Fox-Strangways, *The Music of Hindustan*, Oxford, 1914; A. B. Keith, *The Sanskrit Drama*, Oxford, 1924; R. G. Thakurta, *The Bengali Drama*, London, 1930; Th. B. van Lelyveld, *La danse dans le théatre javanais*, Paris, 1931; Chu-Chia-Chien and A. Jacovleff, *The Chinese Theatre*, London, 1922; A. E. Zucker, *The Chinese Theatre*, London, 1925; L. C. Arlington, *The Chinese Drama*, Shanghai, 1930; M. C. Stopes, *The Plays of Old Japan*, London, 1913; Zoë Kincaid, *Kabuki, the Popular Stage of Japan*, London, 1925; A Miyamori, *Masterpieces of Chikamatsu*, London and New York, 1926; A. Maybon, *Le théatre japonais*, Paris, 1925; E. Fenollosa and E. Pound, *'Noh,' or Accomplishment*, London, 1916; A. Waley, *The Nō Plays of Japan*, London, 1921, New York, 1922; Noël Peri, *Cinq Nô*, Paris, 1921; R. Umemoto and Y. Ishizawa, *Introduction to the Classical Dances of Japan*, Tokyo, 1935; B. Laufer, *Oriental Theatricals*, Chicago, 1923; G. Wimsatt, *Chinese Shadow Shows*, Cambridge, 1936; B. March, *Chinese Shadow Plays and Their Making*, Detroit, 1938; five volumes on Japanese drama, dancing, and music in the "Tourist Library"; and the present writer's *Transformation of Nature in Art*, 2d edition, Cambridge, 1935, and *Why Exhibit Works of Art?* London, 1943. Mr. Alain Daniélou's *Introduction to the Study of Musical Scales*, London, 1943, deals with the metaphysical implications of Indian musical theory, and contrasts the traditional Asiatic and modern Western musical procedures. Besides these books, very many articles on Indian and

Indonesian dancing and dramatics have appeared in *Indian Art and Letters* (London), *La revue des arts asiatiques* (Paris), *Djawa* (Weltevreden), and *Triveni* (India), and others. An article on the "Dance in India" will be found in the last edition of the *Encyclopedia Britannica*. The best account of Chinese music will be found in J. H. Levi, *Foundations of Chinese Musical Art*, Peiping, 1936. Noël Peri's *Essai sur les gammes japonaises*, Paris, 1934, contains an extensive bibliography, and also a discussion of the possibility of "harmonizing" Japanese music; the question, whether such harmonizing of Asiatic music is either possible or desirable is one of those most pertinent to our inquiry. A very useful summary account of Asiatic music will be found in R. Lachmann's *Musik des Orients*, Breslau, 1929; and a more detailed discussion in Curt Sachs' admirable *Rise of Music in the Ancient World, East and West*, New York, 1943. The publication of so many books and articles, almost all within the last twenty years, implies the existence of a considerable public interested in their subject matter. Nearly all of these books and articles are based on solid foundations of knowledge and sympathy; their point of view is neither superficial nor romantic, and their influence has in all probability outweighed any effects of which direct evidence could be easily discovered.

We must also speak of Rhetoric because no serious study or criticism of Indian drama, dancing, or music can be undertaken without some knowledge of the vast literature that has been devoted to the theory of expression by means of words in poetry, as well as in the languages of gesture, music, and even painting and sculpture. In these technical works, which correspond more nearly to what is sometimes called "Poetics"—and let us not forget that, as Plato says, "*all* the arts are kinds of 'poetry' "—than to what is now so awkwardly called "Aesthetics," are to be found the categories and definitions of all the ideas and feelings that can be "registered" or "danced"; and furthermore, an adumbration that can be expressed in works of art of the nature of the final experience involved in what is called the "tasting of the flavor." Works of art, as a whole or in their parts, are characterized by "flavors" (*rasa*), and these flavors are as it were the distilled essences of the actual states-of-mind (*bhāva*) that are registered by those who speak or play in poems, dramas, or dances. For example, the "Heroic" flavor corresponds to the display of "Courage." It is not in order that the spectator may participate in the hero's feelings directly and sympathetically that he must be both sensitive and learned, but that he may taste their qualities, and finally, relish only that one flavor in which all the distinctive tastes of life are fused, just as the tastes of many flowers are confused in what can only be called the taste of honey; and that is the taste of God, the superlative flavor and last end of all expressions; so, as the *Upanishad* expresses it, "Those who sing here to the harp are singing *Him*." And that is true; for, like Dante, the Oriental author is not working primarily for aesthetic ends, but employs his art, however artfully, to attract an otherminded audience to the essential theme of Liberation, which might be called the leitmotiv of all Eastern art.

We have so far maintained that the actual influence of Oriental dancing and music upon the American theater has been slight and superficial, and have attributed this to the widely differing purposes and points of view on which the Oriental and modern civilizations are based. If that is a correct diagnosis, it will still be pertinent to ask in what way such an influence may yet be felt, and in what sense it could be thought of as desirable. Clearly, we cannot isolate the influence of the dance from that of other aspects of Oriental culture as a whole, by which America has already been affected and is likely to be more profoundly affected in the future, as Europe was influenced by Eastern ideas in the somewhat analogous age of the Crusades. On the other hand, it is evident that nothing like an Orientalization of the West is to be desired. For an Oriental, however critical of modern Western civilization he might be, to propose to "proselytize" the West would be only to invert the error of those (and they are many) who firmly believe that the best thing possible for the East would be to imitate our own political and industrial forms and to adopt the material values on which they rest; or that of those who seek to evangelize the East in a very different sense. We need hardly say that influences exerted in this way, and which involve the borrowing of outward forms, lead only to caricature.

Insofar as there is involved a conflict of two contrasted cultures, that is for America just as much an internal as it is an outwardly geographical problem. Here in America metaphysics and religion—the latter already sentimentalized—are fighting an apparently losing battle with scientific materialism and the concepts of economic and psychological determinism; art is no longer valued as a means to "good use" and for its significance, but only as a means to aesthetic experience, i.e. for its effects upon our sensations.

At the same time it is almost universally felt that Western civilization has disappointed the high hopes that were entertained for it in the nineteenth century; it has given men neither peace nor security, and even here the question can be asked, whether we have not missed our way and ought not, in some sense, to retrace our steps. It is precisely at this point that the problem of Oriental "influence" acquires its great significance. It cannot, however, be altogether dissociated from the problem of Western influence upon the East, although this is one with which the present volume is not directly concerned. For whether we think either of these two influences desirable will depend upon our stand in the conflict of spiritual with material values within the limits of our own world. The "Orient," in the present discussion, can only mean the traditional Orient, and not the Westernized East, since we cannot suppose an influence exerted by an effect upon its cause: and there can be no question upon which side the traditional Orient stands. Whatever influence it may exert can be only on the side of the spiritual values; and it is for this reason that it is to be welcomed, not as a proselytizing power, but as an ally, as an "extrinsic and probable proof" and reminder of many things that are already ours but that have been forgotten. Nothing is more usual than for an Oriental to say to a European that there is little or nothing in his culture or sacred books that the latter does not already possess, if he would but remember it; for example, as René Guénon justly remarks, "Hindus may be sometimes seen encouraging Europeans to return to Catholicism, and even helping them to understand it, without being in the least drawn to it on their own account." [10] Only those for whom "spiritual" values are merely "superstitions" to be outgrown as soon as possible will be afraid of or wish to resist an Oriental influence, or to rise up in "defence of the West." For this influence, insofar as it may be deliberately exerted, will never be exerted with a view to persuading Europeans to adopt forms that were not made for them and for which they are not constitutionally adapted: it is generally the European who wants to practise Yoga, and the Oriental who seeks to dissuade him, reminding him that he has contemplative disciplines of his own.

We spoke of a "reminding" deliberately, because it has been always the function of the traditional arts, at the same time that they give us pleasure or supply a physical need, to serve as reminders of the invisible prototypes of which they are "imitations" and in which they "participate." Whoever attempts to understand Eastern art (the same holds good in the case of "primitive" and medieval art) will find that he cannot do so without an understanding of its themes, and that no real judgment of its qualities is possible on the basis of the aesthetic surfaces alone; we cannot know if a thing has been well said until we know what it was that was to be said. As soon as we begin to study Oriental drama, we find that we are involved in a mythology, or in other words in metaphysics; for as Aristotle very truly remarked, the mythologist is a philosopher, and as Plato also said, philosophy begins with wonder.

Our modern antipathy to religion, and our social reluctance to speak of God, are largely the result of what we called above the "sentimentalizing" of religion, and the general endeavor to make of the great religious heroes, notably the Christ and the Buddha, the sort of men we can approve of and also, by an elimination of the marvelous features in their "lives," the sort of men to whom we can attribute an historical reality, and in whom we can therefore "believe"; we are bewildered by the man who can say "I know that my Redeemer *liveth*," but is far from being convinced that he ever *lived*. We have lost the habit of those things that happened "once upon a time"—i.e. *in principio, id est in Filio*, and therefore now and always—and do not realize that the stories of the Solar Hero and the Bride, Prince Charming and Enchanted Princess, Psychopomp and Psyche, *must* end with the words "lived happily ever after"—i.e. eternally—and that nothing more is told of them just because the eternal life to which he awakens her by sword or kiss is actually uneventful and cannot be related in the terms of any narrative. It is just those myths and fairy-tales that we consider only from the angle of their literary value that provide the theses of the Oriental drama; while we have come to think of Epic and Romance, and even of Dante, to say nothing of the Bible, primarily as "literature" and only secondarily, if at all, as expositions of a "theory" essential to our felicity. It is, in fact, precisely our "aesthetic" that stands between us and a real understanding of Eastern art, at the same time that in more scholarly circles what is intended to be an objective application of historical methods becomes aloofness; which aesthetic and aloofness serve us as a mechanism of defense, "lest we should hear, and understand, and be converted." It has been said that "the prostitution of scientific truth may lead to world catastrophe" and that "responsibility for this problem in a peculiar sense lies within the domain of Oriental studies": [11] but it is a question whether much can be expected from the passionless reason of our objective scholarship, which concerns itself so much rather with what men have believed than with what should be believed.

If, then, we were to be seriously influenced by the Oriental theater, we should hardly expect to find the evidence of it in any recognizable imitation of its formulae (even though these might be of use in certain cases), but rather in a change of the dominant subject matter, a shifting from the depiction on the stage of our own all too human behaviorism, to a representation of myths. We should, in fact, be producing "Mystery Plays." But that could only be if we were as much interested in the "mystery" of the inner man as we are in "ourselves," the outer man. One might, of course, point to Wagner as the outstanding European example of a modern producer of "mysteries," and also, needless to say, to the Passion Play at Bayreuth. But these are isolated cases, and that of Wagner is more or less vitiated, partly by his own "artistic" personality, and still more by the manner in which the Ring is actually staged, not so much as a myth in which the audience believes or as a rite in which it participates as a spectacle to be enjoyed and applauded.[12] The only drama amongst ourselves that is really what drama means to those who as Hindus are present at a Rām or Krishna Līlā, or as Javanese witness a shadow play, or as Tibetans a so-called "devil-dance," is that of the Mass, performed in church, not as a spectacle, but as a sacrifice.

The problem of understanding the East, and that of enriching our own culture through the closer contacts that circumstances have made presently inevitable, is then as much one of our own inner life as it is of the external adaptation of what may seem at first to be new and strange ideas. On one side of us, although a side that has been more or less deliberately suppressed in the current world of an "impoverished reality" and that lives more by facts than by meanings, there is *no* barrier that separates East from West; there is *no* fundamental doctrine of the Philosophia Perennis that cannot as well be supported from Oriental as from Western sources. On the other side, that which is represented by "scientific humanism," with its denial of the reality of any knowledge not based on sensibility, and by the social values that take for granted the existence of castes of workers and fighters from whom no great measure of intelligence or culture can be expected, East and West are still at cross purposes. For the East, *"chaque occupation est un sacerdoce,"* [13] and livelihood is the accident of calling, while in the West it is far more his wages than his work that interests the workman.[14] In the East it is through devotion to one's natural calling (Plato's τὸ ἑαυτοῦ πράττειν, κατὰ φύσιν) that perfection is attainable; the West ignores that there are no degrees of perfection, and that an excellent carpenter must be more nearly perfect, *as* the Father in heaven is perfect, than an incompetent physician could ever be. It is proverbial that the Oriental craftsman loves his work: but the industrial workman loves his play; and there is an issue that can only be resolved on that level of reference where the distinction of work from play elapses.[15] The natural end of work is the production of utilities; and there is, perhaps, no field in which the East can better co-operate with the West than in that of the conflict with production for profit, of which the consequences are so degrading to the workman and so often injurious to the consumer.

Again, I refer to the Crusades: it may very well be that when we are able to look back upon the present century as we can now upon the history of Europe, we shall see in its ultimate cultural forms as many factors of Middle and Far Eastern origin as we can now recognize to have been of Islamic origin. What Arabian, and indirectly Persian culture was for the Middle Ages —of which Dante is the universal demonstration [16]—Indian and Chinese may become for us. If there is still a bridge to be built, Meister Eckhart and Jalālu'd Dīn Rūmī are its piers, already standing. Meister Eckhart, who spoke of Plato as "that great priest," and Jīlī, who saw him in a vision, "filling all space with light," are of one mind. The very possibility of an "influence," indeed, presupposes an already existing kinship; none could be exerted where no foothold could be found. Would it be easy for a European, if there had been no Plotinus, Dionysius, or Eckhart in his cultural background, to understand the *Upanishads?* or, had there been no "Companions," no "Fidèles de l'Amour" in the West, no Dante, easy for him to penetrate the Sūfīs, with their "What is love? Thou shalt know when thou becomest Me"? [17] Without some hidden affinity, could the English De Morgan and George Boole or the New England Transcendentalists have assimilated so much of the Vedanta? Or how could the sophisticated world of mid-nineteenth-century France have been moved by Indian mythology,[18] the visible quintessence of her wisdom?

The assimilation of Eastern ideas should be a slow, and for the majority an almost unconscious, process. It will imply at the center an agreement on principles; since it is only at that level that there can be a total agreement: but such an agreement will still permit of the greatest possible differences in application, which must always be appropriate to the constitution of those who live on principle. Thus the evidences of Asiatic influence may never be conspicuous, even if far reaching. We cannot avoid the conclusion that any real assimilation of Oriental art must have an ultimately religious basis; or that while it may be taken for granted that an influence of some kind will be felt in any case, it must depend on something like a change of heart in ourselves whether the influence is for evil, or for good. The Christian West is the natural heir of the view of art implicit and explicit in the Greek Paideia, viz. that only those arts are acceptable and fine that serve the needs of the body and the soul at one and the same time. Thus the East and the Classical and Medieval West are at one in holding that we cannot give the name of art to anything irrational, or consent to judgments of art based on likes or dislikes. It is to a renewal of this agreement that the influence of Oriental art, and especially that important part of it that has to do most obviously with showmanship, may lead, if only in connection with all showmanship we ask ourselves, with Plato, "Of *what* is the artist such a skilful exhibitor?" [19] That is the question.

*Pearl S. Buck*

# CONCLUSION:
# EAST AND WEST

IT HAS long been a fashion to say that the East is "spiritual" and the West "material," but, like many common things that are heedlessly spoken, it is not true. This particular saying is not always heedlessly spoken, either. It is repeated by the frustrated on both sides of the world. Those Westerners who have not had what they wanted out of life have taken refuge in thinking themselves too sensitive for their environment, too fine for the appreciation which they would like and do not get, and they have declared their environment too crass and their neighbors too coarse to understand their delicate qualities. It is natural that these should think wistfully of the East which they do not know but which they have heard is less material-minded than the West.

But there are frustrated souls in the East, also, who out of a sort of inverted pride and a certain jealousy of the extreme material prosperity of the West, have declared that such prosperity was beneath the peoples of the East, who think more of their souls than of their bodies. Out of a secret conviction of inferiority one will hear some men from the East then cry out against that materialism of the West and proclaim their own spiritual superiority.

All of this is nonsense. The East is neither more nor less spiritual than the West, and the West is neither more nor less materialistic than the East. Indians and Chinese love their comforts and their food and their wealth as well as any American does and will do as much to get them. I do not find, East and West, any difference in this sort of thing.

231

Extremes of wealth and poverty are more vast in India, and probably in China, than they are in the United States or in England today. The people of India take their religion hard, as most oppressed peoples do, but China takes religion very lightly indeed, and, by and large, the Chinese are a practical and materialistic people, with a shrewdness which often makes them disliked in other Eastern countries. I do not doubt that even in India the people will pursue religion far less heartily when their bodies are better fed and industries provide jobs as well as labor aids.

This may be said of all men alike—they prefer to have food rather than to starve, to have shelter rather than to be homeless, to be healthy rather than diseased, to live long rather than short lives, to be happy rather than sorrowful. Given the choice between a comfortable life on earth and a possible heaven afterwards, people, East and West, will choose a good life on earth.

Then where did this myth about the spiritual East and the material West come from? It has its roots in a sort of truth, and this truth can be simply stated. The East, generally speaking, will not sell all it has for more of anything. People over there like to enjoy life. They will not work so hard that they have no time for simple pleasure in living, in eating, in sleeping, in playing with their children, and in talking with their wives and familes. They will not take on two jobs if they can pay their bills with one, for two jobs eat up their time and distract their minds. They do not want to think constantly about work. They enjoy work less than other things. This is not to say they are lazy. They are not in the least lazy. They put an enormous amount of energy into their skills and pastimes. But to work merely to earn more money than they need is to them not sensible. They are ambitious, but not most of all for money, because all that they want cannot be bought with money. Peace cannot be bought with money, and fun cannot be bought with money, nor laughter, nor time to smoke and drink tea, nor time to make flower gardens and write poetry, or to walk on the hills carrying a bird cage, or to play with children.

In the West money does seem necessary for what people want. A car, two cars, a house, two houses—one in the city, one in the country—gadgets, labor-saving machinery, fine furniture, all these things are desirable but expensive, and so money is the first requisite. Men spend their lives in making money to buy things.

Competition, too, is keen in the West and not very keen in the East. To have more cars, more houses, better houses, finer furniture, more expensively dressed wives and daughters than one's neighbor has, these are desirable in the West and again money is needed. But the average man of the East would reason that he cannot ride in more than one car or live in more than one house at a time, nor sleep in more than one bed, and he does not want other men or women envying his wife and daughters, nor does he want to envy others theirs, so why does he need so much money?

It is not that one man is more spiritual than the other, or more material. It is simply that the values in East and West are different. The man in the East wants more out of life itself than the man in the West does. He wants plenty of peace and pleasure for himself, and he will not work more than enough to get him as much peace and pleasure as he wants. If anything, the East is more materialistic than the West. The East, being so old, knows how short life is. Man's years pass so quickly, and the time for keenness of the senses is over so soon. Therefore enjoyment of life cannot be put off, for in old age the senses are dulled, and man can enjoy but a little. He can eat only a little food and drink only a little wine and the day is over for passion. To waste one's youth, therefore, in making money would to the man of the East seem the sheerest folly.

But one cannot live among the people of the East without feeling something more than this, too. Again this something is not spiritual, in the sense of being other-worldly. It is, rather, intensely human. There is in all the old countries of the East, so much older and more crowded than other parts of the world, an extraordinarily delicate consideration of the human individual. Can this be true, one may ask, when one sees the suffering of beggars and of the diseased and poverty-stricken? Even so, there is consideration beyond anything we of the West know. I mean that there is a deep sense of the importance of psychological understanding between persons and peoples. The real materialism of the West lies in its ignorance of the importance of such psychological understanding. The average citizen of a western country is apt to scoff at anything so intangible as human relations. The feelings, the state of mind, the personal peculiarities of an individual are dealt with impatiently if at all. The result is an amount of personal frustration and unhappiness which is really astounding, in view of the material comforts and aids of our civilization.

"Man cannot live by bread alone," is a saying of the Orient which we of the West have never believed or understood. We have shallowly interpreted it as meaning that we need religion as well as factories, but that is not what it means. The people of the East know it means that a man is not necessarily happy because he has bread to eat and possessions enough. They know it means that he has certain needs of the heart and the mind that must be satisfied, too. He needs appreciation and understanding and tolerance and patience. He has a psychic life as well as a physical one.

The peoples in crowded old countries of the East have lived so closely together that they know the happiness of all depends upon the happiness of the individual, and individuals can only be happy when they are allowed personal freedom to be themselves, inside the security of the close human unit of family and community, and therefore each individual must be dealt with by others as an individual. Grandfather has grandfather's needs. He is old and talkative and somebody must listen to him talk and answer him and make him feel welcome and respected. And little grandson is small and does not know how to behave yet and so too much must not be expected of him and he must be allowed to have enough of his own way to keep him happy, and yet not so much that he is a nuisance to other people, and he must be taught, without frustrating him too much, that he must consider the needs of others and not only himself.

All this is done not from a religious or spiritual motive, but from plain common sense. Everybody is happier if all are happy, and the end of life is to be as happy as one can be. It is practical to make others happy, for the sake of one's own happiness, not because God wants us to do so.

The emphasis on human happiness is, I believe, the greatest gift which the East has to give the West. The free peoples of the East are certainly the happiest in the world, even as the slave peoples there are the saddest in the world. For the people of India have the same conviction about happiness as the people of China—

they also would like to be happy, but none can be happy without freedom.

But human happiness is not only dependent on human freedom —it is dependent, too, on knowing how to enjoy life and the simple gifts of life, on good family life and pleasant community fellowship, on all the human relationships, first of all. To understand human relationships and to know what is required in each is the beginning of happiness in the nation, the peoples of the East believe.

The Chinese early defined the human relationships and the duties required. These requirements emphasized psychological understanding rather than material support. The material support was to be only so much as was necessary to remove fear and suffering from the mind.

We of the West need to have happiness restored to us, not through a new spiritual rebirth, in the sense of a new religion, but through a plain and simple return to what makes people really happy. The East is right about it—what makes a human being happy is to feel himself wanted and understood and appreciated. The fabulous courtesy of the East is not a ritual, but simply oil to grease the machinery of human relationships.

And the people of the East need from us the physical aids which will make them still more happy—science to heal diseased bodies and to remove a crushing labor and to provide more food.

There is nothing incomprehensible in the East or in the West. We are like men digging a tunnel through a mountain. We have begun at opposite ends but the goal is the same—human happiness. We ought to meet somewhere one of these days, and find that each faces the other's light.

# APPENDICES

## FACTS AND CURIOSA OF THE EAST-INDIA TRADE

*Collected by Arthur E. Christy*

Some readers might have turned to this book for "new light" on the history of the Indies trade. Much research remains to be done and numerous books must be written before the history of that trade is fully known. Furthermore, the intent of this book is not to explore commercial and economic relations. What follows represents, therefore, merely a very modest contribution to the primary materials available in print, a suggestion of the varied documents which are still to be explored by historians, and an effort to capture if only briefly the lure of the East-India trade.

The samples of documents in various collections of East-India trade records which follow have been quarried from libraries and archives in Europe and America. To give the historical background of each document, or to discuss its significance, would expand an appendix into another book. The reader is therefore requested to judge each document in the light of its inherent worth, mindful that no isolated item can ever represent the whole truth regarding great social issues or the various stages in the long history of Oriental-Occidental relations. Finally, it is hoped that the facts and curiosa which follow will both entertain the reader and suggest to researchers many engaging problems as yet unexplored.

*Appendix A* contains samples of broadsides preserved at the Bodleian Library, Oxford, which reveal the disruption of English industry by the importations of the East India Company (founded by Queen Elizabeth in 1600), preceding the passage in 1700 of the first Act of Parliament to restrict the trade and to protect home industries. The broadsides are for the most part dated about 1699 and represent the climax of the protests of various guilds. The problems of cheap labor and economic competition from the Orient continue into our own day. In the light of these broadsides, one can readily understand why an Englishman of the eighteenth century wrote of Indian cotton goods as that "tawdry, piesotted, flabby, low priced thing called Callicoe . . . made by a parcel of Heathens and Pagans that worship the devil and work for a half-penny a day."

*Appendix B* contains transcripts of documents which reveal the rivalry of English and American merchants, after the latter formally entered direct trade with Canton and other ports of the Indies in 1784. It is not to be assumed, however, that in the seventeenth and eighteenth centuries American colonists were not supplied with the spices, fabrics, and other commodities of the trade. In varying degrees the English East India Company met the demands. But the colonists also took matters into their own hands. The logbook of the ship *Prudent,* which made a voyage to Colombo in 1806, now in the large collection at the Essex Institute, Salem, Massachusetts, contains the following stanza:

> Yankee doodle had a Wife,
> She was hard of hearing;
> He put a Swivle on her Back and
> Sent her a Privateering.

Much research remains to be done on this phase of American Colonial history. The documents presented in this section are from the records of the English East India Company, preserved in London, and deal chiefly with the rivalries and the smuggling of the early national decades. They record the observations and fears of English traders and consuls in various parts of the world to which American ships had penetrated.

*Appendix C* contains samples of the unpublished records of the American-China trade during the so-called Clipper Ship era. Selected not only to illustrate the conduct and profits of the trade itself and the speculative "adventures" of very small investors, they also offer a list of the commodities and reveal the volume of trade handled by a large Boston company during a typical year. The relations between American captains and supercargoes, and the Hong merchants of Canton and their associates, are also suggested. No fact stands out more clearly in the logbooks and journals kept by the American traders than their dependence on the good will and honesty of the Chinese merchants appointed by the Emperor to the Cohong, through which all foreigners were required to transact the major part of their business. The need and expediency of securing the services of the best available merchant were great. Since silks, porcelains, and teas were the articles in greatest demand, orders were usually manufactured or packed while the ships awaited their cargoes. The trustworthiness of the Chinese contractors and security merchants could almost determine the success or failure of a voyage. It is consequently not surprising to find in many a journal frank commentary on the character of the merchant with whom the American trader had dealings. Houqua, for many years the head of the Hong, was frequently described as "very rich" and "just in all his doings, in short a man of honour and veracity," who had more business than any other of the eleven members of the Cohong. Youqua, some recorded, generally "sends good cargoes" but was "pushed for money at times." Consequa was reputed to be "rich—roguish—ingratiating—polite," a man who sends "some excellent cargoes—some bad cargoes," but who in general was "not attentive enough to business and a man with whom you cannot talk with safety, as he will promise everything & perform what he pleases." Nevertheless few men had greater influence than the Chinese members of the Cohong in laying the foundations of good will between two great peoples of the East and West in the beginnings of their intercourse.

*Appendix D* reveals both the romantic adventures and the sufferings of American seamen. The cruelties of the Barbary pirates which led to war are illustrated. Less well-known is the fact that more than half a century before Commodore Perry opened Japan to American commerce, Yankee captains had sailed into Nagasaki and traded with the Japanese. Captain James Devereux of Salem, Massachusetts, sailed his ship, the *Franklin*, to Japan in 1799 and thus deserves an honored place as the first individual in the maritime history of his country to take an American crew into a Japanese harbor. The second ship was the *Margaret*, famous in its day and belonging to the great Derby interests of Salem, which visited Japan in 1801. The conditions were unique and are a part of the history of European empires overseas. The Dutch, having supplanted the Portuguese in Japan, were permitted at infrequent intervals to send one ship from Batavia to Nagasaki. On occasions when Dutch ships were not available, those of foreign nationals were chartered and sailed under their own crews, but with a Dutch supercargo to represent the Dutch East India Company. It was under these conditions that the first two American ships to visit Japan were engaged. The documents taken from the records of these voyages show the restrictions and formalities imposed by the Japanese, and also the impressions of a first-hand observer.

The reader is reminded that a number of the documents are the work of amanuenses who transcribed the originals for company records. This fact may explain infelicitous or awkward constructions in language. In others, the un-

familiar diction which appears represents the contemporary patois and ter-
minology of the East-India trade, or of generally uneducated seamen whose
use of place names does not conform with that of modern geographies.

The editor herewith expresses his general thanks to the officers of the
indicated institutions, from which various documents have been borrowed,
for the many courtesies extended to him.

# APPENDIX A

## BROADSIDES ON THE EAST-INDIA TRADE AND THE RESTRAINING BILL BEFORE PARLIAMENT

From the Bodleian Library Collection, Oxford University,
Folio 0658.

### I

### PRINCE BUTLER'S TALE

*Representing*
The State of the Wooll-Case, or the East India
Case Truly Stated

When first the Indian Trade began
    And Ships beyond the Tropicks ran,
    In quest of various Drugs and Spices
    And sundry other strange Devices,
Saltpetre, Drugs, Spice and like Trading,
Composed the bulk of all their Lading.
Bengals, and Silks, of Indians making,
Our Merchants then refus'd to take in,
Knowing it wou'd their Country ruin,
And might prove to their own undoing.
Nor did they carry Gold or Bullion,
To fetch home what Supplants our Woollen;
Nor were this Nation fond to wear
Such Indian Toys, which cost so dear:
Then were we clad in Woollen Stuffs,
With Cambrick Bands, and Lawn Ruffs,
Or else in Silk, which was Imported
For Woollen Goods, which we Exported;
Which Silk our English Weavers bought,
And into various figures wrought.
Then scarce a Child was to be seen,
Without *Say* Frock, that was of green,
Our Hangings, Beds, our Coats, and Gowns,
Made of our Wooll in Clothing Towns.
This Nation then was rich and Wealthy,
And in a State which we call'd healthy.

But since the men of Gath arose,

238

And for their chief Goliath chose,
And since that mighty Giants Reign,
Whose chiefest *Aim* was private Gain,
This Trade was drove on by such measures,
As soon exhausted much our Treasures.
For then our chiefest Artists went
With Patterns, and with Money sent,
To make and purchase Indian Ware

For which this nation pays full dear.
Then by great Gifts of *finest* touches,
The Lords and Ladies, Dukes and Duchess,
So far prevailed, as set the Fashion,
Which Plague-like soon spread o'er the Nation.
Our Ladies all were set a gadding,
After these Toys they ran a madding;
And nothing then wou'd please their fancies,
Nor Dolls, nor Joans, nor wanton Nancies,
Unless it was of Indians making;
And if 'twas so, 'twas wondrous taking.
This Antick humour so prevail'd,
Tho' many 'gainst it greatly rail'd,
'Mongst all degrees of Female kind,
That nothing else could please their mind.
Tell 'em the following of such fashion,
Wou'd beggar and undo the Nation,
And ruin all our Labouring Poor,
That Must, or starve, or beg at door,
They'd not at all regard your story,
But in their *painted* Garments glory;
And such as were not Indian proof,
They scorn'd, despis'd, as paltry Stuff:
And like gay Peacocks, proudly strut it,
When in our Streets along they foot it.
This humour strangely thus prevailing,
Set all the poorer sort a railing.
Or else with grief their Case bewailing.
The *richer* seeing what was doing,
And how the Nation ran to ruin,
To King in Council did complain,
In time of Charles the Second's Reign.


II

THE CASE OF THE JOYNERS COMPANY,

*Against*
*The Importation of Manufactured* CABINET-WORK
*from the* EAST-INDIES

*WHEREAS* great Numbers of Artificers, Members of the said Company,
have been bred up in the said Art or Mystery of making Cabinets, Scrutores,
Tables, Chests, and all other sorts of CABINET-WORK in *England*, in which
of late Years they have arrived to so great a Perfection, as exceeds all *Europe*.
BUT several Merchants, and others, Trading to the *East-Indies*, and to
several Ports and Places thereabouts, have procured to be made in *London*,
of late Years, and sent over to the *East-Indies*, Patterns and Models of all

239

sorts of Cabinet Goods; and have Yearly return'd from thence such great Quantities of Cabinet-Wares, Manufactured there, after the *English* Fashion, by our Models, that the said Trade in *England* is in great Danger of being utterly Ruined, being ingross'd by the said Merchants, and others, that Trade to and from those Parts, to so great a Degree, that they not only supply these Kingdoms with such Commodities, so Imported, but also spoil the EX-PORTATION of the said *Joyners* and *Cabinet-Makers* Work to Foreign Parts, so that their Journey-men and Apprentices, in a manner, will be useless; which, if not timely prevented, will Reduce the said *Joyners, Cabinet-Makers,* and Thousands of other Poor Artificers depending on them, as the *Carvers, Turners, Copper-Smiths, Glew-makers, Sawyers,* &c. to a deplorable Condition, who must perish for want of Work, or be maintain'd by their several Parishes.

AND in lieu of abundance of Foreign Commodities, which the said *Joyners* and *Cabinet-Makers* are obliged to use in their Trade, fhe *English* Woollen Manufactures were Exported, so that the Kingdom in general were Gainers thereby.

AND the Youth of this Nation, that now are, and daily come to Handy-craft Trades, will be under the like Misfortune, if, when their Trades are brought to Perfection, their Models are carried to *India*, and Manufactured there.

THE following Goods, Manufactured in *India*, have been Imported within these Four Years, *viz.* Two Hundred forty four Cabinets, Six Thousand five hundred eighty two Tea-Tables, four hundred twenty eight Chests, Seventy Trunks, Fifty two Screens, Five hundred eighty nine Looking-Glass Frames, Six hundred fifty five Tops for Stands, Eight hundred eighteen Lacquer'd Boards, Five hundred ninety seven Sconces, and Four thousand one hundred twenty Dressing, Comb, and Powder Boxes.

Besides several Sales lately made, in which were great Quantities of the said CABINET-WORK; as also in other Sales daily expected.

*Wherefore 'tis hoped the Wisdom of this Honourable House will interpose for the Relief of these poor Artificers,* &c.


III

THE CASE OF THE FANN-MAKERS;

*Who have Petitioned the* Honorable House *of* Commons, *against the Importation of* Fanns *from the* East-Indies

THE Petitioners are several Tradesmen, and Artificers, who are concerned in the Manufacture of Fanns, in which great Numbers of Men, Women and Children, used to be constantly Employed, some in making the Sticks, Papers, Leathers, and in Ordering and Stiffning of the Silks, others in Painting, Varnishing, and Japanning, and in preparing other Materials wherewith Fanns are made, by which there used to be Yearly consumed great Quantities of Silk, Paper, Leather, Wyer, and several Tunns of Whale-bone, Tortoise-shell, Ivory, Box, Ebony, and other sorts of Wood, which were Imported from *Turky, Russia,* and other Foreign Parts, to the Increase of His Majesty's Customs, and to the great Benefit and Advantage of our Woollen Manufacture, for which such Foreign Goods were bought in Exchange; so that by the making of Fanns here at home, not only the Woollen Manufacture, and the King's Customs are greatly advanced, but abundance of Poor People are continually kept at Work. All which Advantages to the Common-wealth are now likely to be destroy'd, by the Importation of vast Quantities of Fanns from the *East-Indies,* from whence there have been lately brought over above a 130000, tho' scarce half that Quantity hath been Entred in the

*Custom-house,* the rest having been Fraudulently conveyed on Shoar by the Seamen and others, without paying any Duty; and as for the Duty which is paid, 'tis but inconsiderable, in comparison of the Duty which arises from the Commodities Imported from *Turky, Russia,* and other Foreign Parts, which are consumed here about the Fanns; and besides formerly great Quantities of our own Fanns have been Exported, for which a considerable Duty used to be paid to the King; so that 'tis hoped that this Honourable House will think fit to Prohibit the Importation of *Indian* Fanns, and Fan-sticks, as well as Silks and Callicoes; for that thereby, not only the Woollen Manufacture, and His Majesty's Customs are considerably Lessen'd and Impair'd; but also Multitudes of Poor Artificers and their Families will be reduced to a Deplorable Condition. And many of them for want of Work are already become a Burthen to the several Parishes where they Inhabit.

## IV

The Case is since Re-printed, and Sold by A. Baldwin in War-wick-Lane, London.

# A Short Abstract of a Case which was last Sessions presented to the Parliament: Being a true Relation of the Rise and Progress of the East-India Company, shewing how their Manufactures have been, are, and will be prejudicial to the Manufactures of England, and what endeavours have been used for and against any Restrictions. Together with some Remarks and Query's thereon.

THat for several Years after the *East-India* Company was Establish'd, they were afraid to bring in Manufactur'd Goods, which they knew were very prejudicial to our own: But now, by their great Stock and Interest, they are got over these Fears, and bring in vast quantities, opposing all kind of Restraint, tho they are convinc'd, and have declared their Manufactures are prejudicial to this Kingdom.

That as their Manufactures increas'd, our own were discouraged, and *Wooll* reduced so low, that an *Act* was made for *Burying in Woollen,* and the Manufacturers at the same time reduced to great Necessities, and many ruined thereby.

That during great part of the late War, the *East India* Trade was under some Discouragement, and while it was so, our *English* Manufactures flourished very much, and extended to several Places, where, before the People were out of Employment, *Wooll advanced*, and bore a good Price, and all other Provisions raised proportionably.

That the *English Manufacturers* finding the *East-India* Traders endeavouring to get an Establishment by *Act* of Parliament, and knowing how fatal it might prove to their Manufactures, unless they were in some measure restrain'd, made their Application to the Parliament, and in Two succeeding Sessions a Restraining Bill was past in their Favour in the House of Commons, and a Third being drawn up in a different Method to the Two former, was stopt thereupon.

That the Proposal of advancing *Two Millions* for the Supply of the Government, was the great Inducement for the Establishment of the *New Company;* And the Reasons the Manufacturers did not then so vigorously complain and sollicite against the Establishment, as formerly they had done, proceeded from the Fair Promises given by the *New East-India Men*, and the Hope of a more favourable Opportunity; being unwilling to disturb the Loan, so necessary then to be raised.

That the Manufacturers being deceived by these *East India* Traders Fair Promises, and finding that the late great Importation and Wear of their *Indian* Manufactures are increasing, and have already, in a great measure, ruin'd the *Canterbury* Trade, and obliged the *London* Weavers to fall upon all sorts of Woollen Manufactures, to the Prejudice (and may in a short time prove to the utter Ruine) of several Places where such Manufactures have for a long time been *established*, are therefore come again to represent their *Deplorable Case*, and Pray the Consideration of this *Parliament*, and hope they will be pleased to consider it as well as either the *Old* or *New East-India* Companies Cases.

### *Remarks.*

This appears by a Printed List, which is Sold by Edw. Loyd at his Coffee-House in Lumbard-street.

Since the Presenting the *Case* above mentioned, There has from the 20th of *May* 1699, to the 4th of *September* 1699, arrived in *England* from the *East-Indies* and *China*, Ten Ships, which have brought in above Five Hundred Thousand Pieces of Manufactured Goods, which are by very intelligent Persons computed to be worth about One *Million* of Pounds *Sterling*, which vast quantity has already reduced the *Manufactures* of this Kingdom (to which they are opposite) to a very low Price, which has in a great measure ruined the *Manufactures* in *London, Norwich*, and in divers other Places, as is ready more fully to be made appear.

Vide Loyd's List. Near 2 Millions sent to India.

That there is now gone to the *East Indies* and *China*, Fifty Ships, which are computed at near 400 Tuns *per* Ship, one with the other, and by a modest Computation are reckoned to have carried with them near *Two Millions* of Bullion, which is about Forty Thousand Pounds *per* Ship.

242

That all these Ships, or as great a number, are expected and may make a Return in Two Years' and their Cargo may reasonably be supposed and valued at *Six Million*, it being common to make about Treble the First Cost. And it is reasonable to suppose that *Five Millions* will be in Manufactures. And how far this may further dammage and ruine the Trade of this Kingdom, is submitted to consideration.

## Two Queries.

If the increase of the *Woollen Manufactures* in *Ireland* was judged Prejudicial, and would *inevitably* sink the value of the *Lands* in *England* and *Ruin* our Trade; because the *Irish* could under-work, and so under-sell us, as the *Act* for restraining that Trade sets forth. Will not the *East-India Manufactures* do the same, and deserve the Consideration of the Parliament, as well as the *Irish?*

Whether the great Complaints made in *Flanders,* and other Foreign Parts of the decay of their Linnen Manufactures; and their setting up Woollen Manufactures do not (as the *Author* of the *Essay on Ways and Means* tell us) proceed from the expence of *East-India* Linnens, which are here worn in their stead; and whether their late Prohibition of our Woollen Manufactures, do not proceed more from that Cause, than from the late *Act* made for the more effectual restraining the Importation of *Flanders* Lace?

## V

### Reasons Humbly Offered

### To the Consideration of the Lords Spiritual and Temporal, On Behalf of the BILL to Restrain the Wearing of East-India and Persia Wrought Silks, &c.

THAT the Advocates for the *East-India* Company rather blind and amuse the Matter controverted, than explain it; for the Dispute is not with or against the Trade in general, but that Branch only which is certainly destructive to *England* in the Value of its Land, Productions, Manufactories, Navigations, Land-carriages, and to the extream dispeopling thereof. All which we have and can make good.

*England's* own Productions, is the Foundation of all its Wealth, Navigation and Merchandize; and the due Improvement thereof, especially in the Wooll, is what ought to be principally regarded and promoted, and the Packs in the Honourable House of Lords bespeak no less.

That *England* had never recovered the Mischiefs former great Importations of *India* wrought Silks brought upon us, had we not been beholden to the Invention of Worsted Crapes, which for several Years was a universal Fashion, and cut out the *East-India* Goods and recovered the Trade for Wooll, when many Growers thereof at that first Invention, having Six, Eight, some Ten Years Wooll before hand; and it did likewise greatly increase the Trade in Number, that now want Employment both at *London* and other Parts.

That English Wooll being first Improved by Manufactory in several

Counties and Towns, and afterwards by Navigation and Merchandize to *Spain* and *Italy*, brings home unwrought Silks and Spanish Wooll, for the Employment both of Silk Weavers and Clothiers; which Spanish Wooll is again, with our own, Manufactured and Exported to *Turky* and other Parts, and the principal products thereof are raw Silk, and Grograin and Cotten Yarn, Unmanufactured; which again Employes Multitudes of People, that, as well as the former, live and consume the Productions of our own Lands.

That the passing this Bill into a Law, will in a few Years greatly increase our numbers of People in this Kingdom, and will so invigorate the Minds of all Fabricators both in Silk, Wooll, and Grograin Yarn, that have any thing of Stock or Credit by Faith and Hope, to contend with all other Disadvantages, tho' Mony should be as scarce as at present; whereas the contrary will discourage (those of great Ability) to that degree, that the Out-Parishes of *London*, *Tower-Hamblets*, and all the Wooll Manufacturing Towns in *England*, will not be able to support their Poor.

That *East-India* wrought Silks, &c. is Destructive to all the before mentioned Advantages, to the Dispeopling of the Kingdom.

That nothing is so great and unnatural a force upon Trade, as sending our Woollen Manufactures to *East-India*, in regard they are not worn there, but sent to *Persia;* to the extream prejudice of our *Turky* Merchants and that Trade. So that the Consumption of Woollen Manufactories is not increased thereby.

That the more wrought Silks comes from *East-India*, the less raw Silk doth come both from *India* and *Turky;* and nothing is so valuable an Exchange for our Gold and Silver as raw Silk.

That the passing this Bill will give the *East-India* Trade either to the Scotch or Dutch, is so Frivolous as deserves no Answer, for it must produce the quite contrary Effect.

That our Entertainment of so many thousand Strangers argues a necessity for passing the Bill, unless we intend to maintain them without Working, or Starve them.

That whatever Reasons induced the French King to part with his Weaving Subjects, 'tis plain, that whilst he had them, he took great Care for their Preservation; for by his *Edict* 26th of *October* 1686. He not only Prohibited the Wearing all sorts of *East-India* Silks and Callicoes; but likewise under a severe Mulct, forbid the Imitation of figured and flowered Silks, by Printing or Staining any thing in likeness thereof, and under the same Penalty commanded all them Prints and Tools for so doing, to be utterly demolished, and never to be made again. By which tis plain that King had another Opinion of this Trade and People, then the *East-India* Doctor, that in his Superfine Spun Linse-woollse Discourse would render it otherwise to us.

That part of the Act for Navigation looks strangely Unreasonable if this Bill deserves not to Pass, when for the sake and profit only of Throwing and Dying of Silk, 'tis prohibited so to be brought both from *East-India* and several other Parts, for the Weaving part thereof is at least four times the Value to *England* than both Dying and Throwing is.

That Manufacturing of Silk is as Reasonable and as Natural, and no more Foreign to *England* than to *France, Holland* or *Flanders*, tho' of later attainment; and it being so greatly benefiical (as it certainly is) deserves and requires to be the more tenderly Cherisht and Supported.

That at the price Provisions sell in *England*, 'tis impossible for English Manufacturers, either Clothiers, Silk Weavers or Silk Throwsters, to work Cheaper than they do.

That 'tis the Interest of all Fabricators, to Work and Sell as Cheap as they can Afford, and Trade will in that Case certainly adjust it self, and they that do not will Suffer for it: But we believe not, that our Noble Ancestors plac'd the Wooll-packs just under the Throne, to make Wooll as little worth as it possibly could.

That neither *Italian, French,* or *Dutch* Silks can prejudice us in our

PLATE 21    Early European Impressions of Oriental Acrobats and Freaks. *From Joan Nieuhoff*, Die Gesandtschaft der Ost-Indischen Geselschaft . . . an den Tartarischen Cham und nunmehr auch Sinischen Keyser, *Amsterdam, 1669.*

PLATE 22  Flemish Lace Showing Influence of the East-India Trade, c. 1700. By permission of the Victoria and Albert Museum Collection.

PLATE 23   Polychrome Delft Tiles, Manufactured c. 1700. *By permission of the Rijks Museum, Amsterdam, Holland.*

PLATE 24    The Island of Deshima in Nagasaki Harbor, Japan, to which European traders were restricted. *From a print in the Peabody Museum, Salem, Massachusetts.* See page 237.

PLATE 25    Altar mural in Church of the Ascension, New York, by John La Farge, with background sketched in Japan. *See page 44.*

Trades, so much as *India* Silks will and does, we Working upon more equal Terms with them.

That Passing this Bill may occasion the *East-India* Company to Import the more *China* and *Bengal* raw Silks and Cotten Yarn, to the greater Employment of Shipping and our Manufacturers, which the other will destroy.

That the Great Mogul will be no more displeased at this, than the Great Turk was, when those Merchants left bringing over *Turky* Manufactured Silk, Hair Grograins and Tammies (which in our Memory were the general Wear of our Grandmothers and Mothers) and now instead thereof import us only raw Silk Grograin and Cotten Yarn to *Englands* great Advantage.

That what is commonly called *East-India* Silk, the principal Substance with which it is made, is their fine Cotton-Yarn, of which sort of Yarn the Company never brought much, if any unwrought; and it being softer in feeling than our English Worsted, better gratifies the Fancies of our nice Females. And except in that respect, our Grazetts and Autherines are as good a wear as they, if made to the Value. And these *India* Silks, are by the Draper or Mercer, sold as dear, or dearer than English Silks or Stuffs.

That skilful Seamen are made by our *Newcastle* and Coasting Trade, in such small Vessels as are continually plying, to serve our numerous Manufacturers with Coals, Corn, Butter and Cheese and other Necessaries, whilst Trading to *India,* consumes them more than in an ordinary manner; and if it be for the sake of their bringing wrought Silks, they'll dye in a bad Cause; for in respect to Navigation, raw Silk from *Turkey,* is five times more bulky than wrought from *India.*

That if for the gain of the *East-India* Company, our Manufactures must be destroyed, or work at their Prices, that have all the necessaries for Life, six times as cheap as *England* can afford, and want neither Cloaths nor Fuel; the value of Land, and all its productions and Rents, must sink answerably thereto.

That we cannot believe, that good Policy for *England* which is for *Holland,* they living in a small spot of Ground, are obliged in reason to leave Trade more free, and lay their Taxes on the Consumers only: But we that are blest with a large Tract of fruitful Land, rich Mines, productive and laborious Cattle, convenient Ports and Navigable Rivers, must with the Manufacturing our own Productions improve our Land, by feeding our People, support our Trade, Traffick, Navigation and Land-Carriage, and by all Lawful ways encrease our People; and if for the sake of any one of these, the others are prejudiced, the Publick must suffer Diminution thereby; but if in Conjunction all are Advanced, this, and this only, will procure a healthful Constitution in the Body Politick; and when the other parts of the World can agree on a free Trade, it will be time for us to consider; and till then, make the best Improvement of the Blessings of Almighty God.

That the Sentiments of that great Member of the *East-India* Company, Sir *Josiah Child,* may judge betwixt us in the 43d Page of his Discourse concerning Trade, says, That whatsoever advances the value of Land in purchase,

That improves the Rent of Farmes,

That encreaseth the bulk of Foreign Trade,

That multiplies Domestick Artificers,

That inclines the Nation to Thriftiness,

That employs the Poor,

That encreaseth the stock of the People, must be procuring causes of Riches.

We shall conclude with the undeniable Maxim, of the said Sir *Josiah,* which he lays down in his Preface to the said Book.

That a Foreign Expence, especially of Foreign Manufactures, is the worst Expence a Nation can be inclinable too, and ought to be prevented as much as possibly.

[The East-India Company's Rebuttal]

# FIVE QUERIES HUMBLY TENDER'D, RELATING TO THE BILL FOR PROHIBITING THE CONSUMPTION OF EAST-INDIA SILKS, BENGALS AND PRINTED CALLICOES.

I. Why Should *East-India* Silks and *Bengals* be Prohibited which to the Nation are Three Times as Cheap again as *Dutch, French* and *Italian* Silks.

II. Why *East-India* Silks, *Bengals* and Printed *Callicoes,* that Pay Twenty *per Cent.* Customs more than *Dutch* and *Italian* Silks, and Five times the Freight of *Dutch, French* and *Italian* Silks.

III. Why *Persia* Silks Purchased with *English* Cloth and Stuffs more than *Dutch, French* and *Italian* Silks bought with our Money.

IV. Why should Painted Callicoes from *India* be Prohibited, when We must in their Room Print *Dutch, French* or *German* Linnens, which will Cost the Nation Three Times the Price.

V. Why should we Enrich our Neighbours by Prohibiting *East-India* Silks and wearing of theirs, when at one time or other they may Employ the Costs of those Silks against Us.

## VII

[An Earlier French Decree Restricting the Trade]

# A DECREE OF THE KINGS COUNSEL OF STATE, CONCERNING COTTEN LINNEN-CLOTH, PRINTED IN EAST-INDIA, OR PAINTED IN THE KINGDOM; AND OTHER CHINA AND INDIA SILKS, STUFFS, AND FLOWER'D WITH GOLD AND SILVER.

## Given the 26th of October, 1686. Extracted out of the Register of the Council of State.

The King being informed, That the great quantity of Cotten Linnen-Cloth, printed in *East-India,* or painted in the Kingdom, and other *China* and *India* Silk, Stuffs, and Flower'd with Gold and Silver, have not only given occasion of Transporting out of the Kingdom many Millions, but also have diminished the Manufactures of old established in *France,* for the making of Silk, Woollen, Linnen and Hemp-Stuffs; and at the same time the Ruin and Destruction of the Working-People, who by want of Work, having no Occupation nor Subsistance for their Families, are gone out of the Kingdom. The which being needful to provide a Remedy for, and for that effect to hinder the Course and Sale in the Kingdom of the said painted Linnen-Cloth, and *India* and *China* Silks and Stuffs, nevertheless granting to the Owners a reasonable time that they may sell them; Having heard the Report of Monsieur *le Pelletier,* Counsellor Ordinary of the King's Royal Counsel, and Comptroller-General of the Finances; his Majesty in his Counsel hath ordered, and doth order, That from the beginning of the Day of the Publication of the present Declaration, all the Manufactures established in the

Kingdom for Painting of the White Cotten Linnen-Cloth shall be abolished, and the Moulds serving to the Printing of them shall be broke and destroy'd. His Majesty doth forbid, most expresly, the re-establishing thereof; also to his Subjects the Painting of the said Linnen-Cloth; and to the Engravers the making of any Moulds, serving to the said Impression, under the Penalty of losing the said Cloths, Moulds and other Utensils, and three thousand Livers Fine, personally paid and without diminution; one third part to the Informer, the second part to the Hospitals of the Place, and the third to the Farmers of the Revenue. And as concerning the painted Linnen-Cloth, and other *China* and *India* Silk, Stuffs, and Flower'd with Gold and Silver, his Majesty hath granted, and doth grant (to the last of *December* 1687, next) to the Merchants and others, the Permission of Selling them as they shall think fit: The said time being expired, his Majesty doth forbid to all Persons, of what Quality and Condition whatsoever they are, the Exposing and the Selling thereof; and to the Particulars the Buying thereof, doth order, That those found in all Ware-Houses and Shops shall be burnt, and the Proprietors condemned to the like Fine of three thousand Livers, paid as abovesaid. His Majesty doth permit, nevertheless, the Entry, Sale and Retail, of the said White Linnen Cloth in his Kingdom, paying by them the Taxes, according to the Declaration of the Counsel the 30th *April* last, which shall be executed; and that of the 15th of the present Month, to the last of *December*, 1687, next Year. His Majesty doth command to the Lieutenant of the Policy of the City of *Paris*, and to the Intendants and Commissaries of the Provinces and Generalties of the Kingdom, to cause the present Declaration to be executed, being published and affixed in all the Places where need shall be, that no Body should be ignorant thereof. Done in the King's State-Council held at *Fontainbleau*, the 26th Day of *October*, 1686.

Signed COQVILLE

# APPENDIX B

[Abstract of a Letter from the British Consul in New York to Lord Carmarthen of the East India Company. East Indian Office, London. *Home Miscellaneous Series*, Volume 337]

New York the 3d of April 1788

My Lord,

Inclosed is duplicate of the Letters I had the honor of writing to your Lordship by the Speedy on the 5th of March; since which, no Packet hath arrived from England, nor hath any Occurrence taken place in this Country, worthy your Lordship's particular Notice or Attention. The States which have not yet in Convention deliberated upon the proposed New Constitution, continue in great party heats; and those which have, by small majorities, ratified the same, have violent minorities raging against it, which leave it a matter still of doubt, whether ever the said Constitution will take place to any purpose, if at all, in this distracted Country.

Observing the Number of Ships and Vessells that have made Voyages from these States to India, and the many more that are preparing to Import Tea & other Articles from the East, I lately desired a Gentleman in whom I place much Confidence, to take a suitable opportunity of asking a principal Merchant in this City, who is largely concerned in India Voyages, Whether he was not apprehensive that the Markets of this Country would be overdone with Tea & other Articles from India? The Answer was, "By no means" for, "Whatever we import from India more than is Wanted here, we can readily dispose of in England and Ireland"! "I sent (said this Merchant) 250 Chests of Tea to England last October, and they sold very well"! Of this being *a fact* I now have no doubt, though I was much surprized at hearing of it; If thus, the Vending of Tea and other Articles of India, brought from thence in American bottoms, be, as I shd. think it must be, detrimental to our India Company, to the Navigation, and to the general Commerce of the Nation, it would not, I apprehend, be difficult to prevent such Importations from this Country; but however that may be, I think it my duty to lay this Annecdote before your Lordship. . . .

Your Lordship's most faithful,
and obedient Servant.
J. TEMPLE

II

[Copy of a Letter from John Ross, a British Merchant at Gibraltar, to an Official of the East India Company, dated July 15, 1804. East India Office, London. *Home Miscellaneous Series,* Volume 337]

Dear Sir,

This letter will treat on a subject that I conceive if properly followed up may be the means, when removed, of very beneficial Interests to the Commerce and Navigation of Great Britain. And as you continue Chairman for part thereof it is left to you whether it can or ought to be made or entered into as a National consideration. On the commencement of the late Spanish war the Americans traded considerably from America to the Spanish Islands and Settlements in the West Indies and South America, as well on their own account as on Spanish account, being well paid for it and brought the produce of South America and its Islands to different parts of Europe—a great deal to old Spain but more considerable parcels to the different shores of the Mediterranean. This trade was apparently carried on for American account and to avoid our Navigation prize law. They went so far as to unload the Spanish produce in *North America,* transfer the property in a public manner by Sale or otherwise, and afterwards carry it to Spain to its original destination as well as to all parts of Italy and the Levant. This part of the Navigation I fancy they could not be deprived of when the property appeared ostensively to belong to themselves. This Trade is yet considerably followed up but as we have now no right to interfere therein, it may or may not be an object for further consideration in a future war with Spain. Their distant produce found on board Neutrals should be confined to be destined to the Country the Neutral belongs to for his Consumption. This was only done in part by our Prize Act—an American should not be permitted to carry Havannah Sugars, Buenos Ayras Hydes &c in time of War to a distant Market from *his own Country* for Sale.

The principal object and the most serious one I shall now treat on. Previous to the commencement of the late War with France in 1793 and for some Years afterwards, Britain supplied not only the European part but also the Barbary Shores of the Mediterranean and chiefly from Britain with all East India produce whatever, by which means some thousand Tons of Shipping were employed and the Trade by returns must I fancy have been very interesting to those concerned in it. The War spreading after to the Italian and other States of the Mediterranean checked the British Navigation and the Mass of Commerce and Carriage has since been carried on by the Americans. The facility by which the Americans procure their products in the East Indies may yet be unknown and I am not competent to explain it fully; but such part as has come to my knowledge I will now relate—The Americans proceed not only from the different parts of America with a good many Dollars and North American produce suitable to the different (chiefly) British

248

parts or Settlements in the East Indies. They buy there from the Company's servants such Goods as are supposed not suitable for the British Markets (but I believe to this I may add they also buy equally such Goods as are suitable) and such if they had not bought them would have found their way to Britain in British Navigation and from Britain to the Mediterranean. However they buy as a cover a small part of their Cargo from the Company's Servants— they afterwards contrive to agree for other parts with the Natives on the Coast where there are few or no Europeans and after having completed their Cargo they at times go back to America, from thence to the Mediterranean, or come direct from the East Indies hither. It has been here very customary of late to make large collections of Dollars for the Americans returning out of the Mediterranean to call for them, and from hence they go many of them direct to the East Indies. One we had lately consigned to us destined to Bencoolen for a Cargo of Pepper; part he was to buy of the European Factory and the rest being acquainted he was to agree with the Natives and meet them and receive from them on the coast the remainder of his Cargo in a Contraband or Clouded way. It is really incredible the American Navigation at present to the Mediterranean chiefly with East and West India producers. We have had several called in here from the Red Sea, the Cape of Good Hope, St. Helena &c &c with East India Cargoes—all gone up the Mediterranean and the Americans being now so used to the Trade, as they pay a greater price to the Factories or Settlements that they find means to trade entirely with the Natives and those who, I believe I may say, are considered under the protection of the British East India Company. East India Pepper for months past has been used *here* as low as 88 / st. per Eng. Cwt; Mocha Coffee direct from Mocha at about 100 /. Considerable quantities of low priced Muslins and Callicoes and some hundred thousand pieces of Nankeens with a variety of Drugs and other articles.—Now to remedy this and to encourage the British Navigation and Commerce, would it not be right to follow the Spaniards plan—that is, all strange Vessels whatever in time of peace that are found trading with the Islanders or with those on the Continent of South America are confiscable unless that trade is carried on by particular Licence and from a public port of Trade. It is very probable that the Americans in the East Indies receive every sort of encouragement and conveniency from the British Forts and Settlements where they go to Trade— and as this Trade has been only carried into effect but a very few Years and it now appears very considerable indeed—if it goes on to increase it may affect materially the Interest of Great Britain. I leave this subject to your serious consideration, to treat on in any manner you think proper, with this addition, that I do not wish to be called on to substantiate facts in any way whatever. If you however should consider it of national importance and it is taken up as a subject by the East India Directors, it may probably turn out beneficial to them and to us to have an East Indian store established here of such products not suitable for Britain that might come here direct in British Navigation and be sold in the Mediterranean. However this is a large object; too much so for us to have any chance of a direction.

I am &c

JOHN ROSS

III

## [Extract from a Letter of Sir Alexander John Ball, Governor of Malta, to J. Turnbull, Esq., dated March 18, 1806. East India House, London. *Home Miscellaneous Series,* Volume 439]

Dear Sir,

In the course of my enquiries into the sources of Commerce in the Mediterranean, I have been informed, that the Americans have lately entered into a speculation, that may prove very prejudicial to the interest of the East India Company unless it be soon counteracted. They load with opium at Smyrna, which they carry direct to China, and undersell us. In two or three years we shall entirely lose this branch of Commerce. Would it not be policy in our East India Directors to represent to the Chinese Government, that the Cargos of the Americans from the Levant may contain the seeds of the plague, and cause an irreparable calamity to the Empire, and that the only remedy for it is not to permit cargos from the Levant in American bottoms, that have not been landed in America and performed a rigid Quarantine? If they be allowed to perform a quarantine in the Mediterranean they will go to some Ports in Italy, where they can purchase clean Bills of Health without having performed the rules prescribed by the Quarantine Laws. If we can get this established, we shall then trade with the American upon nearly equal terms.

The Americans are beginning to undersell us in the West India Produce. I think I perceive the day fast approaching, when we shall deem it good policy to allow English Ships to sail direct for the Levant to China with opium and other Articles, and perform the quarantine in their Ports, and that we shall likewise grant licenses to English Ships to carry our West India Produce direct from there to the Mediterranean on paying a sum, that may prove a source of Revenue. This would be a popular measure with our Planters, and unless something similar be adopted, in a very short time there will not be a loaf of our Sugar consumed in the Mediterranean except at Gibraltar and Malta.

[Signed] ALEXR. JN. BALL

IV

## [Abstract of a Letter from Captain Welden, Late Commander of a Ship in the East India Company's Service, to the Chairman and Deputy Chairman of the East India Company. East India Office, London. *Home Miscellaneous Series*, Volume 706]

Encloses an exposition of the contraband Trade in Teas, from the United States to the British American Provinces from information collected by himself on the Spot in 1820 and during a second visit in 1823.

An extensive and lucrative contraband Trade in Teas and India & China Manufactures has long been carried on by Merchants of the United States with the Canadas, New Brunswick and Nova Scotia—is now systematized and increased to a degree highly injurious to the Revenue—discouraging to the British Merchants & Ship-Owners, detrimental to the interest of the East India Company, and augmenting the Revenues, extending the Commerce, and enriching the Merchants of the United States.

The American Merchants supply the Colonies with Teas, and the Manufactures of China at half the price the regular dealer can procure them from England.

When, by the late War, the illicit trade was interrupted, the poor people were obliged to substitute Coffee for Tea. Since the peace they have returned to Tea and the consumption of Coffee has gradually decreased in proportion as the facilities for smuggling, increased.

In 1820, Captain Welden was informed that small quantities of Teas &c were imported from England, to mask a much larger illicit importation from the United States, without which the retail dealer could not gain a livelihood. To investigate the subject thoroughly, he proceeded to the frontier

Stations: where he witnessed a daily traffic carried on between the two Countries to a very great extent and with great facility and security. The boundary line is too extensive to be guarded—and during a great portion of the Year an impenetrable fog screens the Smuggler.

The river St. John affords the utmost facility for carrying on an illicit traffic &c from Boston &c. with New Brunswick.

On a second Survey of the boundary lines in 1823, he was astonished at the increase and systematic conduct of the trade from Boston, and from New York in particular, which presents a frontier of 400 miles. Teas are conveyed by the grand Western Canal uniting the Atlantic with Lakes Erie and Ontario.

The small Town of Buffalo on Lake Erie was destroyed in 1813. In 1823 it had risen from its ashes and assumed the appearance of an old established Commercial place—Every. Store is a Tea Warehouse, and every Storekeeper a Smuggler supplying the British Coast of Lake Erie with Contraband Goods, whence they are forwarded to the remotest parts of Upper Canada.

Rochester on the Genesee River, two miles above its junction with Lake Ontario, 8 years ago consisted only of a few log houses—the Western Canal came to its doors—and now Warehouses and a busy population cover a large extent, depending chiefly on an illicit trade with the opposite Shores of Lake Ontario.

In July 1823 several thousand Chests had been brought to Rochester by the Canal and the Niagara River, without any land carriage.

Lake Champlain running Northward a considerable distance into Lower Canada, affords convenience for Smuggling Teas &c particularly from New York and Boston.

The extent of the illicit Trade will appear from a comparison of the lawful importations with the estimated annual consumption.

The legal importation of Teas into Canada on an average of 9 years from 1814 to 1822 is 270,540 lbs per annum. In 1814 the quantity was 487,376 lbs and gradually decreased till 1822 when only 134,379 lbs were entered. Up to August 1823, only 373 Chests had been entered; and the legal importation was not expected to exceed in that year 500 Chests or about 33,000 lbs. The consumption is estimated at 12,000 Chests per annum, the average legal importation is only 4,000 Chests, so that 8000 Chests must be smuggled each year.

The legal importation into New Brunswick from 1816 to 1822 has been 620 Chests per Annum:— the consumption is estimated at 2,000 Chests, so that 1,400 must be smuggled.

The legal importation into Nova Scotia from 1818 to 1823 has been 1,100 Chests per Annum: the consumption is estimated at 2,500 Chests—thus 1,400 must be smuggled.

The value of Silks, Nankeens &c—smuggled into the British provinces is estimated at £100,000 Currency, or £90,000 Sterling.

The above estimates are from Customs Books &c but combining this with intelligence collected in circuit exceeding 3,000 Miles from Public Officers, & from persons engaged in the illicit Trade, Capt. Welden calculates that 16,000 Chests of Tea at least, and Silks &c to the amount of 500,000 Dollars are annually smuggled into the provinces,—& it will increase with the rapid increase of population.

If measures be not adopted to rescue the Trade from its present course before it is so organised and established as to leave no hope of it again flowing in a legal Channel, the consequences will be fatal. America derives from this source a Revenue of £90,000 per annum. The Trade employs 2,500 Tons of her Shipping, besides the Vessels employed in Smuggling to the injury of the Navigation of England. The Americans have represented to the Chinese, that England being incapable of carrying on this Trade with the Colonies or Foreign Europe, has relinquished it to them.

# APPENDIX C

## I

[Regulations of the Canton Trade. From the Journal of Captain Benjamin Shreve, *Shreve MSS.*, Peabody Museum, Salem, Massachusetts]

The following remarks were furnished me by Edward W. Waldo who was Clerk to Capt. Thomas W. Ward to Canton in the *Minerva.*

On arrival off Macao, you will procure a Chinese Pilot at that Island, and be obliged to pay him in advance Forty to Sixty dollars, which is "old Custom." He is generally an ignorant fisherman, totally unacquainted with sailing your vessel, and to be trusted no further than to direct you to avoid "Chow Chow" water.

Your vessel remains at Whampoa, thirteen miles from Canton Factories, to which you will proceed in the Ship's pinnace: on getting there you will provide yourself as soon as convenient with a Factory, and after a day or two, select the Hong Merchant, who is to "secure" your Ship and Cargo, and do your business. . . . It would be prudent however with them, to keep your Specie under your own control. Consequa is the most of a Gentleman, of any of his Countrymen, knows more of European Manners and Customs and *formerly* did the Business for most of the Southern Typans, but has since lost credit, and become poor: he will give you better satisfaction in his *Dining parlour* than in his Hong. Kingqua is a new man, and when I was there was a Silk Merchant out of the Hong. He has been "squeezed" until he is now very poor and but little known. After securing with one of them, you will contract with him for sale and purchase of your Cargo, Teas, Nankins, Silks, & Cassia.

You should be cautious to stipulate for his *Chop* on all goods purchased out of the Hong, and need not let him know the amount of *specie* you have for these purchases. You mention in your Contract *prices* for the *Goods* and may make penalties for non-performance. Teas are purchased on long Credit, and is the article the Hong Merch^t best likes to sell you (you will of course speak often of "Tea Pigeon"). It requires a long acquaintance to ascertain its quality, and you must rely in a great measure on the Honour of your Hong Merchant for its goodness. But see well to its weight & packing yourself. There is generally a great quantity of *old Teas* in Market, which can be purchased at half, or even less price. These sell in our Market almost as well as the best. They must be skin and black teas only. Green soon loses its fine flavour by age (if you except young Hyson not over a year old). There will be much of this trash in the Market now after Three Years war, which you must be careful not to get palmed on to you for good. Nankeens are purchased on a credit of three or four months, unless much in demand, when they command the cash—You purchase them by their chop which is extremely various, they usually permit you to select what pleases you best, first Chop two thirds, second chop one third. You should unroll the package for inspection, and see the inner pieces are as good as the outer.

Nankeens vary in price very much, often a few American arrivals at Macao enhance the price 10 pct for a *few days*. Silks you must order soon after arrival, as it takes two months to manufacture them, they are always a Cash article. Sinchows, a kind peculiar to China, a strong, thick silk, and a staple article alwa᷒ᵣₛ. Satins—Lustrings & Sarsnets, single width and double width. They may be Black—Coloured & Fancy. You must critically examine these goods, and refuse all that are not of the proper Quantity and Quality.

Cassia Lignen, you always want for dunnage—and you only get that, which is *new* & fresh, packed in all sizes to fill every *inch* of your vessel. These are the staple goods you procure from the Hong Merchant, for your Cargo, and generally of a better quality and higher price than what you purchase of China St. Merchants. These fellows are nearly all Sharpers and Rogues, but you will find yourself almost endued with new senses, after awhile, to detect their roguery. You purchase of them China Ware, Silks, Nankeens, Teas, &c. Sinchong is the great Porselain Merchant, you purchase your principal ware of him. Satins, Sinchows, Sewing Silks, Crapes, Lustrings, Sarsnets, and a great variety of other silks you can purchase much cheaper (than of the Hong) of *Eshing, Washing,* Namchong, and a great number of China Street Silk Merchants. These kinds suit our market much better than the higher priced, and will always answer your *private trade* to more profit. Sewing silk should be soft, and not hard twisted, put up in *pound* and not Catty bunches. With respect to the fancy Sarsnets the more flimsy the better for our market when *thin* Silks are no objection. You make contracts with these people, & take from them "Musters," which you keep to confront with their goods when produced. You should well examine their quality and quantity and refuse all not as good as warranted. I found Eshing perfectly honest and honourable in all my dealings with him, but still trusted only to myself. The rest with a few exceptions were "Quisi." You can purchase of any of them Lackered Ware, Tortoise Shell Combs, Cassia, Grass Cloth, Hkfs, Umbrellas, Straw Carpeting, Artificial Flowers, Beads, Fine Paintings of Botany and Natural History, Silk vests—sprigged with silver & gold, and a thousand little articles that can be purchased cheap, and sell well here. My lackered Ware sold for two hundred per cent. The articles most wanted are Tea Caddies at a dollar, Backgammon Boards same price, Dice, Segar Boxes half a dollar & seventy five cents—Loose Boxes, same—Fish Counters, same—Wine stands twelve cents and small articles to fill up the packages—they may be Black or Red. Silk vests ready made—such as you have seen in Havana worn by Spaniards, could be purchased for Eighty Cents, and sold here for two dollars & half. Straw Carpeting that will fill up the wings of your vessel—cost seven dollars for twenty-five yards—sold for twenty. Artificial flowers—wreaths—Beads &c sold at still greater profit, and so will Books of Botany & Natural History—and many other articles not remembered. The prices of articles when I was there were very high, Nankeens 1st Chop Fifty four and a half dollars. . . . The second chop are less price than the first but sell equally well here, of course you get as many of them as possible.

Silks—Sinchows 30 yds $16.50 per piece. Satins 1st Chop 20 yds $19. 2nd Chop 30 yds $19. Lustring 30 yds $15. Sarsnets 30 yds $14.50—15 yds $7.25. These prices are for Hong goods—of course the very best quality. At the same time out of the Hong Sinchows $15. Lustrings $13, Sarsnets $12, Crapes $7 to $9. Sewing silk $3.50 per lb and other silk Goods in proportion.

Be very careful to get all your silks edged with *white* instead of Reds.

The currency of Canton is

10 Candareens make 1 Mace
10 Mace            "    1 Tale

Weights 100 Catties make a Picul of 133½ lb.

You can bring Tale into Dollars by adding two Cyphers and dividing by 72.

Salem March 16, 1805

## [A Modest Adventure. From the Shreve Papers, Peabody Museum, Salem, Massachusetts, Relating to the Voyage of the *Governor Endicott* to Canton, 1819-21]

Salem, May 5, 1819

Mr. Shreve,

I send by you thirty four Dollars, and would thank you to buy for Mrs. Tucker, the following.

4 Turtle Shell Combs

Flat {3 doz. large size blue & white tone China }
Plates {4 doz. 2nd size    do.    do.    do. } Gilt edge

In case the Dollars sent should not be enough to buy the above, then get only so much China Ware as there be Money to pay for, besides the Cost of the Combs. And oblige Yr. Aff.

GIDEON TUCKER

If there should be money left after buying the above, and enough to pay for another dozen Plates, then please get 1 dozen large size Plates.

G. T.

[Supplementary Letter]

Mr. Shreve,

I send sixteen Dollars more which please add to the $34 delivered you this morning, to purchase the articles for Martha.

I am &c.

May 5                                                          G. T.

## [A Typical Investment of American Capital. From the *Gerry Papers*, Marblehead Historical Society, Massachusetts]

### MEMORANDUM NO. 1.

An order addressed to Capt. Saml. R. Gerry Master of the Ship Cowper, for an investment at Calcutta, on account of Daniel P. Parker which is to be varied in the quantity of some of the articles according to circumstantial or conditional instructions as stated below.

Dollars

2,500 —In Salt Petre. Buy the 2d quality of this article. If the price should be over Seven and three fourths Rupees per maund I prefer your omitting this article unless it is necessary to have it for ballast, or unless you hear of war in Europe—should you omit the purchase of Salt Petre on my account, you will of course increase the investment in other articles.

2,000 —In Indigo. Buy the medium qualities say that which will cost 60/ to 110/ Rupees per maund, the best bargains are made in broken Indigo of strong copper colours of medium qualities. The Oude which is of the most inferior quality you will not buy at any price, and you will omit this order altogether if the prices should be 10 pr. cent above the prices named above.

4,000 —In Cowhides. Buy the full amount of this article unless a great advance has taken place since Jan'y 1830. Green [?] Salted hides are the safest article, all hides should be bought with great care and caution. In buying green salted hides care should be taken to ascertain that they are real green salted hides, as Dry hides cured with Cherram are sometimes offered as green salted. The Deca hides are not so valuable, and are usually very unequal in quality, great care should be taken to have the hides packed in such a manner as to preserve them on the passage, from damage by worms or heat.

1,000 —In Goat Skins. Buy Madras, Patna or Calcutta giving the preference in the order I insert them, if you are obliged to buy Calcutta, reject the small ones, they are of little value.

1,200 —In Ginger. Buy the full extent of this order provided the price is not above 4 cents pr. lb. on board, and buy $600 at the current price.

2,000 —In Gum Shellac. Liver and Orange, but principally orange, omit a part if the price should be very high, only about 30 or 35 cents in this market can be calculated on, notwithstanding it is much higher at this time.

1,000 —In Gum Copal. You may calculate this article will be worth 25 or 30 cents in America, and if the price in Calcutta will allow it to be laid down in Boston with $25 pr. ton freight Duties &c added at the above prices you need not fear to buy the articles, but if very high at Calcutta, omit it—30 Rupees per Maund is a very high price—20 or 24 is the usual price.

1,200 —In Gunny Bags. I have put down $1,200 in this article which it may be well to invest unless you should obtain freight at $25 per Ton to fill the Ship without buying them, in which case only you may omit them and invest the amount in some other articles. Part in Bales and part for stowage between decks.

300 —In Munjeet. You will buy this article unless you can fill the Ship without it, it should be secured into Hhds. or compressed into Bales, first a cotton wrapper and a Gunny bag over. You will need some of this article in strong bags with cane poles, to lay your cargo on, and to dunnage at the sides and between decks.

| | | |
|---|---|---|
| 500 | —In Senna Leaves good quality | |
| 500 | —In Tumeric | If you buy these articles, buy |
| 300 | —In Sal Amoae | no more than is put down |
| 300 | —In Malabar Cardam | against the several articles. |
| 300 | —In Gum Arabic | I mean $30—more or less de- |
| 300 | —In Gum Senegal | pending on the prices and |
| 300 | —In Crude Borax | your wants to fill the ship. |
| 300 | —In Blue Galls | |

Balance of my funds in silk goods as under viz.—

¼ in small choppas (good quality) 45/ or 50/ Rupees for 20 ps.
½ in Medium size choppas fair quality 80/ or 100/ Rupees for 20 ps.
¼ in Medium Bandannas assorted say 90/ or 110/ Rupees for 20 ps.
½ chocolate
¼ reds
⅛ yellow
⅛ blue

Silks should be packed in cases of about 40 pieces each assorted.

# APPENDIX D

## THE YANKEE SAILOR AND HIS ADVENTURES

### I

[John Poll. From William Bentley MS. *Miscellanies*, American Antiquarian Society, Worcester, Massachusetts]

While at Mocha, I had many interviews with John Porl, or Poll, who was a boy belonging to the Ship Essex, Captain Joseph Orne of Salem, which

[The Canton Trade During a Sample Year. From the Augustine Heard MSS., Baker Library, Cambridge, Mass.]

## STATEMENT OF THE AMERICAN TRADE WITH THE PORT OF CANTON SEASON 1832 & 33

### Imports

Bills on London [£] 1,043,988 at 4/4 ½ per dollar

| Quantity | Unit | Item | Value | Amount |
|---|---|---|---|---|
| | | Dollars and Bullion | @ 62 | |
| 10,154 | pls | Quicksilver | @ 62 | 629,548 |
| 7,061 | " | Lead | 4½ | 132,102 |
| 29,356 | " | Iron | 2¼ | 15,887.25 |
| 9,789 | " | Copper S. Am. | 21 | 205,569 |
| 7,418 | " | Spelter | 4.10 | 20,413 |
| 100 | Bxs | Tin plates | 6½ | 650 |
| 380 | pls | Turkey opium | 600 | 228,000 |
| 2,183 | " | Ginsing Crude | 58 | 116,614 |
| 324 | " | do Clarified | 60 | 19,440 |
| 104,517 | " | Rice and Paddy | 2.15 | 234,711.55 |
| 10,189 | r* | Broad Cloths | 30 | 305,670 |
| 1,912 | " | Camlets | 23 | 43,976 |
| 15,162 | " | Chintz | 3½ | 53,067 |
| 7,880 | " | Long Ells | 10½ | 82,740 |
| 61,953 | " | Long Cloths | 4¾ | 294,276.75 |
| 16,273 | " | Cambrics | 2 | 32,546 |
| 20,156 | " | Domestics | 2¾ | 55,429 |
| 138 | " | Velvets | 8 | 1,104 |
| 6,394 | " | Bombazetts | 8 | 51,152 |
| 28,319 | Doz | Handkfs | 1¾ | 42,478.50 |
| 100 | pcs | Linens | 18 | 1,800 |
| 2,554 | " | Cotton drillings | 4½ | 11,493 |
| 2,203 | pls | Cotton Yarn | 42 | 92,546 |
| 1,928 | r* | do Prints | 3½ | 6,748 |
| 13,203 | " | Sand Otters | 6½ | 85,419.50 |
| 494 | " | Sea Otters | 43 | 21,242 |
| 11,903 | " | Fox Skins | 1 | 11,903 |
| 514 | " | Sable | 10¢ | |
| 4 | " | Seal | 2 } 10¢ | 1,833.30 |
| 17,739 | " | Muskrat | | |
| 1,810 | " | Beaver | 6½ | 11,765 |
| 205 | " | Sea Otter tails | 4½ | 922.50 |
| 2,602 | pls | Pearl Shells | 5 | 13,010 |
| 5,600 | " | Sandal Wood | 5 | 28,000 |
| 49 | " | Cochineal | 280 | 13,720 |
| 6 | " | Shell Scraps | 30 | 180 |

[$14,772.516
682,519

### Imports

| |  | |  |
|---|---|---|---|
| 200 | Music Boxes | | 6,000 |
| | Coral Beads Perfumery Clocks Watches and Sundry Articles not enumerated put down by the Importers at Dollars | Dollars | 26,000 |
| | Balance | | 2,907,936.35 |
| | | | 9,204.14 |
| | | | 8,372,175.49 |

### Exports to the U. States

| Quantity | Unit | Item | Weight | @ rate | Amount |
|---|---|---|---|---|---|
| 13,665 | ch* | Bohea | Pls 8,199.00 | @ 11.Ts | 90,189.00 |
| 31,614 | " | Souchong | 22,499.10 | 20. | 449,982.00 |
| 4,723 | " | Pouchong | 2,361.50 | 25. | 59,037.50 |
| 2,563 | " | Pecco | 1,281.50 | 55. | 70,482.50 |
| 201 | " | Congo | 130.65 | 22. | 2,874.30 |
| 55,766 | | Chests Black | | | 672,565.30 |
| 57,363 | " | Young-Hyson | 33,385.95 | 47. | 1,569,139.65 |
| 14,248 | " | Hyson | 6,839.04 | 49. | 335,112.96 |
| 6,614 | " | Gunpowder | 5,291.20 | 58. | 306,889.60 |
| 31,736 | " | Hyson Skin | 15,868. | 27. | 428,436.00 |
| 5,939 | " | Imperial | 4,157.30 | 55. | 228,651.50 |
| 4,872 | " | Tonkay | 3,020.64 | 30. | 90,619.20 |
| 114,772 | ch* | Gum Total 170,538 | | | 3,631,414.21 / 5,043,630.84 |
| 19,811 | | Crape Shawls Embr'd. | | @ 4¢ | 79,244 |
| 59,065 | " | Do Damask | | 1.75 | 103,363.75 |
| 4,559 | r* | Crape | | 6 | 27,354 |
| 24,174 | " | Blk Hkfs | | 5.75 | 139,150.50 |
| 3,105 | " | Pongees | | 7 | 21,735 |
| 13,172 | " | Sinshaws | | 9 | 118,548 |
| 19,909 | " | Sarsnetts Black | | 7 | 139,363 |
| 2,380 | " | Do White | | 7 | 16,660 |
| 3,300 | " | Levantines | | 8½ | 28,050 |
| 3,051 | " | Satin Levantines | | 12 | 36,612 |
| 7,201 | " | Satins | | 14 | 100,814 |

## Exports to the U. States

| | | | | |
|---|---|---|---|---|
| 60 | rˢ Satin Damask | | 17 | 1.020 |
| 1,091 | " Camlets | | 9½ | 10,364.50 |
| 9,645 | " White Pongees | | 11 | 106.095 |
| 39,096 | " Suchan | | 3½ | 136.856 |
| 1,630 | " Mix'd Lustring | | 7 | 11.410 |
| 72 | pls Sewings | | 420 | 30.240 |
| 144 | " Raw Silk | | 350 | 50.400 |
| 31,500 | rˢ Blue Nankins | | 85 | 26.775 |
| 7,428 | pls Cassia @ 12¢ 59,136, 121 | | | 107.286 |
| | pls. S .. [?] oils | 150 18,150 | | |
| 14,444 | Bxs Fire Crackers @ 2¼. 32,499 | 10,296 | | 42.795 |
| 396 | pls Camphor @ 26¢ | | | |
| 635 | " Vermillion @ $35 [---?] | | | 27.835 |
| 5,613 | " Sr. Mts. [?] 1683.90 @ 15¢ | | | 25.258.50 |
| 3,997 | pls Sugar | | 9 | 35.973 |
| 10,368 | Rolls Floor Matting | | 4 | 41.472 |
| 100,000 | Groce Pearl Buttons | | 12 | 12.048 |
| 645 | Boxes China Ware | | 20 | 13.080 |
| 725,030 | Fans & Fire Screens | | 03¢ | 21.750.90 |
| 3,155 | rs Grass Cloth | | 6 | 18.930 |
| 300 | " Gauze | | 5 | 1.500 |
| 1,898 | pls Tin | | 15¾ | 29.893.50 |
| 8,000 | pcs Yellow Nankins | | 50 | 4.000 |
| | Fire Works, Window Blinds, Bamboo Canes, Musk, Cassia Buds, Gamboge Glue and Sundry Drugs | | | 12.825 |
| | Sundry Articles not enumerated | | | 69.100 |
| | | | | 490,521.90 |
| | | | | 6,091,412.49 |

## Exports to Europe

| | | | | | |
|---|---|---|---|---|---|
| 1,312 | chˢ Gunpowder | 1,049.60 | 58. | 60,876.80 | |
| 1,777 | " Imperial | 1,243.90 | 55. | 68,414.50 | |
| 316 | " Orange Peuco | 126.40 | 20. | 2,528.00 | |
| 32,228 | Chests | | | 634,976.20 | 881,911 |
| 521 | pls Sweetmeats | | 15 | 7,815 | |
| 918 | " Cassia | | 12 | 11,016 | |
| 20 | Bxs Vermillion | | 35 | 700 | |
| 5 | pls Spice oil | | 150 | 750 | |
| 145 | " Galangal | | 3½ | 507.50 | |
| 100 | " Camphor | | 26 | 2,600 | |
| 50 | " Star Aniseed | | 11 | 550 | |
| 50 | " Cassia Buds | | 11 | 550 | |
| 27 | " China Root | | 3½ | 94.50 | |
| 20 | " Turmeric | | 5½ | 110 | |
| 700 | " Sugar | | 9 | 6,300 | |
| 3,970 | rs Silks & Crape Shawls | | | 8,870 | |
| 1,000 | Rolls Window Blinds & Sundry unenumerated articles | | | 1.200 | 41,063 |
| | | | | | 922,974 |

To—

Sⁿ. America, Manila, and Sandwich Islands

| | | | |
|---|---|---|---|
| Cargo of Sh. Don Quixotte Chili & Peru cost | | 76,597 | |
| " Bg. John Gilpin do " | | 52,884 | |
| " Sh. Pearl do " | | 101,692 | |
| " Bk. Flora Brazil " | | 75,000 | |
| " Bg. Griffin Sandⁿ Island | | 40,000 | 346,173 |

The following Vessels were loaded at Manila Mary Frazier, Lascer, Eugene, Caroline, Active, Rasselas, Jnⁿ & Elizabeth & Washington with funds drawn from Canton.

The following Vessels received part of a Cargo at Manila Viz. Don Quixotte, John Gilpin, Fanny, Jeannette, Oneida & Pearl with funds drawn from Canton.     198,816

| | | | |
|---|---|---|---|
| Port Charges | | | |
| on 19 Vessels at Whampoa @ 6000 | | 114,000 | |
| " 28 " " " with Rice 1000 | | 28,000 | |
| " 12 " " Linton [sic?] 400 | | 4,800 | 66,000 |
| Exports to the United States Brought forward | | | 6,091,412.49 |
| | | Dollars | 8,372,175.49 |

## Exports to Europe

| | | | | |
|---|---|---|---|---|
| 3,178 | chˢ Bohea Pls 1,906.80 | @ 11.Ts | 20. | 20,974.80 |
| 7,174 | " Souchong 4,663.10 | | 20. | 93,262.00 |
| 3,349 | " Congo 2,176.85 | | 22. | 47,890.70 |
| 1,653 | " Campoy 1,074.45 | | 22. | 23,637.90 |
| 623 | " Pouchong 311.50 | | 25. | 7,787.50 |
| 3,404 | " Pecco 1,702.00 | | 55. | 93,610.00 |
| 1,428 | " Tonkay 885.36 | | 30. | 26,560.80 |
| 1,577 | " Hyson Skin 788.50 | | 27. | 21,289.50 |
| 4,055 | " Hyson 1,946.40 | | 49. | 95,373.60 |
| 2,382 | " Young Hyson 1,548.30 | | 47. | 72,770.10 |

vessel having been cut off and all her crew murdered, has for a long time interested the feelings of the American publick. His story is as follows. The vessel arrived at Aden for information; here Cap$^t$ Orne found an Englishman, who informed him, that no Coffee was to be procured at Mocha; but advised him to go up to Loheia, and at the same time offered his services as pilot & interpreter; Captain Orne influenced by this advice, accepted his offer, and proceeded to Loheia, where he arrived without stopping at Mocha, & succeeded in procuring some Coffee, but not enough for a Cargo, on which account, after lying there two months, he had determined to go down to Mocha. On the day previous to his intended departure, he had a dispute with the Xeriff Mahmoud, the Governour or petty prince of Loheia. The Xeriff demanded $200. for Port-Charges; Cap$^t$ Orne thinking this an extortionary sum, refused to pay more than $100; but at length the affair was compromised for $150. On the same night on which this settlement was effected, Cap$^t$ Orne & four of his crew being ashore, John Porl, who was cabin-boy on board, was ordered to keep a look-out for the Captain & all hands went below. At about 11 or 12 o'clock, Porl saw a boat approaching the Ship; he announced this to the first officer, who merely answered "that it must be the Captain," yet neither he, nor anyone else, arose to receive him. When Porl came upon deck again, he found two boats, one on each side of the vessel. The Ship was immediately boarded by a number of Caffres and soldiers, during which the Officers & Crew came upon deck and were told by the boarders that Cap$^n$ Orne wished them to go ashore, to which the officers objected as improbable. Porl was then led below and shut up in the Cabin. While below, he heard no groans or struggles, nor when permitted to go on deck, did he perceive any clots of blood or other marks by which he could suppose that the murderous transaction had taken place on board the ship. He enquired of a Lascar, where were his Officers & shipmates, and was told that they had gone ashore. Not satisfied with this answer, he searched throughout the vessel, and not finding anything to relieve his fear and anxiety, he again enquired of the Lascar, who only gave him vague and evasive answers, but told him that no harm should happen to him and in a kind & friendly manner endeavoured to console him in his affliction. A vessel belonging to Sayd Mohammad Ebn Akeel, was lying at the Island of Cameran at this time & Akeel himself was at Loheia and his crew composed part of those by whom the ship was boarded, & the rest either actually were soldiers or availed themselves of their dress as a disguise. The Essex was then taken to the Island of Cameran & there sunk or destroyed. Poll was taken care of by the above mentioned Lascar, who presented him to Sayd Akeel, by whom he was told, that provided he would take the turban & submit to circumcision, his life should be saved. Several of the people about the person of Akeel murmured at this decision & endeavoured to convince him of the policy of putting Poll to death for the general safety. The wife of Akeel however, interceded in his favour & to her was he indebted for his life. He was then carried to Muscat & thence to Dofar, of which last place the Sayd was Sheik or Governour. On board Akeel's vessel he saw two guns, & a number of books, which he is confident formerly belonged to the Essex. He also found a French Renegado in the service of Akeel who was very kind to him & always behaved towards him in a generous & friendly manner; but who when pressed upon the subject of the fate of the unfortunate crew of the Essex, uniformly refused to satisfy his enquiries. Porl feels assured however that they were all murdered, as he has never been able to gain any intelligence respecting them, since the horrid catastrophe took place; whereas had they been enslaved or otherwise disposed of, he would have discovered the fact. This was also corroborated by the testimony of an Arab, who declared that he saw Mr. Carter, the Englishman, whom he well knew, and all the Officers & Crew of the Essex, on the Island of Cameran, with their throats cut from ear to ear! How he became a witness to this bloody spectacle, I could not discover. Poll says that he does not know what became of the money taken from the Essex; he thinks however that a considerable part was retained by the Xeriff Mahmoud & the remainder by the Sayd Akeel. He states that the Sayd Mohammad Ebn Akeel is a sheik of Dofar & is possessed of great wealth. He has several wives, but no children & has adopted Poll as his son, who with the brother of Akeel residing at Mocha, will probably inherit his extensive possessions. His treatment towards Poll has ever been marked with the most parental & affectionate kindness, and though allowing him but little money, has always supplied him with the necessaries & comforts of life. He has given him a slave in marriage, by whom he has two children, to whom he is most tenderly attached. Concerning the destruction of the Essex his recollection appeared to be clear & distinct, but the loss in a great degree of his native language, through the want of practice, (this being the first time he had conversed with any Christians since the murder of his countrymen & shipmates,) rendered it difficult for him to express it in an intelligible manner, and it was only by dint of the most persevering enquiries, that the above incomplete account of that dark transaction was obtained. Concerning his native Country, he has but few imperfect ideas; time & a constant association with Arabs have effaced from his memory the scenes of his early life, & probably pains have been taken by his wily protector to obliterate from his mind all remembrance of his youthful impressions. His conversation & replies however evinced no ordinary talents & his observations & remarks appeared the result of much natural sense & considerable reflection. It may be observed that Captain Austin & myself, offered him every assistance in our power, & used many arguments to induce him to return to his native country & assured him of our protection should he feel so inclined. He answered to this that during the life-time of Akeel, this was absolutely impossible. That his two children, whom he loved better than life or liberty himself, were retained as hostages by his artful guardian, who had also bound him by a most solemn oath, again to return to Dofar. He said that he felt himself strongly attached to his native country & vehemently desired to return thither; but that until the death of Akeel, to which he seemed to look forward as an event that must occur at no very distant period, he must endeavour to forget these patriotick feelings amid the pleasures and endearments of domestick life. He states that about 6 years ago he was brought to Mocha in a vessel of Akeel's. An American vessel, the name of which I could not discover, was lying in the roads at the time. One morning, observing the boat of the American rowing towards them, Poll was ordered below & confined in the Cabin. When the boat had left the ship, he learned that he himself had been the object of their search. He observed that unfortunately the ship was lying to windward of him, but had the reverse been the case, no earthly power should have prevented his throwing himself overboard & endeavouring, by swimming, to have gained an asylum & protection among his countrymen. He was 9½ years old, at the time of the destruction of the Essex, which he thinks must have been in February, 1806. His Mohammadan name is Abdallah Mohammad, to which the name of his patron is sometimes added. The circumspect Akeel, has been careful to educate him in the principles of the religion of Mahammad & taken the most artful means to banish from his mind all recollections of his native local attachments & affections. Poll complained that the Arabs taunt & reproach him with the imbecility of the American Government, in suffering this nefarious & high-handed offence, against the United States & the religion of Christ to go unpunished.

He states that the city of Dofar is a place of some note, but not so large as Mocha, that it is walled & that the inhabitants are generally engaged in petty war-fares with the Bedouin Arabs & on this account are always armed. Large vessels cannot approach very near but the Daous & smaller Craft, anchor within a quarter of a mile of the City. The Dolah of Mocha, being interrogated concerning the effect an attack upon Dofar would have upon the American Commerce in the Red Sea, replied that "Dofar being an independent province & only submissive to the authority of Akeel, any measures that

259

might be taken relative to the apprehension of the villain, or the destruction of his City, could have no effect whatever upon any commerce with the other independent provinces of Arabia."

CHAS. COOK Sr. Commander of<br>Brig Lynn of Newbury

II

# Copy of My Instructions from the Dutch East India Company at Batavia, on My Voyage to Japan.

[By James Devereux, June, 1799]

[From the *Devereux Papers*, Essex Institute, Salem, Massachusetts]

When you get to the Lattitude of 26 or 27 North it will be Necessary to have Everything in Readiness to Comply with the Ceremonies which the Japanese are accustomed to See performed by the Ships of the Company.

1st   You will have all your Colours in order to dress the Ship on her entrance into port.

2d   There must be a table prepared on the Quarter deck which must be Covered with a piece of Cloath & five Cushions for the Officers to sit upon when they Come on board.

3d   It is indispensably necessary to have a list of all the people on board, Passengers & Officers their Stations & age.

4th   All the Books of the people & Officers particularly Religious books must be put in a cask & headed up, the Officers from the Shore will put their seal on the Cask & take it on Shore, & on the departure of the Ship will bring it on board without having opened it.

5th   Before your arrival at Japan you must make the people deliver you their money & keep it untill your departure, this will not be attended with Inconvenience as at Japan Nothing is bought for Cash but they may Change their Specie for [Cambang?] Money & then make their trade, but this must be done by the Captain.

6th   When you are in sight of Japan you must hoist a dutch Pendant & Enseign in their proper places as if you were a dutch Ship.

7th   When the Cavelles are on your Starboard hand & the Isl<sup>d</sup>. of Japan on your Larboard you must Salute the Guard on the Cavallas with 9 Guns.

8th   After that you pass the Larboard side of the Papenburg & Salute with 9 Guns.

9th   You then pass the Guards of the Emperor on the Starboard & larboard Nearly at the Same Time, & Salute with 7 or 9 Guns, the first all Starboard Guns, & the Second all Larboard Guns.

10th   You then advance into the Road of Nangasackey & after anchoring Salute with 13 Guns.

11th   When you enter the Cavelles the Commessaries of the Chief will Come on board & you must Salute them with 9 Guns, at the same time if it is practicable hoist some Colours at the yards as a compliment to them, it is Immaterial what Colours you dress your Ship with, except Spanish or Portuguise it is however Necessary to Recolect that the dutch Colours must be allways in their proper place as if the Ship was of that Nation.

12th   When the Commessaries Return on Shore you must Salute them with 9 Guns.

13th   You must be very Particular in letting the boats which are Round the Ship know when you are going to fire, as if you were to hurt any of them the Consequences would be very Important.

14th   After you have Anchored & Saluted the Harbour, the officers examine the list of your people & Compare them with the number on board, after having received them those who wish it Can go on shore, but before the Japanese land all the arms & Amunition must be sent on shore, & it will be proper that Everything of the kind should be landed as they Search the Ship after she is unloaded. On your departure they will Return it all on board, if there Should by mistake any powder or fire arms left on board, you must be very Carefull that not so much as a pistol should be fired untill they Return the Amunition which was landed. The Agents of the Company will Instruct you Respecting the other Ceremonies to be observed.

### III

[Extract from the Diary of George Cleveland, Who Visited Japan in 1801. *Derby Papers,* Essex Institute, Salem, Massachusetts]

Capᵗ Samuel Derby, (who with Col. Pickman & Mr John Derby, were building a fine Ship at Beckets,) asked me to go with him, on his contemplated voyage as Clerk, and as Capᵗ D. was a very fine man, that I had always Known, I did not hesitate about the propriety of accepting the offer a moment. I spent the Summer of 1800 in Salem, with no other employment than the usual lounging about, of young Sailors, when at home; which is any thing, but profitable. In the Autumn of that year the Ship was launched, and fitted with the usual expedition for her voyage, and on the 25th Nov. 1800, we left Salem harbour bound to the East Indies, and probably a finer, or better fitted, or better manned Ship, never left the port, before. We carried 6 Guns & 20 men. Most of the crew were fine young men in the bloom of youth, and it is very remarkable how many are now living of this Ships company, who sailed from Salem, on that day. As it is an uncommon case, I will enumerate those who are living. S. G. Derby, capᵗ, Thoˢ West 2 Mate, Lincoln Stetson, carpenter, Samˡ Ray, Joseph Preston, Israel Phippen, Anthony D. Caulfield before the Mast, & myself. In addition to these, Wᵐ Messervy was shipped in Batavia and returned to Salem in the Ship and I am uncertain whether a man by the name of Thatcher who left Salem with us is still living or not. Last year a man by the name of Patrick Dwyer who was one of crew, died,—So that at the end of 37 years, nearly one half of the original crew, were living. We soon found on leaving port, what a fast sailing Ship the Margaret was, and this, was more particularly the case, when we fell in with a vessel. I recollect when we were out 11 days, we fell in with the Bark Two Brothers, Capᵗ John Holman, who had left Salem Some days before us, bound to Leghorn. We made him ahead in the afternoon steering the same course we were, and before night we were up along side and spoke him. Capᵗ Holman appeared to be very much surprised & said he thought we were a Sloop of War. The next day we fell in with a fleet of merchantmen convoyed by a Frigate,—As we had to cross the track of these vessels, the Frigate, which was under very short sail Kept all snug until she had got into our wake, when she Set all sail in chase, but we distanced her so much, that in a very short time she gave it up, took in her sails, and rejoined the fleet. On the 19th Dec. we made the Island of St Anthony (one of the Cape de Verd Islands) and had the winds so light and variable, afterwards that we did not cross the Equator until the 4th Jan. making a passage of 40 days from Salem. After crossing the line we had a good breeze from the S. E. and soon ran into variable Winds. The Ship would frequently go 8, 9, 10 & even 11 Knots by the Wind in crossing the trades;—the Sails were all new, and very large, & the night dews, made them very thick,—so that they were equal almost, to a double suit. Nothing took place, that was remarkable. Afterwards in our passage and on the 4th Feb. 1801 we anchored in Table bay (C. of G. Hope). We saluted the Admirals Ship, which was returned. It was the custom of that day to stop at the Cape, outwd. & homewd. bound, to fill water, and procure refreshments, but as many accidents happened by so doing, the practice has gone out of use, and it is rare now for a vessel to stop. If any thing is wanted, on the homeward voyage, Ships stop at St Helena. I found at the Cape, many of my old friends, alive & well;—especially Mr. Onkroyds family, who had treated us so civilly, when there in the Hannah. They complained, of the deceptive and bad conduct of the Cap$^t$ of that vessel, which there is no doubt they had ample cause for, especially in regard to his addresses to a young Lady of the family, whom he promised to come back & marry. I think on the whole she was fortunate in keeping clear of that man, —as she was afterwards respectably married I was told to a Dutch gentleman. We found the most hospitable treatment at Mr. Onkroyds house. On the 10th of Feb. we left the Cape bound to Sumatra and found it difficult to get to the Eastw. as winds and currents were against us; we continued however to make the best of way & after rather a tedious passage we anchored in Bencoolen roads on the 10th of April 1801 after being 136 days from Salem including our stoppage at the Cape. We found at Bencoolen the Ships Belisarius, Cap$^t$ Skerry of Salem & the Mercury, Cap$^t$ Colesworthy of Boston. As nothing could be done at Bencoolen and the Supercargo of the Mercury gave such good accounts of the prospect in Batavia, for such a Ship as ours, he having just arrived from that place; that Cap$^t$ Derby thought it his duty to proceed immediately there. We accordingly left Bencoolen on the 15th of April and arrived at Batavia on the 25th of the same month. We found at this place the Ships Franklin of Salem & Bacchus of Baltimore. Cap$^t$ Derby soon made a bargain with the agents of the E. India company, to take the annual freight, to and from Japan, and as it was the custom from time immemorial that the Japan Ship should sail on a certain day & as that day was some time ahead; it was necessary to find some employment for the vessel previously as it was then very dangerous to the healths of Crews to be lying any time, in Batavia roads. The company accordingly offered Cap$^t$ Derby a freight of Coffee from a port a short distance to the Eastward called Indramao, which he readily accepted. This wore away 12 or 14 days of the time, & added to the profits of the voyage about 2000 Dolls. I remained at Batavia during the absence of the Ship, & as I was very particular in my mode of living I got along very well. I used to ride out about sunset to visit some of the Americans in the Hospital, of whom at that time, there were many. Batavia in those days was much more fatal to foreigners than it is at present. After the English took it, they filled up the Canals,—tore down the City walls, and made many other improvements, so that at this time, I am told, it is quite a different place. It required considerable strength of nerve, to remain any time there, at this period,—as the well, as they were called, looked much more like the subjects of a Hospital, than to be about the Streets. I lived at the great Hotel opposite the great Church; both of which buildings, have been taken down since, in making improvements in the City. The Table was sumptuously supplied, and as for fruit, it was in the greatest variety, and abundance. The business of the Company was carried on with much foolish parade, and unnecessary expence, and it was really ridiculous in the Directors of a Company of Merchants, to be assuming the port and bearing of sovereigns, as they did;—when the plain unostentatious manners, and habits, of their native land, would have been much more, in Character. The warehouses for Storing Sugar, Coffee & Pepper, were on a grand scale; and so large were the accumulations of produce, that the Cargo of 300 Tons of

Coffee, which the Ship brought from Indramao, appeared to increase the bulk of a pile, that was previously stored there, but very little.

Finding that our funds would be so much increased if we returned safe from Japan, that the Ship would not be able to take above half the amount onboard in Coffee; Cap$^t$ D. was at a loss at first to know what to do;—he however finally concluded to send M$^r$ James Stuart, the Chief Mate, to the Isle of France, and there buy a prize vessel, with which he was to return to Batavia in season to meet us when we should get back from Japan. Stuart accordingly sailed as a passenger, for the Isle of France (I think before we left,) taking with him A. D. Caulfield who was one of the Margaret's crew. After discharging the Cargo from Indramao we began to take onboard the Cargo for Japan. This consisted of a great variety of articles, such as the Dutch had been in the habit of shipping for nearly two Centuries. It was composed of Sugar, Spices, Japan & Sandal woods, Rattans, Glass & Glass ware, Cloths, medicines & various other articles; and as every thing was to be done according to a prescribed rule, and we were not to sail until a certain day, in June, we had time enough, to do all things right, as regards receiving, and stowing the Cargo. Having every thing onboard and being all ready, we weighed Anchor at 8 A. M. on the 20th June 1801, with a Dutch Pilot onboard, whom we discharged, two hours afterward. We had as a Passenger, a young Dutchman, who was going out as a Clerk to the establishment, in Japan. He was rather an uninteresting man, and did not add much to the pleasure of our Cabin party. On the 3d day out, we saw 20 Malay proas, lying with their Sails down,—as we approached them, they made sail, and stood to the westward,—we supposed them, a fleet of Pirate proas. On the next day we passed through the Straits of Gasper. On the 7th of July saw the rocks and breakers on the Pratas Shoal, leaving from it N.W. to N. The next day, we made the coast of China, & passed several Chinese fishing boats. On the 9th we were in the Straits of Formosa, and the day following made the Island of that name, the weather thick and rainy.

On the morning of July 16 made the Islands of Cosique and St Clara, which are near the harbour of Nangasacca (our destined port). On the 18th two fishing boats came along side who supplied us with fish. On Sunday July 10 by civil account, at noon, we were so near, that we hoisted 20 different colors; and in the afternoon, entered the harbour of Nangasacca. We had much ceremony to go through, in entering this port, which is considered indispensible; among other things, to fire several salutes. As I was lying in my cot, on our arrival, very sick, with a nervous fever, Cap$^t$ D. endeavoured to get clear of this part of the business,—but it could not be dispensed with, and there was actually fired over my head, while lying in that situation, 49 Guns 6tt [sic] pounds!. As any little noise had previously disturbed me very much, this was more than I could bear, and retain my senses,—so that finally I lost the consciousness of what was passing about me. The day after our arrival I landed on the Island of Decima. (A little Island connected with the City of Nangasacca, by a Bridge; it is walled all round, and here the Dutch residents, are obliged to pass their lives.) As there was no house prepared for us, I went to the Dutch Doctors, Myneer Letzke, who kept House, and had a Japanese woman for his wife, by whom he had several children. This to be sure was but a poor resort, for a person, who was as sick as I was,—but the necessity of the case, and having a Physician at hand, made it more convenient, than to have remained onboard the Ship. I continued with the Doc$^r$ several days; my bed being only a common matrass on the Floor;—Until our own establishment was prepared, when I removed to that, and had the luxery of a Cot swing, and a musquito curtain, which at that time, was better than all the Doc$^{rs}$ prescriptions. After getting into our new habitation I began gradually to improve, but it was a long time before I was well enough to attend to business: during my sickness the Doc. had been in the habit of giving me large doses of laudnum,—and It was long after I had got better,—before I could do without it,—indeed, I finally came to the conclusion that I would not use it any longer, and in consequence, laid awake all night, for several successive nights, until wearied nature at last submitted. Cap^t D. dined every day at the Table of the Dutch establishment, & I remained while on shore, (which was the principal part of the time, we were in Japan,) to get my dinner alone. Francis Hector the Steward of the Ship, was house keeper, Cook, and Servant, and a very good fellow, he was. Provisions were very dear, as every thing came through the hands of a Compredoor & he no doubt put upon them a large profit. My dinner after my recovery was frequently mackerel & sweet potatoes, and even at this day (Feb. 7. 1840) I can remember with what a relish I eat this food; they were both good of the Kind, and in addition, the bread was as fine, as any country could produce. Sometimes we would have pork, or a Fowl, but these articles came very high.

Cap^t Derby, M^r West & myself, carried several articles of merchandize, on our own accounts; this has always been allowed to the Dutch Cap^ts,—but then, the sale of these articles, must be made by the Japanese Government. All the articles were landed on the Island,—opened and displayed in a warehouse & on certain days, the Merchants were allowed to [come] on the Island to examine them. Nothing could exceed the minuteness with which they examined every thing. Among other articles we had a quantity of Tumblers & wine Glasses; these they measured with the greatest care,—run their fingers over every part to determine what inequalities there were on the Surface, and then held each piece up to the light to see the colour. They also made drawings of the different description of pieces. After this investigation was made & it took no little time; they then marked on their memorandums the number of the lot and probably the result of their investigations. Every thing we had to sell, went through a similar ordeal,—so that to us, who were lookers on, and owners of the property, nothing could be more tedious. It was perfectly natural however, that people who did so little, should proceed with a caution, that men who were used to much business, could not spare from other avocations, and that they, should devote much time to small objects, when we should consider it, too valuable. After the goods had been sufficiently examined, a day was appointed for a sale in the City of Nangasacca, and was conducted with the greatest fairness. Cap^t D. & myself went into the City attended by the requisite number of officers & proceeded to what the Dutch call the Gelt Chamber, where we found one or more upper Banyoses seated in their usual state, and a general attendance of the Merchants. We were placed where we could see all that was going on, and receive such explanations, as were requisite, to a thorough understanding of the whole business. The goods being all disposed of, we were escorted back to the Island with much formality, not however, until a day had been appointed by the Great man, for the delivery of the goods. Delivering these adventures, was a great affair, and it was a number of days, before the whole was taken away. No person in this country (who has not traded with people who have so little intercourse with the world,) can have an idea of the trouble we had in delivering this little Invoice, which would not have been an hours work in Salem. We finally after a great trial of our patience, finished delivering goods, and if I recollect right, articles that did not come up to the pattern, were taken at diminished prices.

On the 20th Sep. 1801. we went into the City of Nangasacca, our party consisted of Cap^t Derby, M^r Doeff, D^r Letzke, M^r Egis, M^r Bouquet, M^r Fisher, the Dutch Sailor & myself, besides three under Banyoses & Six Tullocks. The first place we went to in the City was to Facquias, an eminent Stuff Merchant, here we were received with great politeness, and entertained in such a manner as we little expected. We had set before us, for a repast, Pork, Fowl, Meso, Eggs, boiled fish, Sweet meats, Cake, various Kinds of fruit, & Sacky & Tea. The lady of the House was introduced, who drank tea with each of us, as is the custom of Japan. She appeared to be a modest Woman, which cannot be said of many of her countrywomen. The place we next visited was a Temple, to this we ascended from the street, by at least

Two hundred stone steps; we saw nothing very remarkable in this building, excepting its size, which was very large; though in fact we were only admited into an outer apartment, as there appeared to be religious ceremonies going on within. Adjoining this building was the burying ground. In this ground was the Tomb of one of their Governors, which was made of stone, and very beautifully wrought; and on the front stone, there was a long inscription, before which, the Banyoses & Tullocks, falling down on their knees, bowed their heads to the earth. The Tomb was enclosed with a wall of stone, and without the wall, were several images of stone, standing on pedestals. There were several stone lamps, but were not lighted. This burying ground was very extensive, it was situated on the side of a hill,—as most of their burying grounds are; each grave had a stone, with an inscription. The Japanese bury the body in the same position as they sit,—with their legs bent under them; they are put into a Bally, which is not unlike a barrel, and in this manner committed to the earth, which is always done in the night. We next visited another Temple, which was likewise situated on the side of a hill, & reached by Stone steps, & was less elevated than the other. The outside of the building was ordinary, as most of the buildings are,—but the inside, presented a great degree of neatness. It consisted of a great many apartments, in some of which were images, and in one, over a Kind of alter, was a Lamp which was kept continually burning. In another apartment there were several long pieces of boards or escutcheons, painted black with an inscription, to the memory of some of their deceased Emperors or Governors, before each of these was a cup of Tea, which they informed us, was renewed every day. There were a number of apartments, which probably the Priests occupied, as there were many of them, passing in & out. These are dressed like the other Japanese, excepting that their caloys, or outside garments, were all black, & their heads shaved all over.

From this Temple, we went to the Glass House, which was on a small scale, this was the first, & the last Glass House, I have ever been in, (altho' I am 59 years old.) I was surprised to find they had brought the art to such perfection, but they are yet obliged to import fine glass, to supply their wants. From the Glass House, we went to a Lac ware merchants, we were entertained, with much hospitality. From thence we were conducted to a Tea House, or Hotel, where we dined. After dinner, we were entertained with various feats of dancing, tumbling &c. their dancing is much like the Chinese fashion, and other eastern nations, and consists more in distortions of the body, than in anything, that could be called grace. The music consisted of an instrument not unlike a Guitar, accompanied by the voice of the person who played the instrument, this hapened to be an old man, whose distortions of countenence, made it apparent, that it was no small effort, to *make music.* There was also a Drum, & likewise an instrument, shaped very much like an half hour glass. After the dancing came a kind of comedy. This resembled very much their dancing, excepting that the actors spoke,— almost all those, were women, & were said to be people of very loose habits. The last performance was the Tumbling, which was done, with great agility. Towards dark we returned to the Island & so great was the crowd, in the streets, to see us pass, that it was with difficulty we could get along. The number of children we saw, both going & coming, was truly astonishing.

The City of Nangasacca, is surrounded with very high hills, excepting the part, connected with the harbour;—it is not of great extent, but very populous, containing it is said, between, fifty & sixty thousand inhabitants. It is not a manufacturing City, like Jeddo, or Neaco, nor does the lands in the neighbourhood, appear well adapted to agriculture,—but probably so many people are brought together here from having so fine a harbour, and its vicinity to China, with whom the Japanese have a considerable intercourse. The streets of the City are all narrow, and are inconvenient to walk in, as they are covered with loose stones, about as large as paving stones. At short distances, you have to go up, or down, flights of stone steps, which extend across the street, and is caused, by the inequality of the ground. They have no kind of carriages, as it would be impossible to use them, in such streets. At the end of every street, is a gate, which is locked at night,— and if a citizen were to pass the night, in any other than his own street, his name would be taken by the person who keeps the gate; and most probably handed, to the Police Officer. The houses are generally built of wood, and seldom exceed two stories, on account of the earthquakes, which are very frequent. The external appearance of almost all their Houses, are mean but within, they are very clean, & neat, at least, those that I saw. The floors are all covered with mats, & it is considered a piece of ill breeding, to tread on them, without first taking off the shoes. The Japanese dress much alike; the dress of the men consists first of a caloy, or loose gown, which comes down as low as the ancles, over this, is worn a kind of petticoat, which comes as low as the other,—these garments are made of Silk, or cotton; the Petticoat does not go higher than the hips;—over the shoulders, they wear a shawl, which is generally made of black crape, and round the waist, they have a band of either Silk or Cotton; thro' this band, the Officers of Government put their swords, and they are the only persons, who are allowed to carry these instruments. The middle part of the head, is all shaved, the remaining hair, which is left, on each side, & behind, is then combed together, and made very stiff, with gum, mixed with Oil, & then turned up on the top of the head, in a little club, about as large as a man's thumb. This is the universal fashion of dressing the head, both with rich & poor, excepting the Priests, whose heads are entirely shaved. The dress of all classes are in the same fashion, the poor do not wear the silk Petticoat, or crape shawl, and indeed the Cooleys & other labourers, at the time, we were there, threw all their clothes off, excepting a cloth around the middle, when at work. The dress of the women is a Caloy, with large sleeves, very much the same as the mens;— they also wear a band round the waist, made either of Cotton, Silk, or Plush. The females suffer the hair to grow long, which is made stiff with gum & oil, and then is turned up, on top of the head, where it is secured, with various turtle shell ornaments. These ornaments, are the dearest part of a Ladys dress, frequently amounting, to 300 Tale. The shoes & stockings of men & women are alike, the former are made of straw & protect only the bottom of the foot,—the latter, are generally made of thick blue, or white Cotton, & come up, about as high, as the calf of the leg. The stockings are not worn, unless the weather is cold.

The Japanese, to each other, are very polite,—as they generally sit on mats, their usual salutation to each other, is by bowing the head to the earth, and in the street, they stop to bow to their acquaintances; and these civilities are not confined to any particular class in society,—but the poor, as well as the rich, have the same kind manners. As long as we were in Japan I do not recollect of seeing one person, that appeared to be angry with another, but the most perfect harmony prevailed among them. They have great vices as well as great virtues; such as are very common both with male & female, in Eastern nations. Of the religious opinions of Japanese, I know but little, and the Hollanders who reside here, appear to be no better informed. I am told, they believe in the existence, of one supreme being,—in a future state, and in rewards & punishments;—they have numerous Idols, with which their Temples abound, these they consider as mediators, with the supreme being. I have seen them kneel before these Idols, with much apparent humility & piety. They likewise worship fire, many of them, having a Lamp continually burning in their Houses, also, the new & full moon. I have seen some of them with a string of beads on their arms, in the manner of Catholics. They have various fasts and luckey & unluckey days. It is said, that the 5th of their new year, is the day appointed for dishonoring the cross, but of course, we saw nothing of it. They have observed one fast since we were here, which was in remembrance of the dead; the ceremonies were principally in the night; the first of which was devoted to feasting, at which they fancy their friends are present, the 2d and 3d nights, the graves, which are lighted with paper Lamps, & situated as they are, on the side of a hill, make a most brilliant appearance. On the 4th night at 3 o'clock the Lamps are all brought down to the water, & put into small straw barks, with paper sails, made for the occasion, & after putting in rice, fruit &c, they are set afloat. This exhibition was very fine. The Japanese on the death of their parents abstain from flesh & fish, forty nine days, & on the Anniversary they keep the same fast, but do not do it, for any other relatives.

# REFERENCE NOTES

## THE ORIENT AND WESTERN MUSIC

[1] Strabo, *The Geography*, transl. by H. L. Jones (1928), V, 109.
[2] Curt Sachs, *The Rise of Music in the Ancient World* (New York, 1943), pp. 198-271.
[3] Curt Sachs, "The Road to Major," *The Musical Quarterly*, XXIX (1943), 381-404.
[4] Curt Sachs, *The Rise of Music in the Ancient World* (New York, 1943), Section 7.
[5] Curt Sachs, "Towards a Prehistory of Occidental Music," *The Musical Quarterly*, XXIV (1938), 147-52.

## THE ORIENT AND WESTERN ART

[1] Edward F. Strange, *Japanese Illustrations* (London, 1896).
[2] Raymond Koechlin, *Souvenirs d'un Vieil Amateur d'Art de l'Extrême Orient* (Chalon-sur-Saône: Imprimerie Français à Orientale, Bertrand, 1930).

## OUR AGRICULTURAL DEBT TO ASIA

[1] *Indian Journal of Medical Research*, XXIV, 1083-92.
[2] W. H. Sebrell, in E. A. Evans, Jr., *The Biological Action of the Vitamins* (Chicago: University of Chicago Press, 1942), pp. 74-83.
[3] H. J. Webber and E. B. Boykin, "The Advantage of Planting Heavy Cotton Seed," *Farmers Bull.* 285, (1907).
[4] *Yü ti mien hua t'u*, by Fang Kuan-cheng, Viceroy of Chili (1765 A.D.), a large folio of 12 plates in de luxe binding, regarding cotton culture, harvest, spinning, and weaving, with a rhythmic prose introduction by the Emperor K'ang Hsi and descriptive and allegorical poems, one by the Emperor Ch'ien Lung, and brief instructions on cotton culture and use by the Viceroy Fang Kuan-chêng opposite the plate to which they refer. The plates are in white line on black ground, like rubbings. Translated by Kiang Kang-hu and Walter T. Swingle in Ms., 1917.
[5] H. W. Barre and W. B. Aull, "Hot Water Treatment for Cotton Anthracnose," *Science*, n.s., 40:109-10, 1914.
[6] Since 1931 more than a dozen papers concerning *lei kung t'eng* were published in Chinese by Chinese entomologists and chemists. Mr. Hagerty translated all of them under my direction, and thanks to the full information these papers contained, the plant was identified as *Tripterygium Wilfordii*, a member of the family *Celastraceae*. This family includes the American *Celastrus scandens*, which resembles the *lei kung t'eng* in vegetative characters. The Chinese species has very different winged fruits, not showing a scarlet aril as do those of our American vines.
[7] Walter T. Swingle, H. L. Haller, E. H. Siegler, and M. C. Swingle,

"A Chinese Insecticidal Plant *Tripterygium Wilfordii*, Introduced into the United States," *Science*, 93:15-17, January 17, 1941.

[8] Bureau of Plant Industry, Bull. 86.

[9] Carl R. Raswan, *The Black Tents of Arabia: My Life Among the Bedouins* (London: Hutchinson & Co., 1935), Appendix 1, "The Arab and His Horse," pp. 213-39, with diagrams showing 3 principal breeds and 20 leading strains.

[10] Victor Arthur Rice, *Breeding and Improvement of Farm Animals* (3rd ed.; New York: McGraw-Hill Book Co., 1942), p. 52.

[11] Blunt, Lady Anne, *Bedouin Tribes of the Euphrates*, ed. with some account of the Arabs and their horses by W. S. B[lunt] (2 vols., 1879).

Blunt, Lady Anne, *A Pilgrimage to Nejd* (2 vols., 1881).

## THE ORIENT AND CONTEMPORARY POETRY

[1] F. S. Flint, "Eau-Forte," in *Some Imagist Poets* (Boston: Houghton Mifflin Company, 1915).

[2] T. S. Eliot, "Journey of the Magi," in *Collected Poems* (New York: Harcourt, Brace and Company).

[3] Herbert A. Giles, *A History of Chinese Literature* (New York: D. Appleton-Century Company, 1901).

[4] Ezra Pound, *Personae—Collected Poems* (New York: Liveright Publishing Corporation).

[5] Arthur Waley, *170 Chinese Poems* (New York: Alfred A. Knopf).

## LIVING RELIGIONS AND A WORLD FAITH

[1] Wincenti Lutoslawski, Polish philosopher celebrated by William James in his essay on "The Energies of Men."

[2] Rabbi Newman of New York is my authority for the statement that the Jewish population of the world between 1880 and 1940 had approximately doubled.

## UNDERSTANDING AND REUNION: AN ORIENTAL PERSPECTIVE

[1] Cf. my "Ornament" in the *Art Bulletin*, XXI (1939).

[2] Gopala Krishnayya, quoted in G. V. Krishna Rao, *The Chirala-Perala Tragedy* (Madras, 1922), p. 145.

[3] Marco Pallis, *Peaks and Lamas* (1939), p. 380. In this highly civilized, and not merely civilian volume, as also in Aldous Huxley's *Ways and Means*, there can be studied the technique of bringing together again the accidentally divided cultures; the proper task, as was pointed out by René Guénon, in *East and West*, of an intellectual aristocracy.

[4] St. Augustine, *Confessions*, IX, 10.

[5] Xenophon, *Oeconomicus*, XVII, 3.

[6] J. Buhot, "Easter Art and the Occident," *Aryan Path*, Feb. 1932.

[7] B. de Zoete and W. Spies, *Dance and Drama in Bali* (1939).

[8] M. H. Aung, *Burmese Drama* (1937). Cf. D. C. Sen *History of Bengali Language and Literature* (1911), pp. 724 ff.

[9] *Cambridge History of English Literature*, VI, 328.

[10] René Guénon, *East and West* (London, 1941), p. 146. This is the first

of a series of translations of René Guénon's works, all of which have an important bearing on the question of Oriental "influence."

[11] Leroy Waterman in *Journ. Am. Oriental Soc.* 58.410-412.

[12] Cf. Aldous Huxley, *Ways and Means*, p. 205, "A Greek tragedy was much more than a play ... Modern dramas ... are, essentially, secular ... an almost daily stimulant. Abused as we abuse it at present, dramatic art is in no sense cathartic; it is merely a form of emotional masturbation."

[13] A. M. Hocart, *Les castes* (Paris, 1939), p. 27.

[14] R. S. and H. Lynd, *Middletown*, p. 80.

[15] See A. K. Coomaraswamy, "Play and Seriousness," *Journal of Philosophy*, XXXIX (1942), 450-52.

[16] Cf. Miguel Asin, *Islam and the Divine Comedy* (London, 1926).

[17] Rūmī, *Mathnawī*, Book II, Introduction. Cf. René Guénon, *L'Esotérisme de Dante* (Paris, 1925).

[18] See Jean Seznec, "Flaubert and India," *Journal of the Warburg and Courtauld Institutes*, IV (1942), 142-50. Creuzet's illustrations of Indian deities, on which Flaubert relied, are quite creditable: this is especially true for the figure of Bhavānī as ποτνία θεϱῶν and *nutrix omnium*, reproduced by Seznec.

[19] Plato, *Protagoras*, 312 E.

# INDEX

271

273